James Talboys Wheeler

Madras in the Olden Time

Vol. 2

James Talboys Wheeler

Madras in the Olden Time
Vol. 2

ISBN/EAN: 9783337401634

Printed in Europe, USA, Canada, Australia, Japan

Cover: Foto ©ninafisch / pixelio.de

More available books at **www.hansebooks.com**

MADRAS IN THE OLDEN TIME.

BY THE SAME AUTHOR.

HAND-BOOK TO THE MADRAS RECORDS, being a Report on the Public Records preserved in the Madras Government Office from the earliest period to 1834, with an Introduction and notes, 8vo. price Rs. 2-8.

This Report on the Public Records of Madras has received the approbation of the Secretary of State for India, in a Dispatch dated London, 25th of May, 1861. For the opinions of the local journals see the end of the volume.

MADRAS IN THE OLDEN TIME:

BEING A

HISTORY OF THE PRESIDENCY

FROM

THE FIRST FOUNDATION OF FORT ST. GEORGE.

COMPILED FROM OFFICIAL RECORDS,

BY

J. TALBOYS WHEELER,

Author of the "Geography of Herodotus," &c. &c. and Professor of Moral Philosophy and Logic at the Madras Presidency College.

VOL. II.
1702—1727.

MADRAS:

PRINTED FOR J. HIGGINBOTHAM, MOUNT ROAD,
BY GRAVES AND CO., SCOTTISH PRESS.
1861.

PREFACE.

In issuing a second volume of "Madras in the Olden Time" as it is depicted in the old records of the Madras Government, the Compiler has little to add to the Preface which was appended to the former volume. He has continued to adhere to his design of endeavouring to convey to the reader all the pleasure and information to be derived from a perusal of the original records, without the painful labour of wading through a mass of obsolete detail. The present volume brings the annals down to the year 1727. The third volume will so far complete the undertaking, as to fill up the blank which has hitherto existed in the history of the English Settlement, between the first foundation of Fort St. George and the period when Mr. Orme's history may be said to begin.

According to the plan here sketched out, the present series of annals of the Madras Presidency will be brought to a close about the middle of the last century. But it may not be premature to add that the compiler has no intention of bringing his labours to a conclusion at so important a crisis in the history of British India. From 1640 to 1750 the annals comprise little more than the story of a commercial settlement; and may be best gathered from selections from the early records, such as we are now placing before our readers. But the half century immediately succeeding to that period is a period of conquest, of which only a small portion of the history has been told by Mr. Orme, and to which modern historians generally have only done partial justice. India as it was in the days of Clive and Hastings, Hyder and Tippoo, of Coote and Wellington, of Cornwallis and Mornington, is almost a blank so far as a living narrative of the times is concerned. The politician, the moralist, and the military annalist have done their best, but it still remains for the antiquarian to exhume from the records of the time, the story of that eventful period written by the hands of the actors themselves. Such a task however involves far more than an examination of the records of a single Presidency; and the writer must therefore defer placing any definite plan before his readers, until the third and concluding volume of "Madras in the Olden Time," which is nearly all ready for the press, shall have been fairly brought to a close.

MADRAS,
July 10*th*, 1861.

CONTENTS OF VOL. II.

CHAPTER XVIII.

GOVERNORSHIP OF MR. THOMAS PITT, 1701—3.

Page.

Passage of arms between the Bishop of St. Thomé and Governor of Fort St. George—Drunkenness in church—Commercial rivalry between Madras and Pulicat—An "infant" chief watchman—Outrages in the Red Sea—Feastings in honour of the departure of Dawood Khan—Round Robin against a Captain and Chief-Mate—Proclamation of the occasion of Queen Anne—A disinterested Native—Extraordinary administration of the law against coining—Attempt to seize the Company's out-villages—Improper conduct at the General Table—Purchase of Mr. Pitt's silver plate for the General Table. 1

CHAPTER XIX.

GOVERNORSHIP OF MR. THOMAS PITT,
(continued) 1703—4.

Difficulties in the collection of new taxes—Petition of the Natives—Great engagement with Pirates—Diplomatic Department—Duelling—Rumours of coming troubles—Fresh demands for the out-villages—Sea engagement with the French—

Attempted exercise of Ecclesiastical authority in Madras by the Patriarch of Antioch at Pondicherry—Dispute between Governor Pitt and the Foujdar of St. Thomé 17

CHAPTER XX.

GOVERNORSHIP OF MR. THOMAS PITT,
(continued) 1704—7.

Unsuccessful attempt to rear silkworms—Claims of Native Princes to wrecks on the coast—Emeute at St. Thomé between the Moorish Governor and Portuguese Governor—Serjeant Dixon made an Ensign in the hope he might become a Protestant—Salvage of anchors—Wills of Roman Catholics—Eccentricities of the Natives as regards deeds and bonds—Visit of Dawood Khan to St. Thomé—Dawood Khan's dinner in the Company's Garden—Insolent action of Captain Seaton—Disputes between the Right and Left hand Castes—Petition of the Right hand—Desertion of the town—Mr. Fraser espouses the cause of the Right hands—Great dissensions between Governor Pitt and Mr. Fraser 37

CHAPTER XXI.

QUARRELS BETWEEN THE RIGHT AND LEFT HANDS IN THE GOVERNORSHIP OF MR. PITT,
1707.

Agreement between the two Hands of no effect—Mutinous proceedings of the Right hands at St. Thomé—Publication of a general pardon—Rob-

Page.

bery of the "Stones"—Mr. Fraser implicated in the mutiny of the Right hands—Proffers of service from the Armenians, Persians and Patans—Disclosures of the Gusbardar from St. Thomé—Right hands refuse to return from St. Thomé except Mr. Fraser sign the Cowle—Cowle granted by Mr. Pitt rejected—Preparations to attack St. Thomé—Return of the deserters—Mysterious publication of papers—Old differences between the Right and Left hands in the days of President Baker, 1652—Commercial rivalry between the Right and Left hands, the cause of the quarrel between Governor Pitt and Mr. Fraser—Charges brought against Mr. Fraser—Grave rebuke administered by the Court of Directors to all parties... 60

CHAPTER XXII.

GOVERNORSHIP OF MR. THOMAS PITT,
(continued) 1708—9.

Communications between Governor Pitt and the Great Mogul at Delhi—Copy of the Agreement between the Right and Left hand castes—Villainy of the Madras Boatmen—Governor Pitt thrashes a Native—Mr. Pitt's horsedealing—State of the Mogul Empire after the death of Aurungzebe—Shah Aulum opens a communication with Mr. Pitt—Reception of a Husbulhookum—Governor Pitt's Petitions to King Shah Aulum, to the Grand Vizier, to Zulfikar Khan the Commander-in-Chief, and to Zoodee Khan the Lord High Steward—Presents to the lady of Zoodee Khan at St. Thomé—Punishment for robbery—King of Pegu swindled out of Elephants—Five out-villages obtained by Governor Pitt—Very respectful letter of Governor Pitt to Zoodee Khan—Firmaun from Shah Aulum. .. 87

CHAPTER XXIII.

GOVERNORSHIPS OF PITT, ADDISON, MONTAGUE, AND FRASER, 1709—10.

Page.

Changes in 1709, 1710, and 1711 similar to those in 1859, 1860, and 1861—Charges brought against Governor Pitt of having purchased a great diamond—Captain Seaton in disgrace—Sudden recall of Mr. Pitt, and accession of Mr. Gulstone Addison—Death of Gulstone Addison within a month—His property inherited by Joseph Addison the author—Mr. Edward Montague Provisional Governor—Futile attempt to send Captain Seaton to England—Accession of Mr. Fraser—Great storm of 1709—Ambitious project of the Armenians to form an independant Factory at the Mount—Effect of the war between the English and French—Shocking state of the Church yard of St. Mary's in the Fort—Friendly letters of Zoodee Khan to the Governor of Fort St. George—Out-villages claimed by the Dewan Sadatulla Khan—Ineffectual letters of Governor Fraser to Sadatulla Khan and Zulfikar Khan... ... 108

CHAPTER XXIV.

GOVERNORSHIP OF MR. WILLIAM FRASER, 1710—11.

Troubles at Vizagapatam—Evils of money dealings with Native chiefs—Blockade of Vizagapatam by Fuckerla Khan—Minister wanted at Christmas time at Fort St. David—Extraordinary case of breach of promise of marriage—Judgment on the case by the Governor and Council—Sudden recal of Mr. Fraser. 132

CHAPTER XXV.

GOVERNORSHIP OF MR. EDWARD HARRISON, 1711—12.

Page.

Declining power of the Great Mogul—State of the Dekkan—Character of the reign of Shah Aulum—Rupture between the English Deputy Governor of Fort. St. David and the Mussulman Governor of Ginjee—History of Ginjee—Cause of the quarrel between Deputy Governor Roberts and Serope Singh—Mr. Raworth arrives at Fort St. David as Deputy Governor—Gallant action of Captain Roach against the troops of Mohabat Khan—Disorders in the garrison at Fort St. David—Murder of Serjeant Parsons—Appeal of Governor Harrison to Zulfikar Khan—Senseless retaliation against Serope Singh, Rájah of Ginjee—Native merchants at Fort St. David threaten to leave the bounds—Attempted negociations—Attack on the enemy's entrenchment—Outrage of Captain Courtney upon Ensign Paddle. 149

CHAPTER XXVI.

GOVERNORSHIP OF MR. EDWARD HARRISON, *(continued)* 1712—13.

Protestant Missionaries at Tranquebar—Visit of Bartholemew Ziegenbalgh at Madras—Proposals to erect Charity Schools from the Society for Promoting Christian Knowledge—General letter from the Directors thereon—Neglect of Divine service and disorders at the General Table—Influence of the Foujdar of St. Thomé with the Nabob Sadatulla Khan—Advices sent home of the death of King Shah Aulum, the accession and dethronement of Jehander

Shah, and the accession of Ferokscre—Appointment of the first Nizam of the Dekkan—Curious report on the changes in the Native demand for European commodities—Refuge afforded to wealthy Natives by Fort St. George—Disorderly conduct of Mr. Fleet Aynsworth—Will of Mr. Saunders, an illustration of social life—Pressing demand of the Nabob for the out-villages—Rebellion of Mr. Raworth at Fort St. David against Governor Harrison—Charges against Mr. Raworth—Appeal of Mr. Raworth to arms—Negociations ineffectual—Governor Harrison proceeds to Fort St. David—Mr. Raworth assisted with provisions by the French at Pondicherry—Exchange of firearms—Mr. Raworth's extraordinary surrender—Subsequent death at Paris... 177

CHAPTER XXVII.

GOVERNORSHIP OF MR. EDWARD HARRISON, *(continued)* 1714—17.

Contemporary state of the Mogul power at Delhi—Cheen Kulich Khan appointed Nizam of the Dekkan under the name of Nizam-ool-Moolk—Capture of Ginjee by the Nabob Sadatulla Khan—Love potion administered by a slave—Death of Queen Anne and Proclamation of George I—Testimony of Governor Harrison to the good behaviour of the Capucin Fathers at Madras—Rules for the Charity School in Madras—Sate of the library in Fort St. George—Mussulmans relieved from the support of the Hindoo Pagodas—A false Chaplain—Quarrels between the Right and Left Hands—Public disturbances—Final negociations—Departure of Mr. Harrison and accession of Mr. Collet... 213

CHAPTER XXVIII.

ENGLISH MISSION FROM CALCUTTA TO DELHI, 1715—17.

Page.

Discovery of the dispatches from the Envoys amongst the Madras Records—Want of interest in Native Histories, its cause—Character and objects of the English Mission to Delhi—Oppressions of Jaffier Khan, Nabob of Bengal—Arrival of the Mission at Delhi—Audience with the King Feroksere, and visits to various Omrahs—Contemporary state of Delhi—Difference between the Mogul Mussulmans and the Arab Mussulmans—Declining power of the Moguls—Rvolution of the Seiads places Feroksere upon the throne—Progress of Court intrigues against the Seiads during the stay of the Mission—Troubles of the Mission—Intrigues in the Dekkan resulting in the death of Dawood Khan—Disorder of the King Feroksere cured by Dr. Hamilton—Marriage of Feroksere—General dilatoriness at Court—Disorders in the Tartar Army—Capture of the rebel Gooroo, Bandu the Seikh—Wholesale execution of his followers—Cruel death of Bandu—Business of the Mission painfully delayed—Brought to a sudden conclusion—Last interview with the King Feroksere—Attempt to delay the doctor—Death of Dr. Hamilton 240

CHAPTER XXIX.

GOVERNORSHIP OF MR. JOSEPH COLLET, 1717—18.

State of Southern India—Curious forgery—Reformation in hospital charges to soldiers—Punishment of a Factor for familiarity with the wife of a Sergeant—Foundation of Charity Schools for the children of Portuguese and Malabar slaves—Public rejoicings on the arrival of the Firmaun from King Feroksere—Projected occupation of Divy Island—Operation of the Firmaun as regarded the out villages—Occupation carried out by Governor Collet—Forcible occupation of Trivatore by the son of Diaram, the Head Renter—Captain Roach drives the enemy out of Trivatore—Reward of Captain Roach —Adventures of a pretended doctor—Murder of a Surat merchant and his servant—Pedda Naik removed from his appointment of chief watchman for extravagance and incapacity—Final arrangement with the Nabob Sadatulla Khan as regards the out-villages—Disorders on the West Coast of Sumatra ... 269

CHAPTER XXX.

GOVERNORSHIP OF MR. JOSEPH COLLET, *(concluded)*, 1719—20.

Tranquillity at Fort St. George and tragical revolutions at Delhi—Clandestine arrival of a young Englishman at Fort St. George—Peaceful relations with Sadatulla Khan—Entertainment of Ducknaroy, the Dewan of the Nabob—Patan Merchants induced to reside in Madras—Punishment of a Chetty for hoisting a Gentoo flag—Repeal of Mr. Streynsham Master's law on the marriage of Protestants and Roman Catholics—Ignorance of French and Portuguese amongst the English inhabitants—Reductions in the Garrison at Fort St. George—Restoration of the Pedda Naik—Execution of a pirate—Punishment of the Choultry Dubash for extorting exorbitant fees—New regulation of fees—Foundation of Collet's pettah—Depar-

Page.

ture of Mr. Collet—Contemporary state of the Mogul Empire—Rise of Cheen Kulich Khan—Last attempt of Feroksere to escape from the thraldom of the two Seiads—Failure of the plot—Frightful disorders in Delhi—Downfal of Feroksere—Night conflict in the streets between the Mussulmans and the Mahrattas—Feroksere dragged from the haram and thrown into prison—Child Emperor proclaimed by the Seiads—Murder of Feroksere—Final overthrow of the Seiads by Mohammed Shah ... 298

CHAPTER XXXI.

GOVERNORSHIP OF MR. FRANCIS HASTINGS.
1720—21.

Internal irregularities in the Government of Fort St. George—Havildar at Egmore shot dead by the Company's Chief Peon—Supposed treasonable correspondence between the Chetties at Madras and Portuguese Viceroy of Goa—Quarrel between Governor Hastings and Mr. Elwick—Harsh proceedings towards the Chetties—Suspension of Mr. Elwick—Murder of a Chetty by two soldiers—Proceedings against Mr. Elwick—Extraordinary Will of Mr. Charles Davies—Seduction of a Rajpoot woman—State of the Dekkan—Murder of Europeans at Pegu during the Mohurrum. 326

CHAPTER XXXII.

GOVERNORSHIP OF MR. NATHANIEL ELWICK,
1721—24.

Tranquil state of Fort St. George—Startling defalcations in the Public Treasury—Dangerous illness of the ex-Governor Hastings—Confinement of Mr. Cooke the Secretary—Death of Mr. Hastings—Great storm of 1721—Extortions of the Governor's Dubash—A convivial Hindoo—Illicit trading of the Armenians at Poudichery—Discussions about the old contract with the Armenians—Insults offered to a Member of Council by a Ship's Captain—Victory obtained by Nizam-ul-Mulk over a confederacy of Nabobs—Struggle for the possession of Ginjee—Seige of Shiraz by the Afghans, and consequently failure in the supplies of Shiraz wine—Drunkenness at Fort St. David—Ensign shot by a jealous Gunner—Barbarous usage of a runaway debtor at St. Thomé. ... 351

CHAPTER XXXIII.

GOVERNORSHIP OF MR. JAMES MACRAE, 1725—26.

Early history of Mr. James Macrae—The son of a Washerwomen appointed Governor of Fort St. George—Governor Macrae's opening address in Council—Energetic character of Mr. Macrae's administration—Imprisonment of a Native for reflecting on the character of a Governor—Coinage at the Madras mint—Comparison of the English mint with the Native mints—Mode of acquiring landed property in the Madras Presidency—Petition of Mrs. Maria Pois—Business occupations of Madras Governors in the olden time—Lease of the out villages—Difficulty between Governor Macrae and the Nabob of Arcot—Punishment of Perjury—Counterfeit Pagodas—Yearly payments to the Jesuit Missionaries in China... 382

CHAPTER XXXIV.

GOVERNORSHIP OF MR. JAMES MACRAE.
1726-27.

Page.

Supervision of Native goods by Governor Macrae—Contracts with Native Merchants—Curious story of a forged bond—Oppressions of Mahadin, the Renter of Trivatore—Counter-petitions—Punishment of Mahadin—Economy in Hospital charges—Purchase of Horses for the Governor—Promotion of emulation amongst the younger servants of the Company—Bills of Exchange in the olden time—Attempted poisonings by a woman slave—Restrictions on the sale of poisons—Statements of the revenue and expenditure of Fort Saint George and the other settlements on the coast of Coromandel—Building of a Sawmill—Causes of the declining trade of Madras—Restrictions upon Respondentia bonds—Mode of transacting business with Native merchants—Attempted fraud by a diamond merchant—Proceedings as regards interlopers—Trade with China.... 406

HISTORY OF THE MADRAS PRESIDENCY.

CHAPTER XVIII.

GOVERNORSHIP OF MR. THOMAS PITT, 1701—3.

In the previous volume we brought down the annals of Madras to the siege of Fort St. George by the Nabob Dawood Khan. Before however proceeding with the annals chronologically, we shall bring forward a few extracts for the years 1701 and 1702, which refer to domestic incidents, and which could not have appeared in their chronological order without interfering with the history of the siege. After the date of the raising of the blockade, the events will be arranged as before in order of time.

The first extract refers to the old struggle for the exercise of independent power by the Roman Catholic Bishop of St. Thomé, against the Governor of Fort St. George.

"Thursday, 8th May, 1701. The Secretary is ordered to deliver Padre Friar Michael Anjous, the following paper translated in Portuguese, and he to be present at the reading of the same in their Church on Sunday next.

"Whereas we, the Governor and Council of this place, have been credibly informed that on or about the 12th March last, the Right Rev. Father Don Gaspar Alfonso, Bishop of St. Thomé, as he styles himself, did send a paper to the Padres of Madras belonging to the Church, for the exercising the Roman Catholic Religion, commanding and requiring them to publish the same; the purport of which paper being to require and command the delivering up of sundry papers to the Provisor and Vicar General of St Thomé; which papers wholly relate to a cause depending in our Court of Admiralty; and upon their non compliance with the same, they were to undergo the greatest excommunication.

"In order to publish these our highest resentments against the Right Reverend Don Gaspar Alfonso's proceedings, and the Reverend Padre Friar Michael Anjous compliance with the same, we hereby declare that no Bishop whatsoever of the Roman Catholic religion hath any power or jurisdiction over the Clergy or Laymen of that persuasion, residing under this our government.

"And to prevent the like irregularities for the future, we strictly command and enjoin you Padre Friar Michael Anjous, or whoever shall succeed you as Chief Padre in this Church, not to publish, read, or permit to be read any paper directed to you from any Bishop or ecclesiastical functionary whatever, without first acquainting the Governor of this place, and obtaining his leave for the same, as you will answer the contrary at your peril. And we further require you to publish this our order in your Church in a full congregation on Sunday next. Given under our hands and the seal of the Right Honourable Company. Dated at Fort St. George in the city of Madras, this eighth day of May, 1701.

(Signed by the President and Council.)

Our next incident is quite a domestic one.

"Tuesday, 9th May. Whereas Ensign William Read on Sunday last coming drunk into Church and challenging his fellow officers, it is therefore resolved for such offences, that one month's pay be stopped by the Paymaster, and he be severely reprimanded by us."

The following little anecdote illustrates the commercial rivarly which prevailed between the Dutch at Pulicat and the English at Fort St. George.

"Saturday, 28th June. Serapa and the Joint Stock Merchants informing us that the Dutch, who have now made great contracts all along this coast, are tampering with all our Weavers to seduce them from our service. And whereas it has been the custom in such considerable contracts as have been lately made here, to deposit in the Weavers hands five Pagodas for each loom, to be delivered in cloth at the last payment; the Dutch now, to engross the Weavers and get them from our Merchants, have offered to deposit in the Weavers hands ten Pagodas for each loom. So considering the ill consequences if we should not enable our Merchants to do the same, and that they will inevitably lose their looms; we order that forthwith fifteen thousand Pagodas be advanced to Serapa and the joint Stock Merchants."

The next incident illustrates the Native idea of the hereditary nature of all public appointments.

"Wednesday, 24th December. Angerapa Naik, our Watchman, dying the 29th October last, there has been great application by letters from several Poligars to us in the behalf of Timapa Naik, who contended several years for the place with the deceased Watchman; but finding upon enquiry that it was not his right, besides having murdered some inhabitants of this place, he was rejected. And whereas the late deceased Watchman has left a son an infant, who upon enquiry of the most knowing inhabitants of this place say, that the infant has the right of succession: so that to prevent any more application to us, and fearing that Timapa Naik may procure the Nabob's perwanna, which may occasion disputes between the Government and us; we have thought fit to grant our Cowle to the infant, during whose minority his uncle Tegapa Naik is to officiate and to be Chief Watchman of this place; and accordingly it is agreed that the infant be tasheriffed with the usual ceremony, and a Cowle drawn out."

The losses entailed upon the Company's Government by the proceedings of the Arab Pirates have been already alluded to, and are sufficiently represented in the following extracts. Our readers will bear in mind that it was at this same Judda or Jedda, the Port of Mecca, that the massacre of Christians took place in 1858.

"Saturday, 24th January, 1702. This place Madras having suffered much by ships unjustly seized by the Arabs of Muscat and the Bashaw at

Judda, which has occasioned great clamours amongst the inhabitants of all sorts in this place, chiefly through despair of any assistance from the Government, for procuring satisfaction, for the same; the Governor and Council, to pacify them for the present, proposed the sending a Petition to the king of England, and a Letter to the Company, setting forth their grievances and great losses thereby. Which Petition and letter was read and agreed on as entered after this Consultation.

"To the king's most Excellent Majesty in Council.

"The humble Petition of your Majesty's most dutiful and loyal subjects, inhabitants of the city of Madras on the Coast of Coromandel in the East Indies.

"Humbly sheweth,

That we, your Majesty's Petitioners residing in this place, having liberty of trade in these parts gal, and thence to Persia, where she arrived safe; but on her return, 14th April, she met three Arab ships off Muscat, and took her and carried her into that Port, and made prize both of ship from the East India Company* Merchants of London trading to the East Indies, did in June 1695 equip out a ship called the "London," burthen about 120 tons, Richard William Master, to Ben-

---

* Our readers must bear in mind that the Company's servants at this time had permission to trade on their own account between different ports in the East, so long as they did not interfere in the trade with Europe. This permissive trade they generally carried on with the assistance of the principal Native Merchants of Madras on the principle of a Joint Stock Company.

and cargo, valued at about £5000 sterling. She had ten Europe men on board of her, three of which made their escape, and the others miserably perished in prison, who were most part your Majesty's subjects. And on the 18th June 1700 did send hence a ship called the "Friendship," burthen 100 tons, William Merrice Master, to Surat, who from thence went to Persia, and meeting with two Arab ships in the Gulf, was seized on by them and carried to Muscat, where they sold the ship and cargo, amounting to about £8000 sterling, besides Armenian goods of great value; and imprisoned after a most barbarous manner her ship's company, the master, mates, and several Officers being your majesty's subjects.

"We also in October 1699 sent a ship called the "Diamond," burthen about 100 tons, John Cockroft Master, to Bengal, and there to lade for Judda in the Red Seas; who accordingly did, and proceeded to the aforesaid Port; but losing her passage wintered at Acheen, so that she did not arrive at Judda till March 1701. They were promised by the Bashaw freedom of trade, and the protection of the Port; upon which they landed their goods and sold to the Bashaw and his officers good part thereof; but soon after they were possessed of the goods, they seized the ship and the remaining part of the cargo, which they made sale of; so that with what they had before in their hands, amounting to at least £30,000 sterling. They also seized the Supercargo and Commander, and what other Europe men did not make their escape, and murdered some of them by their barbarous imprisonment, and threaten to sell the persons of those living. All which was upon pretence, that this was the ship that took an Arab's ship off the high land of St. John's near Surat the year before. At which time this ship " Diamond" was at Mocha, and returned thence into this road in September, whilst your Majesty's four Men of War were here ; and being informed that this place Judda is in some measure under the Government of the Grand Seignour, we have represented this great injustice by letter to your Majesty's Ambassador at Constantinople and your Consul at Grand Cairo.

" These our misfortunes, we know not what cause to assign for them, unless it be as is reported through this country, that some of our nation have most industriously endeavoured to fix all piracies committed in these parts on the Old East India Company and their Factors, and on such as reside in their settlements ; inculcating likewise into the Natives, that let them seize what they will of ours, that we have no power to make ourselves restitution, nor will there be any trouble come to them thereon.

" We having here most humbly represented to your Majesty, the most notorious injustices we have suffered from the Arabs of Muscat and Bashaw of Judda, all amounting to at least £43,000 sterling ; for the restitution of which we humbly implore that your sacred Majesty will be graciously pleased to extend your Royal protection to us, in granting us your letters of reprisal, or in such manner as in your great wisdom shall be thought meet.

"And your Petitioners as in duty bound shall ever pray, etc.

The Letter to the Company covering the Petition to the King, contains little more than a request that the latter might be forwarded. The following extract from it is worthy of preservation as exhibiting the feeling of animosity which prevailed against the New East India Company.

"We have too much reason to be jealous that that unhappy misfortune at Judda may be justly attributed to the infamous and hellish contrivances of some of our own countrymen (i. e. New East India Company), who have stuck at nothing in endeavouring to fix the Piracies upon you and your Factors abroad. And if that Bashaw of Judda does what we are advised of, in selling the Commander and Supercargo, why may it not be a precedent for the Arabs of Muscat, and the Moors throughout India, to do the same, and then what will become of all your subordinate Factories. These are also many more dreadful consequences to be inferred from the late resistencies of these nations; and if they be not speedily called to an account, and forced to restitution for what is passed, it will most certainly end in the utter ruin of your trade in these parts."

We now return to the domestic annals of the Presidency. During the actual blockade of Fort St. George, no other entries of any importance appear in the consultation books excepting those connected with the siege. In May however, matters returned to their old channel. The following extracts explain themselves.

"Thursday, 21st May, 1702. We finding that gardens within a mile of the works of Black town to be very inconvenient, they giving great advantage to an enemy for Lodgements, and erecting Batteries against us; for which reason it is ordered that Messrs. Empson and Marshall do take a view of what Gardens have been planted these five years, and report to the Governor and Council the distance they are from the works, and whether any ways incommodious.

"It is ordered that the Paymaster provide scarlet coats and beaver hats for the Portuguese Officers, as a gratuity for their readiness to serve the Garrison, and the same for the English Officers, viz. Lieutenants and Ensigns."

The departure of Dawood Khan was celebrated with four days successive feasting as appears from the next entry.

"Friday, 22nd May. On the 19th instant the Portuguese Militia, on the 20th one Company of Soldiers, the next day the other Company, and this day the Gunroom crew, were handsomely treated with dinners under a large tent spread in the Inner Fort; and the Commission Officers of the respective Companies those evenings supped with the Governor." Again on the 25th, "the Governor and Council and Trainbands were splendidly entertained with a supper at the Company's Garden; they having also been under arms in our late troubles."

The following complaint brought by a crew

against their Commander and Chief Mate is worthy of preservation.

"Wednesday, 8th July. The Governor yesterday receiving a sort of a Letter, with a Paper signed by twenty-nine of the *Phœnix* Ship's Company, commonly called a Round Robin; the purport of the Letter consisting chiefly of complaints against Captain Carswell and his Chief Mate, Mr. Abbis. The Governor immediately sent for the Captain and Purser of said ship, who seemed to be surprised at it, saying that they knew nothing of the matter. Upon which the Governor sent off an order to the Chief Mate, about which the Captain, Chief Mate, and five of the men appeared before us this day; two of the five being the Boatswain and Gunner of the Ship, who complained chiefly of the disability of the Chief Mate, that he knew not how to discharge his duty in that employ, as also of his abusing the men. Their complaints chiefly against their Commander for pinching them in their provisions; he confessing before us that their allowance three times a week is but a quart of rice and gram together for five men a day, but promises that for the future it shall be rectified. So upon the whole examination of this business, we find that the Gunner has been the ringleader, who seems to us to be an impudent, saucy, insinuating fellow, and believe has been the sole occasion of stirring up the men to complain in this malicious manner. The Round Robin as well as the Letter, as he himself confesses, was wrote with his hand; so that to prevent the ill consequence that may attend such clamours, it is resolved that the Gunner and Boatswain are discharged the ship, as also Daniel Bulfinch and Peter Middleston; the two latter, as the Captain tells us, have been very active in this villany; and for the present that the four aforesaid persons be committed to the main guard, till we consider of inflicting such punishment as they deserve."

On the 8th March, 1702 died William III, and in September the same year the news reached Fort St. George, as will be seen from the following entry.

"Thursday, 17th September. In pursuance to an order of Consultation, the Flag was early this morning hoisted, and at eight o'clock was lowered, when there was two volleys small shot and one hundred cannon discharged by the half minute glass, for the death of our late gracious King William the Third of blessed memory. Then the Flag was again hoisted up, when the Mayor, and all the Aldermen in their gowns on horseback, with twelve Halberteers and a Company of Grenadiers marching before them, Proclaimed our gracious Queen Anne at the Fort Gate, Town Hall, Sea Gate, and Choultry Gate, with many huzzas and great demonstration of joy, with three volleys small shot and one hundred and one pieces of cannon discharged. And in the evening the Governor, attended by all the Gentlemen of the Council, with the Mayor and Aldermen and several other gentlemen in palanquins and horseback, to the Company's Bowling Garden, where there was a handsome treat provided; all Europeans of fashion in the city being invited to the same, where they drank the Queen's health, and prosperity to old England, with many others.

The following very disinterested act on the part of a Native Chief deserves especial notice.

"Saturday, 26th. Abdul Labby Khan, Governor of Porto Novo and the country about it, came last night to St. Thomé, having been lately at the Camp at Vellore ; unto whom the Governor sent this morning the Moollah with a compliment, and two bottles of rosewater, which he kindly received, and intimated to him that he was desirous of seeing Madras, which the Moollah was ordered to evade if possible, but not to give a flat denial. And whereas we have always found the Governor of Porto Novo a friend to our Company's interest, and to preserve his friendship, it is agreed that we make him a present of Gold Chains to the value of about 450 Pagodas.

"Sunday, 27th. The Moollah and Brahmin did this day attend the Nabob Abdul Labby at St. Thomé, with the present of Gold Chains, which they privately offered ; but he refused to accept them, telling them he was a true friend to the English, so would take no present, but would always continue the kindness he had for us, and make it his study to do us all the good services that lay in his power."

Our next extracts explains itself.

"Tuesday, 20th October. During the time Dawood Khan lay before this place, we were continually straightened for provisions, at which time the weather being very hot we could not salt up any ; so were forced to keep a great number of

Hogs, the meat for which was very chargeable, besides the great inconvenience of keeping such a number. So to prevent any future danger that may happen from the Garrison wanting Provisions, it is agreed that between this and January next, that the Steward be ordered to kill three hundred Hogs, to be salted up as the Governor from time to time shall direct. And if it should so happen there be no occasion for them, that then they be disposed of to the shipping as opportunity offers."

"Wednesday, 4th November. The President is advised from Masulipatam that the Mogul pitching his Camp near some great mountains, from which of a sudden came so great fall of waters, that it swept away about 150,000 people, with elephants, horses, camels, and baggage, he himself narrowly escaping." (This event is noticed by Elphinstone, who however reduces the number of people who perished to 12,000.)

The following incident furnishes an extraordinary illustration of the administration of the law.

"Friday, 6th. The 29th ult. it was ordered that the three black fellows apprehended, and found preparing to coin Pagodas, should be brought on their trial to-morrow; but finding the evidence against them is so insufficient that they will most certainly be acquitted, and they offering six hundred Pagodas to be acquitted without a trial, it is thought much better to accept the same; not only in regard to the six hundred Pagodas, but likewise their being acquitted on their trial would encourage others to attempt the same; and accordingly it is agreed to receive the said six hundred Pagodas, and banish them the place.

The news of the war of the Spanish succession had now reached the Presidency, and preparations were made to improve the defences. The following entry will illustrate the state of affairs.

"Saturday, 16th January, 1703. Here being a report that there is coming a strong squadron of French and Portuguese men of war for India, against which we are informed the Dutch are making great preparations, and putting their garrisons in a posture of defence; and we fearing our nation is engaged in the war in Europe, and well knowing that the Dutch will give us no manner of assistance, so think it necessary to keep our Garrison in the best posture of defence we are capable of."

This year another series of attempts was commenced for obtaining possession of the Company's out towns of Egmore, Persewaukum, and Triplicane. The first, it will be seen, was checked by a very decided action on the part of Governor Pitt.

"Friday, 12th March. The Governor having news brought him last night, that there had been six or eight Peons, who had tied leaves in the Company's towns, which is the custom of the country when they take possession of any place; Peons were sent out immediately to seize them, but could not find them; but this morning three of them came to the Governor at Egmore, and produced a paper which is an order from the Foujdar of Poonamallee, grounded upon an order he had received from the King's Dewan Mahomed Seid. The Governor ordered them to be carried prisoners to the Fort, where they were put in irons, and intended to be punished for executing an order within our jurisdiction, without first acquainting the Governor therewith." Four days afterwards the three Peons were released, " in consideration that they were but servants, and obeyed only their Master's order; but were severely checked for the same, the Governor telling them that if they or any others presumed to do the like again, they should most certainly lose their heads."

The following entry of the same date explains itself.

" Mr. Richard Pearson writer, who came out in the *Phœnix*, and immediately sent to Masulipatam, where he behaved himself very insolently to his superiors, for which they sent him hither in January last, where soon after he behaved himself very impudently to the Governor, who confined and punished him for it; and afterwards upon his submission, and acknowledging his fault with promises of amendment he was set at liberty; when in few days after, he quarrelled at the Company's General table, where he gave opprobious language to several, and blows to boot. So finding him an incorrigible and debauched fellow, and that keeping him here may tend to the ruin of several of the young men in the Company's service;—it is agreed that he be confined to the inward Fort, and sent for England by the first opportunity; and that he be permitted to come no more to the Company's Table, but that the Steward shall send him such Provisions as the Governor directs."

We have already seen, on the occasion of the visit of the Nabob Dawood Khan to Fort St. George, that the General Table could be magnificently served. The following extracts will prove that even in the matter of silver plate, the show was by no means despicable for those days.

"Thursday, 8th April, 1703. The Company having no plate for their General Table, or any other use, but what is very old and battered, and but very little of it too, which is now agreed to be melted down, and the President who brought out a set of plate with him, and has used it ever since at his own charge : it is agreed that the same now be taken on the Company's account ; allowing for the same, as the Company's silver was lately sold, sixteen Dollars weight for ten Pagodas English standard ; and for the fashioning thereof as it cost in England ; and that the same be weighed off to the Steward, and an account of it brought into Consultation, that so it may be brought into the Books. From the particulars of an account which is given at full length in the Consultations, we learn that Governor Pitt's silver plate weighed 2240 oz. 17 dwts. ; that the metal was valued at £700 sterling, and that the fashioning cost £65. The old plate which was melted down was valued at less than £100. Mr. Pitt's new plate included 66 silver plates, 6 salts small, 1 salt large, 3 castors and mustard spoon, 3 porringers, 16 spoons, 6 forks and 6 knives, 1 ladle large, 12 dishes, 1 teapot, 1 sauce pan, 2 salvers large, 2 salvers small, 1 Monteith, 4 large candlesticks, and 7 covers.

CHAPTER XIX.

GOVERNORSHIP OF MR. THOMAS PITT.

1703—4.

The great event which distinguished the period in our annuals now under review, is one which can be stated in a few words, viz. the union of the old and new Companies into one. With this event the quarrels of the two Companies naturally terminated, and attention was once more directed to the prosecution of trade, the progress of domestic affairs, and occasional communications with the Nabob.

The first incident to be noticed furnishes another illustration of the old difficulty of collecting new taxes from the natives. It will be remembered that on the advance of Dawood Khan a brick wall and other works had been erected for the defence of Black-town, and arrangements were made to meet the expense by collecting a special tax from the inhabitants. It will be seen from the following extracts, that many abuses had occurred in the collection, which were charged upon Serapa Naik, the Chief merchant who had been appointed to superintend it.

" Friday, 9th April, 1703. The Chiefs of the Castes having met daily for some weeks past at the Pagoda to consider of ways and means for raising the money for building the Black-town wall and works ; and having acquainted the Governor a few days past that they had perfected the same ; we summoned all the Castes this day before us, and called over the Roll of how much every Caste was assessed. With which they all seemed to be satisfied, and declared they had given their assent thereunto. Upon which we ordered it forthwith to be collected in such a method as they themselves desired ; which was to be by their own Conicopolies, and two Peons to each Caste.

"Wednesday, 28th. There having been a scandalous paper dropped in the town, relating to the assessing of the Town wall money, written in a counterfeit hand in English ; which we judge to be by some European who has had some insight in the Company's affairs ; the drift of which can be for no other than to raise mutinies and insurrections to prevent the collecting the money for building the Black-Town wall and works ; and there being some particular charges against Scrapa the Chief Merchant ;—we summoned all the heads of the Castes before us this morning, and examined them to every particular, when they positively denied they knew anything of it. Which paper is entered after this consultation.

" To the Council of Fort St. George,

" Gentlemen,

" Finding personal application to some of you, to mediate matters with the Governor about a due regulation in assessing for the Town wall, has been fruitless ; we have in concert with many others, taken this method to lay before you the sentiments of the inhabitants ; hoping your justice in compassion to us, zeal to the Hon'ble Company, and regard to the welfare of this place, will induce you to consider the following.

"That the building of the Town wall was by the Hon'ble Company's order, some of us have been made sensible of, and we believe it ; also that they expect the charges for the same should be borne by the several Castes, which we think a very great hardship ; considering the benefit of Customs the Honorable Company reaps by our Sea and Land Trade ; also the Farms of Betel, Tobacco, and Arrack (which fall sensibly heavy), not to mention the Ground rent of our houses, Pedda Naik's Duty, etc.

"Although these, as aforesaid, are hardships, yet by length of time, being become Sallabad (as we esteem them) there is no great demur made now, and are not recited here as grievances ; so much as an introduction to inform you, that we are wholly dissatisfied in Serapa Naik's being intrusted with the collection of the town wall money, lately ordered by the Governor and yourselves to be received of us ; for his audacious injunctions publicly made to the Conicopolies and Peons (who go about to gather the money) to beat and pull us by the necks with cords to the Choultry, upon refusal of payment ; which has been committed on some who were not in a capacity to launch out so much as demanded.

"Such outrages and insults are seldom inflicted under the Moors, therefore we are amazed at Serapa's presumption in giving such orders under the

English Government ; but they have been redressed (upon a complaint made to the Honorable Governor) by punishing two Peons ; though we are since served almost as ignominiously ; being constrained by those sordid Collectors to stand before our doors a while in the sun, till wrought into a compliance ; and if such sufferings are caused by our backwardness to pay, please be referred to our reasons that makes us so.

"First, Serapa Naik, at a General Meeting upon his summons, told us the Honorable Company having been at a great charge for raising a wall round the Black Town for our security, must be reimbursed, and three thousand Pagodas more added to repay the said Serapa's charges of presents, etc. during Dawood Khan's stay here last.

"Second. Having well considered the Honorable Company's indulgent care to protect us, we shall most willingly acquiesce to refund their cost of the Town wall, but then humbly request may be granted, viz.

"1st. That only the first costs thereof be assessed.

"2nd. That an Englishman be appointed receiver or Collector.

"3rd. That no pretence of presents, etc. made by Serapa Naik, be interwoven with the Town wall money.

"4th. That every caste, knowing what each are to pay, have liberty of themselves to bring the same, which they promise to do within any time limited.

"Third. These four requests being granted

will give a general satisfaction, and save the hire of so many Conicopolies and Peons employed as now appointed in this affair.

"Fourth. And what further induces us to insist on the four requests as aforesaid, are, because we are under some jealousy, that besides the Town wall money, and the 3,000 Pagodas for Serapa Naik, more may still be taken, and appropriated to the present manager's use.

"Ourselves, and fathers before us, have long experienced the quiet and moderate English Government, and hope our children's children after us may enjoy the like. But when some by their characters assume to it abuses ; under a presumption that their being favourities will protect them against all clamours (which we find too true) ; we have only this expedient left, viz. To represent our calamities. And having so done now, we hope a short time will show us the effects of your wisdom, by interposing in matters so destructive to the public good ; otherwise we propose to apply ourselves to the Honorable Company, by sending them a copy hereof, with another memorial of farther complaints of this nature. Dated Madras, April, 1703. In behalf of the Native inhabitants of Madras."

Notwithstanding the denial on the part of the Natives, of any knowledge or participation in the paper, it is certain that subsequently the amount was only partially collected, and that with the utmost difficulty, as may be gathered from many allusions, which need not be reproduced here.

The following quaint but graphic narrative of

an engagement with Pirates is entered in the consultations, dated 31st May, 1703, and is well worthy of preservation as illustrative of the times.

"A Relation of the taking of the Ship "Pembroke Frigate," by the Pirates at Mayotta, March 10th, 1703, by Mr. Edward Fenwick, the Supercargo.

"On the 9th of March last we made the Island of Mayotta, and as we were standing in with the land about three leagues distance, we discovered two ships under sail close under the land. They had sent their boats off before we could see them to make out where we were; they were full of men, and kept rowing about half a mile to windward of us. After we showed our colours and fired a gun to windward, they each of them put out a flag, which we at first thought to be the King's flag, not plainly distinguishing it; but they would not come near us to acquaint us which was the road or the way in; which we were obliged to endeavour the finding ourselves, being in extremity; and with this consideration concerning the ships, that if they should prove Pirates our loading would be of no use to them, so consequently we might expect good treatment from them, as has formerly been shown to others. We steered west and west by south till we came into five fathom water about a league from the shore, and there anchored; which we had no sooner done, and veered away a little cable, but the most frightful and greatest of dangers presented themselves to us, both of the ship and our lives; breakers on all sides within half a ship's length, which, because it was dark and just high water, we did not perceive till we were so near them. Whilst we were in this consternation and hurry what to do, the two boats hailed us, lying at a Grappling right ahead within call ; but would by no means come to our assistance, except we first sent our boat to them. Then we immediately sent our Yawl with four hands, two of which they took into their boat, and put two of their own people into our boat. When they came on board they thought we had been fast ashore, and said they were sorry to find us in so bad a condition ; the loss of our ship being unavoidable as they thought ; we lying on a reef of rocks which run out two leagues on each side of us, and would be dry in half an hour's time, and all round us nothing but breakers. They advised us to let the ship lie till morning dry, and they would all come off then, and see what possibly might be done to save her ; so little hopes had we from them of getting off again ; and indeed we soon perceived they told us nothing but the truth ; for by this time the tide had ebbed very much, and at every hollow of the sea the ship began to strike. Therefore Captain Wooley considering that delaying longer was but running ourselves into greater dangers, and that there was no other remedy but to cut and stand the same way out as we came in ; so desired the two men to go and send our people on board which were in their boats, which they presently did. Then all hands turned to, and immediately hoved a peek and cut away, having a spring upon the cable to cast her. By these endeavours it pleased God everything answered our expectations ; and before we could cast the lead six times were past all danger, receiving no other damage than the loss of our best bower, and about ten fathom of cable. Now after our ship was out of danger, we began to consider the answers made by the two men that came on board, to a few questions we asked them. They said their great ship was a Permission ship bound for Muscat, laden with guns, anchors, cables, etc.; Captain Hillyard Commander. The little ship they said belonged to the Scotch Company, one Captain Drummond Commander, and was bound for Madagascar, to trade for slaves, with small arms, powder, etc. That they had lain there nearly three months before to repair and clean their ships ; and that just as they made us coming in, they were standing out to proceed on their voyage. We acquainted them the great necessity we were in for provisions and water, and that several of our men were down ; to which they answered, they did not doubt but their Captain could assist us with everything, and send their boat betimes to us in the morning. We did not give much credit to what they said, yet there was no way to get clear of them but by fair words and entreaties ; so kept standing off and on all night ; and at 12 o'clock next day, being the 10th, we came to an anchor about a mile from the shore, being low water, at which time we see their two boats lying dry upon the sand. About an hour after, when the water floated them, they rowed towards us ; and being come with pistol shot under our stern, they hailed us, asking if they might be

suffered to come on board, that they were friends
and had brought us fresh provisions. Captain
Weoley answered, one of them might come, yet they
both came rowing on; and when they were under
our quarters, one on each side, they all started up
with their arms guarded, swearing if any of us fired
a piece they would give us no quarter, and if we did
not fire they would do us no harm, nor take any
thing from us. Captain Weoley ordered every
one to fire, which we all did, and they at us;
Captain Weoley jumping down the after skuttle at
the same time, and bidding every one to their close
quarters, some into the cabin and some between
decks. But we not able to keep either of them
long, they firing six shot to our one; and then
perceiving it was impossible for us to do more,
they having two ships very near us, we called for
quarter; which they gave us, disarming us, and
turning us into the head. Then they began to
rummage and rifle the ship everywhere, until their
heat was over. In this scuffle we had two men
killed, Mr. Gold our Chief Mate, and Cornelius
Browne a Foremost man. Of their men they had
two wounded; one of them mortally, the other
shot through both his arms. The rest of the day
they spent searching about the ship, and swearing
to revenge themselves on Captain Weoley, for first
bidding them come on board, and then firing upon
them as they came along our side; likewise to
burn the ship. The next day they carried Captain Weoley on board one of their ships, and
kept him prisoner there; about forty of them
staying on board us till Friday the 12th, when

they put it to the vote whether to burn her
or to give her to us again. If this had been done
the next day after they took her, she had certainly been burnt; but putting it off three or four
days gave us time to make many friends to give
their votes in our favour, that we carried it by
seventeen votes more to save her than to burn
her. After taking several things out of her, they
delivered the ship to us again that night about
seven o'clock; they making the best of their way
to Madagascar and we for Johanna, giving us six
old small arms in lieu of what they took out of
us. But they would by no means clear Captain
Weoley; forcing him to go along with them to
serve as a pilot for the Straits of Malacca, swearing to shoot him if he refused it. They likewise
detained by force Francisco de Cruz our Carpenter; yet one of our men, Martin Hogendirk a
Dutchman, entered himself and went voluntarily
with them.

"These two Pirates are very strong, full of
men, and one sails excellently well. The biggest
carries 40 Guns and near 200 men; she is called
the " Prosperous," and was (as they told us first)
a Permission ship upon a trading voyage, but
surprised and taken about six months before at
Madagascar. The then Commander Hillyard died
soon after of the wounds he received then, but
the new Pirate Captain of her is called Howard.
The little ship is called the " Speedy Return,"
and was formerly commanded by one Captain
Drummond, but now by one Bowen. She carries
12 Guns and 70 men, and is about 100 tons. She

with another about the same burden were sent out by the Scotch Company."

In consequence of this extraordinary relation, those ships in the Madras Roads which were bound for the Straits of Malacca did not proceed on their destination; "which tends," says the consultation book, "to the great detriment of the Port and lessening of the customs; besides it is to be feared that if these Pirates take any of the country ships, it will bring us into new troubles with the Government, out of which we have but a few months past extricated ourselves." It may be mentioned that Captain Weoley made his escape from the Pirates a few months afterwards.

Our next extract is worthy of record as illustrating the mode in which the political department of the Company's administration was carried on in these primitive times.

"Thursday, 12th August, 1703. It being the general report of the country that there will be sudden alterations in the Government by the removal of the Nabob, or Dewan, or both, and we having but two spy Brahmins in the Camp, and here being ——— who tenders his service, being son to Vinkettee Puttee, who procured the firmaun from the king of Golconda for this place, and he seeming to be an intelligible person :—it is agreed he be entertained, if he will serve for five or six Pagodas per mensem, to reside as a private person in the Camp, to give us intelligence of all affairs of importance, but not to be there as a Vakeel."

The following entry illustrates the stringent nature of the laws against duelling.

"Monday, 23rd August, 1703. The Governor having confined Captain Seaton and Mr. Stratford for going out yesterday to the Company's old garden to fight a duel, he ordered them to be brought up this day before him in Council to examine into the occasion of it ; when it was found that Captain Seaton gave the challenge without any manner of provocation, so that it was resolved their confinement should be continued till we had considered what punishment we should afflict on them to deter others from doing the like." The confinement lasted ten days, at the expiration of which Captain Seaton was fined 200 Pagodas and Mr. Stratford 50 Pagodas. Captain Seaton, however, as we have seen on former occasions, had a happy knack of getting out of a scrape as easily as he got into it. Three weeks afterwards we find the following significant entry :—" Captain Seaton delivering in a petition setting forth his contrition for his offence, for which he was fined 200 Pagodas, and prays that we would remit the same ; which, in consideration of his great charge of children, and his promises of not doing the like, is granted him, and ordered that the Secretary do return him the same."

In November this year rumours of coming troubles appear to have reached the Presidency. The Steward of the Fort was ordered to buy up 300 hogs, and feed them up, "so that they may be fit to kill and salt up during the cool weather for the service of the Garrison." We also find the following entry.

"Tuesday, 2nd November, 1703. The Governor received advices this day from the Nabob's Camp, that there was orders given out to the Foujdar of Tripassore to raise forces to come and seize our towns; which we are resolved to defend; and in order thereto, it is agreed that the Paymaster forthwith run up a brick wall round the Choultry at Egmore, in such manner as the Governor shall direct, to lodge such forces as we shall send on all occasions to defend the place; and when the wall is done, to pull down the present Choultry, which is thatched and ready to tumble, and to build a commodious one for that purpose."

Eleven days afterwards the news was confirmed by the receipt of the following letter from the Foujdar.

"Translate of a letter from Tahir Khan, Foujdar of Tripassore, received November 13th, 1703.

"I wish your Honour all health. About three months past I received a letter from Khan Bahadur to take possession of those villages you have, which are under the Poonamallee country. I was loth to acquaint you with this unwelcome news by reason of our friendship; but fresh orders are arrived to the Dewan and myself; and your Honour is sensible that the servant must obey his Master's orders; so that I can defer it now no longer. The occasion of my sending you this is to let you understand that if you will send one of your Vakeels to me, my friendship shall not be wanting to accommodate the matter."

Mr. Pitt's reply was cautious, but sufficiently firm.

"To Tahir Khan Foujdar of Tripatore, November 15th, 1703.

"I received your letter and observe the contents, and can only return this answer. The towns you mention were given us by Assid Khan, the Grand Vizier, whose purwanna we have, in consideration of the good services we had done your king; which was much to the satisfaction of Khan Bahadur who afterwards gave order for the delivering them to us. When we thought it had been in this country, as in all other parts of the world, that whatever the Grand Vizier granted, the king always made it good; or what reliance can there be on the favour of such great men's purwannas. I esteemed you always as you write yourself our friend, and am sorry you are commanded to execute such unjust orders; which will occasion no less than a difference between the two nations—Who is the aggressor let the Great God judge. Our Vakeel is sick; if you send one hither, I will immediately give my answer to what he shall propose."

The following incident of the war with France respecting the Spanish succession, is interesting from the fact that the Mr. Dolben here mentioned, was our old friend the Judge Advocate in the Court of Admiralty, who had been dismissed from his Office, and engaged in a profitable trade. Notwithstanding the report of the Pirates in the Straits of Malacca, he had boldly set out there in the Canterbury, in the pursuit of commerce under difficulties.

"Friday, 14th January, 1704. Last night the Governor received news by a Portuguese letter from Pondicherry, that the two French ships were returned with an English prize called the "Canterbury," belonging to the New East India Company; having met her and Mr. Dolben in the "Chambers" Frigate in the Straits of Malacca; which is this day confirmed to us by a letter from Pondicherry, copy of which is as follows, viz.

"The two French vessels met the "Chambers" Frigate, and another of the New Company's called the "Canterbury" of more than 300 tons, commanded by Captain Kingsford, came from England and bound to Surat. The 19th December, near the Island of Sambelan in the Straits of Malacca at night, they gave each other broadsides. The "Chambers" Frigate had her mainyard disabled, which he got repaired in the night. The next morning she fought again during four hours against the lesser French ship; after which he made all the sail he could to the bank of Parsola. The "Maurepas" (French ship) fought against the "Canterbury" which he took immediately. Monsieur de Fontenay was sent against the "Chambers" which seemed the least, but proved the biggest and best man. We hear from those we have taken, that Mr. Dolben gave 50 guineas to each man, and a promise to each that should be wounded to provide for them, to the end they should behave themselves well."

About this time a Roman Catholic Patriarch of Antioch arrived at Pondicherry, and subsequently, like the Bishop of St. Thomé, executed not a little opposition by endeavouring to interfere in ecclesiastical affairs in the Presidency. In the previous November, a messenger arrived from this Presidency with a complimentary message for Governor Pitt, as will be seen from the following entry in the consultations, dated, 22nd November, 1703.—

"There being arrived at Pondicherry a Patriarch and several Padres, said to be missionaries from the Pope to inspect into ecclesiastical affairs in China; one of which came this day into town, sent with a compliment from the Patriarch to the Governor, with a small present of Jocoles, oil, and wines; who was civilly received, and afterwards took up his lodgings in the Portuguese Church."

The following extract shows a determination on the part of the Patriarch to interfere.

"Saturday, 22nd January. Padre Michael having applied himself to the Government for leave to go to Pondicherry, for that he that calls himself the Patriarch of Antioch had summoned him thither, and he feared that if he did not go it would tend to his ruin; the Governor deferred giving him leave till he had consulted his Council, which was this day summoned and Padre Michael sent for, who earnestly insisted for leave to go. Whereupon he was asked by the Governor whether the Patriarch sent for him as Chief Priest of this Romish Church, or on any other account. He answered that it was as he was Chief Priest. To which it was replied that we could allow of no persons to have any authority over the Priests of this place, so as to send for them away, or return them or any others at their pleasure. And supposing the Abbot to have a hand in this matter we sent for him; who Jesuitically evaded, and denied that he knew anything of the matter. Whom likewise we acquainted with our resolutions that the Patriarch, nor none else, should exercise any power over the Priests that live under our Government. So dismissed them both, strictly enjoining Padre Michael not to stir out of the town; besides that orders should be given the officers not to permit him to go without the gate."

In our next chapter we shall have occasion to produce further illustrations of these intrigues.

The following entry will explain itself.

"Monday, 3rd February. Ensign Harris, who has often been found drunk, insomuch that he has been incapable of doing his duty, for which he has been frequently reprehended; but finding it to no purpose, he was this day broke; but in regard he has a wife and several children, we have permitted him to serve as Serjeant, but that no longer than he abstains from drinking to excess."

Early this year a dispute arose between Governor Pitt and the Foujdar of St. Thomé, concerning an Armenian inhabitant of Madras who had been imprisoned by the latter. It appears that one Coja Timore, an Attorney for an Armenian in Persia, had great demands on an Armenian named Coja Awan who was an inhabitant of Madras. The case was carried to court, but meantime Coja Timore the Attorney had business at St. Thomé, and was followed there by Coja Awan; and the latter by some means unknown, but which we may reasonably infer to have been bribery, prevailed on the Foujdar to imprison the Attorney. Governor Pitt of course sent to the Foujdar to deliver up both as inhabitants of Madras; but the Foujdar insisted not only that a free pardon should be granted Coja Awan, which would have been granted, but also that the papers lodged in the Court should be delivered up to him. To have granted the latter demand, would have been to establish a most awkward precedent; as it would virtually admit of an interference for the future on the part of the Foujdar of St. Thomé in all cases pending in the Madras Court of Admiralty. The following letters will throw some light on the dispute.

" From Mirusman Foujdar of St. Thomé.

" I have power over Chinnapatam, and likewise over St. Thomé, as it belongs to the king whose grant of Chinnapatam ground to the Company was on no other intent than to make the place fruitful, and bring riches into his kingdom, but not to act anything that should prove unjust or prejudicial to the Merchants interest there. I cannot help putting you in mind of the Governors of Golconda and Bijapore, who for their unjust actions and ill behaviour were instantly turned out of their Province, notwithstanding all their resistance, and clapped into irons. What reason therefore has the king to value any one, seeing he turns out whosoever he pleases; and who by his great kindness and justice towards his people, has obtained power of God to conquer wheresoever he comes; and knowing me to be one of his Officers, I wonder at the style you write me. What can I say more?"

The following was Governor Pitt's answer.

" To Mirusman Foujdar of St. Thomé.

" I received your impertinent and insolent letter.—We all know your king to be great, wise and just, and many of his nobles to be persons of great honour; but most of his little Governors, amongst whom I reckon you, to be very corrupt and unjust. We would have you to know we are of a nation whose sovereign is great and powerful, able to protect his subjects in their just rights over all the world, and revenge whatever injustices shall be done them, of which there will be speedy instances given. I am not a little surprised at your saucy expressions, as well as actions in imprisoning my inhabitants, when you know that I can fetch you hither and correct you for both. This is an unswer to your letter.

THOMAS PITT."

Meantime the matter had been represented to the Nabob Dawood Khan and his Buxie. A guard had been placed by Governor Pitt over the house of Coja Awan, who had procured the imprisonment of his Attorney, and who of course remained at St. Thomé; and both the Nabob and Buxie declared that this Coja Awan, was indebted to them for jewels, and required that he should be no further meddled with. Governor Pitt sent very long explanatory letters in reply. Subsequently, as Coja Awan owed a great deal of money in Madras, Governor Pitt resolved to open his house, and to take an inventory of his goods, in the presence of the Armenians, Moguls, and Patans of the place. Accordingly the latter were summoned to appear on the 6th April, 1704; but on that morning, instead of going to Coja Awan's house, a number of them appeared before the Governor. The Armenians begged to be excused on the ground that they had goods at St. Thomé, which the Foujdar would seize directly he heard of their participation in the matter. The Moguls on their part stated that the Buxie's servant had been with them that morning, and charged them in the name of his Master and in the name of the Nabob, not to concern themselves in the matter. The Patans made no appearance at all. Acccordingly they were all ordered to the Town hall, whilst the Governor and Council took the subject into consideration. After a little while the following decision was arrived at. The Armenians and others were told that if they would become security for Coja Awan's debts, or for the delivery up of his person within a reasonable time, well and good; but otherwise they must assist at the opening of the house and godowns, and at the taking an inventory of the furniture, or depart from the place altogether within three days time. This decisive measure ensured compliance; and it was agreed that eight Armenians, eight Moguls, eight Patans, and eight Gentoos should meet on the following Monday at Coja Awan's house, and assist the Registrar of the Court in taking an inventory of his goods. The whole matter seems to have been ultimately settled without further difficulty.

CHAPTER XX.

GOVERNORSHIP OF MR. THOMAS PITT.

1704—7.

The Governorship of Mr. Pitt extended over the unusually lengthy period of eleven years, and, as we have already indicated, was marked by some extraordinary incidents. In the years now under review it will be seen that though apprehensions were still entertained of Nabob Dawood Khan, yet the foreign relations of Fort St. George were tolerably tranquil. This state of things may be generally ascribed to the extreme old age of Aurungzebe, and the inability of the Mogul to subdue the Mahrattas; and it may here be noticed, what is scarcely noticed in the consultations, that Aurungzebe died on the 21st of February 1707, in the eighty-ninth year of his life and fiftieth of his reign. The internal events of the Presidency are however unusually interesting. Mr. Pitt had very great trouble in putting a stop to some disastrous conflicts between the Right and Left Hand castes, which for a long time occasioned an entire stoppage of the country trade, besides leading to the flight of many necessary handicraftsmen from Madras. Mr. Fraser also, who had rendered himself so obnoxious to Governor Higginson as to induce the latter to resign, took advantage of the caste dispute to engage in a quarrel with Mr. Pitt. We however leave our extracts in general to tell their own story.

The first refers to the failure of an attempt to rear silkworms and obtain raw silk in Madras.

"Monday, 1st April 1704. We finding that the experiment of making of raw silk to be very chargeable, the success of which depending entirely upon the well growing of the Mulberry trees, and this country being so excessive hot and dry, there is little hope of effecting the same. It is therefore agreed that all the Necands except two, be returned to Bengal."

The next entry illustrates the losses experienced from the claims of the Native Princes to seize all ships wrecked upon their coast; and sometimes to seize vessels which were not sufficiently manned without any pretence whatever.

"Thursday, 22nd June. In the year 1702, when Dawood Khan was besieging this place, the Governor sent the "Bedford" sloop to Tranquebar for provisions, but meeting with a long passage, was straitened for water, so that they anchored in the king of Tanjore's country, where the people seized the vessel and all the men, and put them in prison, where they lay several months and were used barbarously. The vessel they hauled into a small river, and took out her guns which were four, and also ten candy of China root, and sent it to the king. Upon this the President wrote several letters to his Chief Minister demanding satisfaction; but all the answer could be had, they pleaded the vessel was a wreck, and so of course their right. At which time the Merchants of Tanjore had several effects here, which the President would have seized, but that a Merchant here, one Sanka Ramana who has great dealings to Tanjore, pretended that he would accommodate the matter and procure satisfaction; but not having hitherto done anything in it, the President acquainted the Council that he had a few days back seized goods that came from Tanjore for the aforesaid vessel and cargo. Unto which the Council unanimously assented, hoping thereby to discourage those country people, and those adjacent to us from doing the like."

The Patriarch at Pondicherry and Bishop of St. Thomé still continued their attempts to exercise ecclesiastical authority within the English government.

"Friday, 15th September. The Capuchins here of the Portuguese Church, being under interdictions from the Patriarch and Bishop of St. Thomé, who design to put upon us what Padres they please, which may be the worst of consequences. To prevent which it is agreed, for the satisfaction of many of our inhabitants of that persuasion, that Padre Lorenso a Capuchin, be admitted into town to exercise his functions in their Church."

A serious emeute at St. Thomé between the Moorish Governor and the Portuguese Governor, is thus recorded.

"Monday, 25th. Yesterday in the evening we heard that the Portuguese and Moors' had had a quarrel wherein was killed a Portuguese gentleman Senor John Rebeiro of good fashion, and two

Moors; occasioned chiefly by the Moors Governor going after a treacherous manner to his house who they call the Governor of the Portuguese, whom he had designed to have murdered, or used him barbarously by imprisonment. The Governor of the Portuguese received a slight wound, but upon firing some arms, the Moors' Governor and his people fled; two more of whose people we hear this day died of their wounds, and three or four it is said are in danger thereof.

"Tuesday, 26th. About five this morning the Governor here received a message from the Governor and Portuguese inhabitants of St. Thomé being come to the place of our out guards; who desired admittance and protection, which was accordingly granted them; and in the evening one of their chief inhabitants, Senor Matthias Cavallo, waited on the Governor and acquainted him with the whole matter; being much as before recited, only that the original of the quarrel arose from a Moor offering to take a candle from a young woman as they were walking in procession at their feast."

The following incident is very curious, as illustrating the proselyting spirit that prevailed.

"Saturday, 12th May 1705. There being never an Ensign now in the Garrison, the Governor proposes Serjeant Dixon and Serjeant Hugonin for Ensigns, one in each Company. The objection against Dixon is from an obsolete order of the Old Company that no Roman Catholic should bear command in the Garrison; but in regard that they have since employed Commanders Supercargos to India that have been professed Roman Catholics, we hope it may warrant us in making this person an Officer ; he being likewise one of the best soldiers we have in the Garrison ; and it is not unlikely but his preferment may make him return to the Protestant religion. It is therefore agreed that the two aforesaid persons be made Ensigns, and that the Secretary draws out their Commissions accordingly." If Ensign Dixon did turn Protestant on account of receiving an Ensign's commission, he must have proved a valuable convert.

The next extract will prove interesting to local antiquarians.

"Monday, 30th July. The President proposes the hedging and ditching of the Island round, in order to the improving of it for pasture for cattle, which may be of great use to this Garrison at all times, and more especially in times of trouble from the country."

The following entry will explain itself.

"Tuesday, 28th August. We having had for above two years past great complaints of ships losing their anchors in the road, and galling their cables : which we impute to the road being very foul by the many anchors lost, which the muckyard men and all others are discouraged from sweeping for, by reason of the Company having half salvage, and they at all the charge. So to prevent so great a misfortune of any ships driving ashore, it is agreed that all people are free to sweep the Road, and to have whatever they can take up, of anchors or anything else for their labour; and no pretensions whatever to be made upon them for account of the Company or any other; which is to be notified by the Secretary putting up a paper in all languages at the Sea Gate."

The following curious incidents in reference to the wills of Roman Catholics are very significant. The Roman Catholic inhabitants of Madras had been accustomed to prove their wills before the Capuchin Friars; but complaints had reached the Governor and Council that advantage was taken of this circumstance to convey a large portion of the effects of deceased Roman Catholics to the Partriarch of Antioch at Pondicherry. Accordingly it was ordered that for the future all wills should be approved at the Company's Court. The following successful attempt to evade this law, may be best described in the words of the original entry in the consultations.

"Tuesday, 7th May, 1706. This day was read a Petition of Donna Johanna Teseira, widow of John Baptista deceased, who was many years an Alderman of this city; who, by the instigation of the Padres, a little before his death removed to St. Thomé; and leaving a will which his widow proved in the Portuguese Court there, and the estate divided according to the tenor thereof, and the Portuguese customs and laws. But since his death his daughter having married a Portuguese inhabitant of this place, who supposing that his wife had not her just dividend of her father's estate according to the English laws; her husband Gregoria De Arangeo has commenced a suit against the widow in the Mayor's Court, and has attached some moneys in this place, against which she prays relief. And that whereas her husband died at St. Thomé and the will proved there, and that all papers and accounts relating thereto remain in that Court according to custom, which they will not permit to be sent hither to make her defence. So upon mature consideration of the whole matter, and the apprehensions we have of the ill-consequences of interfering with the proceedings of the Courts of other nations; and considering that the daughter of the deceased was content with her dividend before she married, and gave discharges for the same :—It is unanimously agreed that an order be directed to the Mayor's Court to dismiss the cause, and withdraw any attachment they may have issued out against the effects of John Baptista deceased, and leave the whole matter to the Portuguese Court at St. Thomé, where all relating to this affair has been hitherto transacted."

The eccentricities of the Natives with regard to deeds and bonds, are fully illustrated by the following entry of the same date.

" There often arising in this place great disputes and demands upon accounts and bonds of ten, twenty, and thirty years standing, so that it is next to impossible to decide the same; and it being generally amongst the Natives, most of which stick at no manner of villany, for swearing, lying, forging, or any other vile action to gain their end; to prevent which it is ordered that from the 1st of January next ensuing, no bond, bill, or account shall be sueable for in any of the Courts of Justice or the Choultry of this city, that are of a longer standing than seven years; provided it can be proved that within the space of the aforesaid seven years, both parties have been resident on the place six months at one and the same time, and no demand has been made of the debt in the Mayor's Court and an action commenced for the same."

We must now retrace our steps a little to describe the movements of the Nabob Dawood Khan. In June 1705 advices had reached Governor Pitt, that Dawood had been on a visit to the king Aurungzebe, and had returned to the Carnatic with additional honours and powers. In March this year the Nabob was in the neighbourhood of Fort St. David, and a letter was received from the Agent and Council there expressing their apprehensions of Dawood Khan, and requesting to be informed whether they should make him a present. Governor Pitt replied,—" We believe it necessary to give the Nabob a present if he comes to your place, and hope to the amount of three or four hundred Pagodas may do, and we would not have you to exceed five; but if you hear he intends to come to St Thomé, it would be very well if you could evade it, and send him only a present of some liquors; telling his people that you have no orders from Madras, and that the Governor of Madras will be grateful to him for his civility to you; for if you should present and we too, both may be considerable, whereas good part of one, if not all, may be saved if you can manage it as before directed."

In April Dawood returned to Arcot and Governor Pitt complimented him with one hundred bottles of liquor. Five months aftewards we meet with the following entries in the consultation books which will explain themselves.

"Monday, 23rd September. The King's Dewan who is now at St. Thomé, who has all along shown great friendship to the Company's affairs; and now being sent for up to the Court to supply the place of his brother deceased, who was Lord Steward of the King's Household:—we think it for the interest of the Company to make him a present to the value of about two hundred or two hundred and fifty Pagodas in gold chains, or other things that may be most acceptable, leaving it to the Governor to advice therein.

"Thursday, 31st October. This day the Governor received advises that Nabob Dawood Khan was come to Poonamallee, and from thence designed for St. Thomé; upon which we immediately despatched our Moolla and Brahmin to him with a compliment.

"Saturday, 2nd November. The Nabob arriving yesterday at St. Thomé, and this morning our Moolla and Brahmin returning to us, saying that the Nabob receive dvery well the Governor's compliment, and did intend to come and stay some days at a Garden house a little to the southward of the town; which was ordered to be cleaned up for his reception if he continued that resolution, which we were resolved should not be encouraged to by any invitation. They likewise told us that they believed he came not with a design to give us any trouble, which they infer from the small force he brought with him, which were not above five or six hundred horse and foot. He also showed an earnest desire to dine with the Governor."

This intelligence was not wholly satisfactory. Dawood Khan had the whole country at his command, and might have ordered other forces to follow him from Arcot. Moreover he spoke many kind things of the English nation, which the Moors " usually do of all people, when they are carrying on the worst of designs against them." Accordingly two members of Council and the Secretary were sent to pay their respects to him at St. Thomé; but were directed to give no answer about the dinner, and to say they had no instructions upon the subject. The next day, being Sunday, the three gentlemen proceeded to St. Thomé, and met with " extraordinary kind reception." Dawood Khan presented them each with an emerald ring, worth about thirty or forty Pagodas a piece; and also sent a jewel to Governor Pitt of the value of a hundred or hundred and fifty Pagodas. But amidst all this ostentation he ardently pressed for an invitation to dinner; and though the deputation postponed their answer, yet Governor Pitt considered it expedient to send an immediate invitation to the Nabob, upon the condition however, that he would not bring with him more than twenty of his guards. Dawood Khan made the necessary promise, and the Governor made the necessary preparations for the dinner. The result is fully recorded in the consultations as follows.

" Monday, 4th November. Narrain and the

Moolla went to wait on the Nabob at St. Thomé as ordered this day, and the gentlemen of council to the Garden, whither he came about noon; when Narrain discerning that a considerable part of his forces followed him, at least 200 horse and foot, told him he hoped he did not expect the Governor should admit them all into the Fort, who he was confident would not admit any more than what was agreed on. Therefore he desired the Nabob to keep his promise, to which he answered that if he went all those must be admitted with him. So lighted at the Garden and bid Narrain go and acquaint the Governor with his resolution, and that if he would not be received with all his Company, it should be the same thing to him if we sent the dinner to him where he was at the Garden. With which message Narrain came, and soon after the Secretary confirmed the same; when the Governor positively refused to receive him with more than twenty men. So ordered the dinner immediately to be carried to him to the Garden, with all other necessaries; whither the Secretary and Narrain returned, who were to acquaint the other gentlemen with the Governor's resolution; and that the Guns he intended to fire they should acquaint the Nabob were for the King's health, his own, and such of the Great Ministers of State as were his friends. About five in the evening the English gentlemen returned from the Garden and gave the Governor the following account. That the Nabob first seemed out of humour at the answer that was sent him, when it was believed he would not dine there; but after some pausing he dissembled his resentment and sat down to dinner, and ate heartily, and tasted the liquors sent him which he liked very well. After dinner the present was set before him, which at first he seemingly refused, but afterwards accepted of it; and soon after he rose up and returned to St. Thomé."

The following entry records another scrape of Captain Seaton's.

"Thursday, 27th February, 1707. The Governor lays before the Council the insolent action of Captain Seaton, who on Sunday last marched part of his Company (and had all had not the Governor commanded them off) over the Company's calicoes that lay a dyeing; notwithstanding there was much more than room enough to have marched the men clear of them as usual. And afterwards when the Governor sent for him to demand his reason for doing so base an action, he had the impudence to tell him he did not understand it. Upon which, when he came for the word in the evening, the Governor told him that he was suspended till he had advised with the Council; for that he thought him not fitting to serve the Company any longer, nor would he bear any more with his insolencies. It is agreed that he stands suspended, and that the consideration of breaking him be referred to another time." A year afterwards Captain Seaton having appealed to the Directors on the strength of his twenty years service, and pleaded some extenuating circumstances, was reinstated in the command of the garrison.

The following curious entry will explain itself.

"Tuesday, 17th June. The Governor produces a letter from Robert Berriman of Fort St. David, wherein he declares that he had contracted marriage with Mrs. Wilson who lately died here, to whom he had made several presents, which were found in her lodgings at her death, when the Paymaster took an account of her effects. So considering the low circumstances of Berriman, it is agreed that upon his taking his oath to the list of the things he demands, that they were presented her upon account of the intended marriage, that the Paymaster delivers him the same."

We now have to draw attention to the quarrel which broke out between the Right and Left Hand Castes,* and which is fully described in the following extracts.

---

* The distinction between the two Hands is said to be of recent origin, as no mention is made of them in any of the ancient books. Moreover it is almost unknown in the North, and is indeed chiefly confined to a part only of Southern India. In the latter districts, most of the Hindoo castes are thus separated. The left-hand includes the whole tribe of the Vaisya or merchants, the Panchala or five castes of artisans, together with some other mean tribes of the Sudras, and especially the caste of Chakili or cobblers. The Right-hand includes the most distinguished castes of the Sudras, but its strongest bulwark is the Pariah caste, which still glories in the title of "Friends of the Right-hand."

The opposition between the two hands arises from certain privileges to which they both lay claim. The matter is generally some trifling violation of mamool or custom, but not unfrequently leads to bloody disputes. Dabors mentions a contest so dreadful, that many of the

"Thursday, 26th June, 1707. There having been lately a dispute between the Right and Left Hand Castes, that live in the Pettah, about passing some streets on occasion of their weddings, insomuch that the Governor was obliged to order Guards to lie out to keep the peace. To prevent further disturbance it is agreed that Mr. Raworth the Paymaster takes with him the Gunner, and Scrampa and Narrain, Heads for the Right Hand Caste, and Colloway and Vinkettee Chitties Heads for the Left Hand Caste ; and that they survey the Pettahs, and consider of what method may be taken to prevent any further disputes of the like nature, and report the same to the Governor and Council.

"Thursday, 17th July. Mr. Raworth and the Gunner, as also the Heads of the Right and Left Hand Castes, report that they had surveyed the Pettah, and produced a draught of all the streets and buildings in the Pettah, which showed us what streets were chiefly inhabited by the Left Hand Caste, being Bridge Gate street, and that which is called the Chief Peons street ; wherein lives but few of the Right Hand Caste. So to preserve the peace between the two aforesaid Castes for the future, we hereby order that those few of the Right hand Caste in the aforementioned

---

peaceful inhabitants began to leave their villages, just as if a Mahratta invasion were impending. This terrible commotion arose from a member of the Left-hand sticking red flowers into his turban. To this day nothing but the strong arm of the police prevents Madras itself from being frequently the scene of similar disturbances.

streets sell their houses, and go and live in the streets amongst their own Caste ; and that those two streets are peculiarly appropriated for the Left Hand Caste to pass in at their making their weddings and Festivals ; and that none of the Right Hand Caste give them the least disturbance in that precinct at their utmost peril. And it is further ordered that neither Caste may pretend ignorance of these limits, that the Paymaster sets up four Stones at the cost of the Left Hand Caste, according as we have directed him in the draught, and insert thereon in English and Gentoo the purport of this our order."

"Thursday, 14th August. The Governor acquaints the Council that on the 12th at night some disaffected persons to the Government had placed papers on the Stones set up in our Pettah, which stinted the bounds of the Left Hand Caste ; which papers were wrote in the Malabar language and now produced.

"Since the foundation of this city no such thing has been known. By the authority of the Government and prevalence of money this Pillar was erected, in contempt and derison of the Right Hand Caste, who will forfeit the rights of their caste if they do not destroy the others like dogs and tumble them down. If it be demanded by whose order this was written, it is by the will of the King of England and the Company, who will not fail to bring these things to pass ; and this by way of caution."

"The persons unknown also laid at the foot of the Stone, a sort of an enchantment as is esteemed in this country, pieces of skulls with rice and other mixtures. From the translate of the paper it is easily to be inferred that some Europeans have had a hand in it; there being expressions that these people are wholly strangers to. Of which we having considered are come to the following result, that a paper be fixed on each stone in all languages, as also on the Gates in the English and Black town; that if any person shall come and inform us of what person or persons have fixed the aforementioned paper on those Pillars, they shall have one hundred Pagodas reward, and his pardon if concerned therein. The Heads of the Right Hand Caste were sent for before us, who being charged with having a hand in writing these papers, which they denied; agreed that a month's time be given them to find out the person or persons who wrote them; and that if they do not find them, they are to be fined such a sum of money as the Governor and Council think fit; and this they were acquainted with.

"Tuesday, 19th August. The Governor acquaints the Board that on Sunday last, being the 17th instant, that the Right Hand Caste with a Wedding went in great pomp through the street which was ordered lately by the Governor and Council for the Weddings of the Left Hand Caste; and that upon hearing of which, he sent out a party of soldiers who seized nineteen of them, who are now in prison in the Choultry, who he resolves to punish and make examples.

"The Right Hand Caste came to the Fort this day in a considerable body, and delivered in a Petition as entered after this consultation; with the heads of which we had a long debate, and what they said tended, as well as the purport of their Petition, for us to retract what we have done, and that we would give up the Left Hand Caste a sacrifice to them.

"The Petition of the eighteen sorts of people of the Right Hand Castes belonging to Chinnapatam.

"Humbly Sheweth,

Whereas upon the first settlement of the English in this place, the liberty was granted your Petitioners' Castes to have their streets and habitations from Tom Clarke's Gate and the Bridge Gate, both within and without; and to the Left Hand Caste was granted from Mud Point Gate, both within and without; two streets which was kept and observed by each Caste till broken by the troubles which happened to the French at St. Thomé. At which time several people retired hither, and without knowledge or permission from the Government, built their houses one amongst the other in both the Pettahs; which being complained of to Sir Willliam Langhorn, and the ill effects of the falling out of the two Castes being taken into consideration, it was ordered that they should not live together; but that the Right Hand people should go to the place that was first granted them to inhabit, and that the Left Hand should go to theirs. Accordingly to which order the Right Hand people did obey, and likewise some of the Left Hand people; but others did desire leave to stay till the rains was over, which was granted, but after to retire to their own streets; which to this day they have not done, but rather have encroached more upon your Petitioner's liberty. Likewise the Weddings that were made by the Left Hand people that lived amongst your Petitioners, were ordered to be kept always in their own streets; but if it happened that they did make any Weddings in your Petitioners' streets, it was to be done privately in their own houses, without any music, or any such ceremony. But they now very unreasonably desire your Petitioners' streets, which never was done before; and they having complained to your Honour, but upon what account or reason we do not know. Now in the streets wherein the Stones are erected, there are one hundred of your Petitioners houses, with several Wells, Churches, Gardens, and Choultries; all which belong to your Petitioners the Right Hand people. Being very many, being twenty-one Castes in all of these people, we cannot tell every one's mind. The country people have sent letters to us, but what they can do for us we do not know. We all living under your Honour's protection, are afraid to disoblige your Honour, therefore stay very quiet. From the beginning of the world to this day it never was known that any Government did take away your Petitioner's streets, and give them to the Left Caste people, which they know to be true. Now they (the Left Hands) having made many false complaints to your Honour, which is the occasion of all this trouble; for the streets where the Stones are erected are the first streets of the Right Hand Castes for all strangers that come from the country. For these streets that your Honour has given to the Left Hand Castes is a very great dissatisfaction to all the Right Hand Caste people. Therefore your most humble Petitioners desire your Honour would be pleased to take into consideration, and they shall as in duty bound ever pray."

"Friday, 22nd August. The foregoing consultations of late mention several passages relating to the Right Hand Caste and Left. Of the former many have deserted us, and the others have locked themselves up in their houses in town; which, chiefly consisting of Boatmen, Washermen, Fishermen, and other necessary handicrafts, the Governor summoned all his Council except Mr. Fraser; who he was jealous had betrayed us in what we had done, as to settling the dispute between the Castes. And the Governor gave us this instance of it. That when on the 19th past, he acquainted the Board of the insolence of the Pariahs who went through the Left Hand streets with a Wedding and what he had done thereon; when immediately Mr. Fraser according to his custom made a long senseless speech, the purport shewing that he was now against what had been transacted in consultation about the Castes; which no notice was taken of, as coming from him. But then the next minute the Right Hand Caste delivered their Petition, which was presently read, and entirely agreed with the purport of what just before Mr. Fraser spoke. When the Governor immediately charged him with making or reading of it, which he then denied in great confusion, and the same was taken notice of by Messrs. Raworth and Frederick present in Council. So the Governor this day laying before the Board the worst of consequences that might attend the Company's affairs, as well as our own persons, to have one amongst us to betray our counsels; of which the Council being equally sensible, desired Mr. Fraser might be sent for; which was accordingly done. When he was charged with what before mentioned, and told by the Governor that it was impossible that he could make a speech so coherent with a Petition that was just after delivered in, without having made or read it; to which he made no other defence than that we should prove it if we could. The Governor at the same time charged him with directing the Malabar inscription that was put upon the Stones, which he denied with strange asseveration and execrations, but to the making or reading the Petition only a plain denial. So after he told us he had no more to say in his defence, the Governor desired him to withdraw, which he refused to do, but afterwards obliged him to it.

"When we debated the nature of his offence, and the ill consequences of any of the Council encouraging Petitions against our proceedings in general, or such in particular as he himself seemingly agreed to, without the least hesitation to anything that was done relating to the castes :— the Governor to prevent his doing further mischief, pressed the necessity of his being suspended the Company's service ab officio et beneficio ; alleging that no inconveniency could accrue from it, for that his abilities were so little considerable, that all of us knew in our consciences that he

never merited rice and water from the Company;
but yet with his malice, pride, and envy, he has
often made strange progress in mischief, and
wholly incapable of doing good. And it is not
amiss to insert one or two passages, though
foreign to this present matter. Some time past,
upon a suspicion that there was a difference between the Governor and Mr. Raworth, an impudent Dubash, that was often trusted with Mr.
Fraser's whispers, came up to Mr. Raworth in his
chamber, and told him that he heard there was a
difference between the Governor and him, and that
he treated him as he did others; but if he would
stand against him and come and join with Mr.
Fraser and his party, he was sure they would be
able to suppress him: upon which Mr. Raworth
treated him as became him by kicking him down
stairs. About five years past there came from Goa
a Theatine Padre, an Englishman, Milton by name,
who often passed between this place and Fort St.
David, and several times came to the Governor for
leave to build a Chapel here or at Fort St. David;
which he positively refused him, considering that
the worst of consequences must attend it, or that
it would be to the great dislike of the Company to
have an English priest here of the Popish religion,
for that being such he ought to die by our law.
Yet nevertheless one Joseph Hiller, a great consort
of Mr. Fraser, bought a piece of ground here
(without any leave or knowledge of the Governor)
for Milton; on which he immediately erected a
fabrick after the model of a convent, and had made
considerable progress therein, before the Governor,

who was going to the Garden one morning, knew anything of it. When he immediately sent for Padre Milton, and demanded of him how he came by that ground, and who gave him leave to build on it; who answered Mr. Hiller bought it for him. Upon which the Governor ordered him immediately to desist from building, and by six at night to depart the place; which he accordingly did to St. Thomé; where a little time after, Mr. Fraser and others went to dinner with him, and has often been seen conversing with him at that end of the town. Thus whenever the Governor has frowned upon any one for crimes and misdemeanors, whether white men or black, it is well known they were always cherished by Mr. Fraser; who has been the pest of the Government, as well as the ridicule and scum of the place. Yet notwithstanding all before mentioned is well known to be great truths to every man that sits at the Board, who desired the Governor to leave him out in the sorting Summons, for that he was so impertinent and troublesome that no business could be done; yet they were generally unwilling to suspend him the service, till the Governor solemnly averred that he would sit no more with him in Council, nor give his opinion in any affairs more of the Company's where he was present; which induced the Council unanimously to suspend him the Company's service officio et beneficio till their pleasure was known in this matter; which the Secretary is ordered to acquaint him therewith, and that we will give him a copy of what we write home to the

Company relating to him, that so his defence and answer may go therewith."

The following extract from a General Letter from the Court of Directors, dated 4th February, 1708, will show how Mr. Fraser fared, notwithstanding the abuse bestowed on him by Governor Pitt.

"The charge against Mr. Fraser we have considered, and would hope no Englishman, especially none of our servants, would be guilty of such pernicious practices, which strike at the root of the well being of the place; and are more inclined to this opinion, because we find in the consultation of the 22nd August, that the Council were generally unwilling to suspend him, which we cannot think they would be if they apprehended he was justly taxed; and that it was Mr. Pitt's solemn averring he would sit no more with him, that prevailed with them. We have therefore reinstated him, as thinking it not fit to give so much countenance to any Governor whatsoever, as to approve his single opinion, against all the rest of the Council, in a case of this nature, which if it was true does not fully appear to us to have been proved; though we shall always lodge a power in our President and Council to suspend any of the Council or other subordinates, when they have or think they have a just reason; and if it be of great crimes they are charged with that deserves confinement, we shall approve it."

For the sequel of the dispute between the Right and Left Hands we must refer our readers to our next chapter.

CHAPTER XXI.

QUARRELS BETWEEN THE RIGHT AND LEFT HANDS IN THE GOVERNORSHIP OF MR. THOMAS PITT.

1707.

The quarrel between the Right and Left Hand Castes, which resulted in the flight of the former to St. Thomé, is one so extraordinary in its nature, and so illustrative of the character of the people, that we have deemed it advisable to tell the whole story as much as possible in the language of the Records, only abridging those portions which are mere recapitulations. These extracts are all taken from the consultation books during the latter half of 1707, and are arranged in strict chronological order

"Monday, 25th August, 1707. This morning early the Governor summoned twelve of the principal of the heads of each Caste, who were shut up in a room to adjust matters now in dispute between the Castes; which they acquainted him about noon they had done. Upon which at four this afternoon the Council was summoned, when the number of each Caste appeared; when unanimously and in a most solemn manner they declared they had agreed on the following terms.

"1st. That none but the Right Hand Caste

should live in the Pettah commonly called the Pedda Naik's Pettah.

"2nd. That the Pettah called Mootel Pettah should be inhabited by none but the Left Hand Caste.

"3rd. That whereas there are a great many of the Left Hand Caste in the Pedda Naik's Pettah, and so likewise of the Right Hand Caste in Mootel Pettah, it is agreed that each Caste commence removing their Houses on or before the 1st of December to their respective Pettahs before mentioned; and that the same be all completed on or before the 1st of June, 1708; and if any that have houses in either of the Pettahs can agree upon the sale or exchange thereof, they are at liberty to do it, or pull down and carry the materials to the Pettah appointed for them to live in.

"4th. That no Weddings by either Caste shall be made in the streets in the Pedda Naik's Pettah lately in dispute between them, till that Pettah be wholly inhabited by the Right Hand Caste.

"5th. That in Mootel Pettah they shall keep their Weddings there according to custom, till the Right Hand Caste are removed out of it.

"6th. That in neither of these Pettahs before mentioned, no one shall sell his house but to one of his own Caste.

"7th. That whereas there are Boatmen, Laskars, and Fishermen that have their houses by the sea side in Mootel Pettah, it is agreed that they remain there as they now are, without giving any molestation to the Left Hand Caste.

"8th. That as we ordered in Consultation of the 17th July Stones to be erected for stinting the limits of the Left Hand Caste making their Weddings in the Pedda Naik's Pettah, and a suitable inscription thereon;—we now at the request of both Castes agree that the inscription be cut out; but the Stones remain for such inscriptions to be made on them as the Governor and Council shall think fit hereafter.

"To all the foregoing articles the Governor and Council do now agree; with which the Right Hand Caste are ordered to acquaint their people that are now withdrawn, that they now return to their obedience without further delay; which they readily promise to do.

"Wednesday, 27th. Notwithstanding that all matters seem to be so fairly adjusted before us on the 25th past between the two Castes, we have seen no good effect of it by the people returning to their duty. So the Governor ordered this day to to be brought before him in Council, Serapa, Nara Verona, Sunka Rama, and Andee Chitty, —and charged them as chief instruments in raising the present rebellion; and the information of which he had had from one of their own Caste, who was in the conspiracy, who said they had a great difficulty to stir up the poor Handicrafts; and that the Pariahs who are the most numerous, refused to stir unless they sent with them one of their heads of the Caste with one thousand Pagodas to pay their subsistence, which they accordingly complied with; and the Governor was informed who had contributed thereto;

and when they proposed it to the Boatmen, Washermen, and Fishermen, they likewise refused, saying they would not leave the livelihood they had there for an uncertainty ; but with much persuasion they prevailed with them, upon giving them a note under their hands that they would pay them in proportion for the days they were absent, according to what they usually got here ; and that they would allow Batta or subsistence money to all that should desert us (of which the Governor had daily intelligence from St. Thomé) which was paid them. They (the four Natives summoned) denied all ; knowing that whoever of their Caste came in as evidence against them was in no small danger of their life. So the aforementioned prisoners the Governor ordered to be kept in safe custody, and used suitable to their crimes.

"Friday, 29th. This day were before us Serapa, Nara Verona, Sunka Rama, and Andee Chitty of the Right Hand Caste, and Colloway Chitty, Vinkettee Chitty, Petombee Chitty, and Cornapa Chitty of the Left Hand Caste ; when having a Brahmin present, they swore to be true to the Company's interest, and to lay aside all animosity between them relating to their castes, or any other dispute ; and that they would use their utmost influence to compose the present differences on that account ; as also to stand by the agreement made in Consultation the 25th instant ; and for the security of Serapa and the other three, four of the Right Hand Caste, the Pedda Naik, and ten Cuomities were bound for their personal appearance.

"The Governor acquainting that none that had deserted were come in since the agreement between the two Castes, which he imparted to their fear as well as shame. So advised that a paper might be published in the nature of a general pardon; which he now produced, and was read, and accordingly agreed to, and ordered to be set up in the Gates and Mettows in the Gentoo and Malabar, and one in English at the Sea gate as follows:

"Whereas some wicked and evil designing people of the Right Hand Caste, seduced by others as wicked in the Government,* have went about for some sinister ends to make an insurrection and rebellion in this Government; and the better to effect their hellish designs, have deluded the poor and ignorant with a false notion that we, the Governor and Council, had favoured the Left Hand Caste to prejudice theirs; whereas nothing was done by us but by the advice and consent of the principal of their heads; and since this dispute has happened, matters have been thoroughly canvassed by twelve of each heads of the Caste, and all differences adjusted and finally ended before us in Council; yet nevertheless, we hear that some people are still carrying on their ill designs to disturb the peace and tranquillity of the Government, which induces us to publish this our order and intentions.

"That whereas we have always showed great tenderness of the welfare of our inhabitants, and

---

* A hit at Mr. Fraser.

took especial care to provide for the poor and labouring people, who three or four of the rich and crafty have imposed upon them, so as to make them desert us, and to terrify them from returning to their duty, give out the Government will punish them suitable to their crimes.

"We therefore have thought fit to publish this our General Pardon to all such who have been concerned in this insurrection; promising and declaring that such who return to their habitations and duty on or before the 10th of September next, are pardoned hereby to all intents and purposes, as if they had not been concerned therein; and such as do not comply herewith, their houses and estates shall be seized for the Company's use, and their persons when and wherever apprehended; within the Company's jurisdiction, shall be proceeded against with the utmost rigour; and more particularly such who shall after the date hereof contribute any money or otherwise towards the upholding, maintaining, or employing any that shall not come in by the time herein limited. Sealed with the Company's seal, and dated at Fort St. George, this 29th day of August, one thousand seven hundred and seven."

Nothing appears to have transpired between the 29th of August and the 10th of September specified in the General Pardon; but on the latter date we find the following significant entry.

"Wednesday, 10th September. The Governor summoned the Council to acquaint them, that he was just then informed that in the night the Stones were stolen away; which we considered of, and though the impudence of the action deserves the strictest enquiry and punishment, and the immediate erecting others, yet it was unanimously agreed that we desist from doing either till these troubles are over; though obliged the Pedda Naik to give twenty thousand Pagodas for his personal appearance, who must doubtless have a hand in it, or at least knows of the taking away the Stones.

"Those of the Right Hand Caste that have deserted, retiring to St. Thomé, have sent for the heads of their Caste out of the country, who wrote us this day a most saucy and impudent letter, the translate of which is entered after this consultation, wherein is a clause that they cite former Consultations; which is a plain indication that some of our people had the penning of that letter; and though they quote is as a precedent for us, it is a sign they do not understand it, we having acted in this matter exactly according to that clause.

"From Dellaway Donne Paulo Chitty, etc., of the Right Hand Caste, of the four corners and fifty six countries of the world, to the Hon'ble Thomas Pitt, Esq. and Council.

"From the first foundation of Madras it was never known that the Left Hand Caste should be adhered to by wrongly informing your Honours to the prejudice of the Right Hand Caste; upon whose assertions you have erected Stones in our streets, and given the same from us; concerning which an address was made to your Honours by way of Petition, upon perusal whereof you directed that your Petitioners were at liberty to stay or go where they pleased, which you repeated three times. Accordingly they came to St. Thomé, from whom they wrote your Honours; and we hearing the matters are come hither.

"From the beginning of the world it was never before known that the Left Hand in the fifty six countries thereof, ever erected a Stone in the Right Hand Street, nor was it ever allowed by any Government.

"One of your predecessors with Timmia and Verona did appoint certain streets for the Left Hand Caste, and directed how they should act, as upon your Consultation does appear; upon examination whereof advantage would accrue to the Company, which you have hitherto omitted to do.

"From your first settlement justice and equity have been distributed with an equal hand in your place; which has occasioned many to resort to you, and to increase in wealth under your protection; but upon this occasion of erecting Stones we must have recourse to the customs of the country; this we write to a charitable people who we know will observe the same.

St. Thomé, September 9th, 1707.

"Sunday, 14th. The Armenians, Persians, and Patans, perceiving that the Governor and Council was not fairly dealt with in this dispute between the Castes; and that the persons who are employed and confided in to accommodate it, are of the Right Hand Caste, all of whom had been either active or passive in raising this difference; and knowing we had no other, they came in a body of fifty or sixty, and tendered their service. When the Governor summoned what of the Council were to be found, and we accepted of their service and mediation; who promised to-morrow to go some of them to St. Thomé, to which place the Right Hand Caste have retired and sent for several of their heads out of the country, who are come to them; and they promised to take with them Narrain our Brahmin and Moolla, when they will demand of them the reason of their desertion, and accommodate matters as well as they can, and as soon as possible.

"Monday, 15th. The Governor with the Secretary being writing a General Letter to the Company in the Consultation Room, there came a Gusbardar, or messenger, to him from St. Thomé, who was sent by the Nabob to turn out the old Governor there, and put in a new one. He had been here two or three times before, and seemed to be concerned at the troubles we had about the Castes; which he said were frequent in the country, and sometimes grew to such a pitch that the Government found a great deal of trouble and difficulty to quell them; and he said that, by some discourse he had had with them, he found them very impudent and saucy; and that the source of our troubles was not from them in St. Thomé, but from our own inhabitants that remained in town, who not only gave them directions, but also sent them their subsistence. He also added, saying to the Governor, you are likewise betrayed by some people that sits with you at this Table. So asking him by the Linguist what he meant, he answered that yesterday, talking with three or four of the heads of Castes, they told him that the Second of

Council (Mr. Fraser) was of their side; and that without he was restored to his employ they would not return on any terms; but if he would come they would meet him anywhere, and return with him without insisting on any pardon; for that they were assured he was their friend, and that he never consented to what the Governor and Council had done in favour of the Left Hand Caste, and that he was against putting up the Stones; which belief in them had gained him such a reputation amongst the mob, that they went up and down the streets in his hearing, crying out "Chinna Captain," "Chinna Captain," which implies in their language the Second. On which the Governor asked him (the Gusbardar) whether he had heard such discourse more than once from the heads of the Caste. He answered three or four times, and the mob crying out as before mentioned. Upon which the Governor told him that in the evening there would be several of his people there to talk to them, when we desired him to aver what he was told before by the heads of the Castes; to which he readily answered he would. This man seemed to be a very sober judicious person, a stranger in these parts of the country, and could have no manner of interest in saying what he did. There was present at this discourse the Secretary whom the Governor ordered to take Minutes; and for Linguist was present the Moolla Narrain, and Paupilia Brahmin; who all averred that whereas they had been several times to St. Thomé about this business, they had often heard the mob cry out for the Chinna Captain.

"Tuesday, 16th. The Governor summoned this Council, when he reported to them what discourse he had with the Gusbardar, as entered in a diary note of yesterday, in the presence of the Secretary, Moolla, Narrain, and Paupilia Brahmin, who all confessed the same. The three latter now acquainted us that yesterday in the afternoon they accompanied several of the Persians and Armenians to St. Thomé, in order to accommodate this difference between the Castes; who were stopped by the mob at the Gate, whilst they sent in word to their heads for admittance; where they continued near two hours, and no answer but several affronts; and whilst there heard the mob cry out, as the Gusbardar told us, for the Chinna Captain, and who asked Narrain and several of our people why he did not come, for nothing could be done towards their return without him. The heads of the Right Hand Caste at St. Thomé wrote several letters to those of their Caste remaining here (at Madras); threatening their lives and being turned out of their Caste, if they did not come to them. This much intimidated the poor people, but those of any substance little regarded it, since that we kept so good guards to defend them from the threats; and what is to be observed and generally believed that all the people who have left us are not worth five thousand Pagodas. Narrain likewise acquainted us that all the heads of the Right Hand Caste remaining in town, met last night and wrote a letter to our inhabitants of their Caste in St. Thomé; the purport of which was to let them know they were satisfied in all matters relating to their Caste; and therefore whatever ill consequences attend further disputes, they cleared themselves of it and laid it wholly at their doors. The messenger that carried the letter just now arriving was brought in before us, who acquainted us that they at St. Thomé had returned no answer to their Caste in writing, but bid him tell them that they would accept no Cowle than what was signed by Mr. Fraser, and that the Stones must be brought to St. Thomé or put into the Pagoda. We were also at this time speaking of a report that had run about town for two or three days, that the Castes were rose one against the other at Fort St. David, where several had been killed, amongst which four or five of our soldiers and an officer mortally wounded. The Governor said he believed it not, though he had heard of it. Mr. Frederick said he had heard it from several, but being also told it by his dubash, who said he had it told him from Mr. Fraser's dubash, who was sent for, when denied it. But the other confronting him with naming the time and place, where and when he had told it him, caused the Governor to give credit to it, and punished him immediately for spreading false reports. This was done to encourage the Right Hand Caste, and doubtless by order of his master, or some of his accomplices; whose chief dubash one Fango, a crafty profligate villain, is actually now at St. Thomé, holding with the Right Hand Caste in all their counsels. So hearing all before mentioned in this day's consultation, and what passed yesterday with the Gusbardar, rivets in us a belief that the

Right Hand Caste has got Mr. Fraser among them for their tool, or they durst not have adventured to have done what they have. So considering that if this quarrel between them increases, it will be an unspeakable prejudice to the Company, and effectual ruin to the place; and to agree to their insolent and saucy demands may in futurity be attended with the like ill consequences:— to prevent all which it is agreed to send for Mr. Fraser, when the Governor charged him with what before mentioned, and telling him, from which we are sufficiently confirmed, that he was at the head of this vile and base action, which occasioned the dispute between the Castes, that no less than threatened the destruction of the place. To which he answered that it was all a grand suppose, and flatly denied all. So being ordered to withdraw we considered of the whole matter; when it was unanimously agreed that Mr. Fraser, who is now removing out his lodgings in the Fort to a house in the town, that he be continued therein and confined, without permitting any one to come to discourse him, but in the presence of the sentinel. The Captain of the Guard was sent for, to whom the Governor gave a charge accordingly."

"Tuesday, 23rd. The Governor and Council having granted a pardon to the Right Hand Caste (now at St. Thomé) being at the request of several Persians and Armenians, who desired that Doctor Lewis and Padre Michael may go with them to deliver the pardon and accompany them in their return. Accordingly the refractory members of the Right Hand Caste came out of St. Thomé all together about nine this morning. But when they came near the town, they took disgust at something or other, the certainty unknown to us, and returned again to St. Thomé; the Pariahs surrounded the inhabitants and forced them to go with them. So Narrain, being in hopes of giving them satisfaction, went with them, who they abused in several respects and confined; but was the next day discharged upon a threatening letter from the Governor that he would fetch him by force."

The pardon which had proved so nearly successful in bringing the Right Hand Caste from St. Thomé was as follows.

" A Cowle granted by Thomas Pitt, Esq., Governor of Fort St. George, and Council to the Right Hand Caste.

" Whereas you deserted us by reason of our giving your streets to the Left Hand Caste, which we have again returned to you; and whereas you say we have given a writing to them on that account or any other, we say it is forged and false, if any such one be produced. Therefore you may depend upon this Cowle, and return to your duty, and enjoy your ancient privileges according to salabad; giving this before the Great God above and Jesus Christ that we will righteously perform, and that none shall be punished on this account hereafter. Given under our hands and the Hon'ble Company's seal in Fort St. George, this 22nd of September, 1707."

The failure of this pardon seems to have driven Governor Pitt frantic, if we may judge from the following extraordinary resolution, which he arrived at the following day.

"Wednesday, 24th. We finding no likelihood of putting an end to these troubles between the Castes, for that the insolency of the Pariahs daily increases, a particular instance of which we had yesterday by their forcing the inhabitants to return, and imprisoning and abusing Narrain. The Governor proposed the attacking of St. Thomé the 26th at break of day (where they are harboured) and put as many of them as possible to the sword, but no inhabitant of any Caste else; which was unanimously agreed to in Council, and preparations immediately made accordingly; resolving to march two hundred and fifty soldiers, two hundred talliars, and two hundred peons, as also eighteen hundred peons which the Left Hand Caste have raised since the troubles for their security; and the Governor disposed matters to effect the same.

"Thursday, 25th. The preparations being made for attacking our Pariahs in St. Thomé to-morrow morning, which alarmed several inhabitants, more especially Armenians, Moors, etc. who nightly importuned us to desist; for that many ill consequences would attend it, and that they were sure we could not effect our ends in cutting off the Pariahs, who would certainly fly into the country; besides our Pedda Naik who pressed us to desist from our intended enterprise; saying that the new Governor of St. Thomé would be there to night, with whom he was well acquainted, and could prevail with him to turn them out of the town, or else he would be obliged to bring the Governor twenty or thirty of their heads. So considering the numerous importunities, we deferred our design two or three days to see whether milder means would oblige their return.

"Wednesday, 1st October. The Governor acquainted the Council that he observes the new Governor of St. Thomé is weary of our mob, and seems to endeavour what he can to persuade them to return. Yesterday our people going in hopes to have brought them back, they then insisted upon signing a paper amongst themselves, and that those we sent should join them; which they refused, telling them they could not do it without the Governor's leave; the purport of which paper is that they may have leave to rebel when they please; the translate of it is as follows.

"All the inhabitants of the Right Hand Caste of Chinnapatam have entered into an agreement in the presence of the Right Hand Caste of the country, viz.

"Whereas the Left Hand Caste have broke the sallabad by erecting Stones in our streets, upon which we deserted the place, and are come hither; since which the Governor and Council have taken away the Stones, and given us their Cowle that all shall be settled and go according to sallabad, which we will unanimously endeavour to maintain; and notwithstanding, should the Governor act contrary to his Cowle, or that the Left Hand Caste should take upon them more than their duty, we jointly agree to stand by one another for the saving our credit; and whoever of us act contrary to which herein mentioned shall be turned out of the Caste, and the iniquities shall light upon them as befalls such who sacrifices a cow, woman Brahmin, and their mother before the River Ganges. Dated October 1st, 1707."

"So upon our shewing a detestation and abhorrence to give leave to their signing such a paper, it was laid aside; and, as the Governor is credibly informed, that that paper, as well as others we have received during these troubles from the Right Hand Caste, were drawn up and framed by that notorious miscreant Timapa, a fellow adapted to all manner of villany, and always a great favourite and privy counsellor of Mr. Fraser, and a companion of his chief dubash."

"The heads of the Castes and mob which deserted us, having accepted of our pardon the 22nd last month, and still every day starting new demands, and refuse to return, we unanimously agreed this day to send to them our Moolla and Brahmin, to demand of them their final answer, whether they would return upon our pardon or not, and if not to demand it of them.

"Thursday, 2nd The Moolla and Brahmin returning last night from St. Thomé, acquainted us that according to our order they had demanded our pardon given our inhabitants that are fled there; who have refused to return it, promising that they would come back to-day, but that it was not a good day; but to-morrow or next day they would not fail, if those of their Caste here came to meet them. At last, as will be seen by the following entry, the refractory Right Hands were induced to return.

"Saturday, 4th. This evening about seven o'clock the Governor of St. Thomé, being a Gentoo and of the same Caste that deserted us, came with our people that went hence this morning, and brought back all the deserters. The heads appeared before the Governor and were dismissed to their habitations, with assurances that their pardon should be kept inviolable.

"Monday, 6th. Muttombee, the Governor of St. Thomé, having to all appearance taken a great deal of pains to effect the returning of those that deserted;—it is therefore agreed that the following present be made him; the amount of which, in a seasonable time, to be paid the Company by the Right Hand Caste.

"Scarlet 1 piece... Aurora, 1 piece... Ordinary Red, 1 [piece.
Green 1 piece... Looking Glasses... Swords 4,
1 Pair Pistols..... 6 Pair Spectacles. Knives and pen-
1 piece of Serge. [knives.

"The deserters or rebels returning the 4th at night, who for some time refused to accept our pardon, or any proposals but what should be made by Mr. Fraser; for which reasons therein he was confined; after which they never so much as mentioned his name, so that none can believe but that they moved by his direction; but being returned again, agreed that his confinement be taken off, and he set at liberty; when the Captain of the Guard was sent for, and the Governor acquainted him therewith."

A fortnight's quiet passed away, and the storm having subsided, we find the following entries.

"Monday, 20th. The Washermen that deserted upon the late dispute between their Castes, who on their return freely declared that they were forced away by the heads of their Caste, who had combined with the Belljawarr; besides they complained of great injustices that they had received from the heads of their Caste, and desired they may have other four heads; and they would not only pay what the Washers pay, but also sign a paper that they would not desert again on any pretence whatever. Upon which they presented four heads of their own choosing, which we approved of and tasherift them when the whole body signed the paper as agreed on.

"Tuesday, 21st. The officer at Bridge Gate bringing in this morning to the Governor a Cajan letter that he found hung upon a post near the Gate, which when translated seemed to be from a body of the Right Hand Caste; the purport of which was to disown the villany which had been done in the name of their Caste, and charging the contrivers of it to be Narrain, Scrapa, Timapa, Sunka Rama, and Andee Chitty; upon which we sent for the five persons before mentioned, to whom our Brahmin read the letter, which as we expected they disowned knowing anything of it. So we agreed that they five should go to the Pagoda with our Brahmin, and there send for the heads of all their Castes, to whom they should read the letter, and find out if possible the truth and author of it. But in the evening the five persons with the Brahmin returned, and acquainted the Governor that they had all been at the Pagoda, where the letter was read to their Caste, who disowned they knew anything of it.

"Wednesday, 22nd. This morning was brought in four papers that were fixed on the outside of

the bastions of the inward Fort; the purport of
which being full of the most opprobious language
against the Governor; charging him to be the
author of the Cajan letter read yesterday. The
authors of which are doubtless the five persons,
Narrain, etc., who we in our consciences believe
were the sole contrivers of the late rebellion, and
are not a little nettled in fearing that that villany
will in a little time be proved upon them.

"Thursday, 30th. The Governor produces a
paper in the Gentoo language signed by President
Baker, Agent Greenhill, and Mr. Gurney, dated
in the year 1652,* for composing differences
amongst the Right and Left Hand Castes; which
he had from the latter, and doubtless the other
had the same; by which it appears that the Governor and Council now acted as they did then;
the translate of which is as follows.

"In Fort St. George belonging to the Right
Honorable English Company, before the Honorable President Baker, agent Greenhill, and Mr.
Gurney, were present Connaree Chitty, and
Sheshadree Naik, inhabitants of Chinnapatam.
There having of late been several differences and
disputes between the Castes about their streets,
which this day is settled; and in case it be not
observed by each Caste in regard to their Weddings and Burials, the first breaker of it shall forfeit a thousand dollars.

---

* This reference is worthy of especial notice. It
refers to a period within thirteen years of the foundation of Fort St. George, and of which no records are
preserved in the Madras Record Office. The earliest
record in Madras bears date 1670.

"The Right Hand Castes are to reside in the particular streets appointed for them, where are to live or come none of the Left Hand Caste; and the same with the Left Hand Caste, where are to be none of the Right Hand Caste.

"The Great street from before the Fort as far as Taggapa Chitty's Garden, and all the streets to the westward of that street, are allotted to the Right Hand Caste; and the Great street from Mr. Porter's reaching to Malley Carjun's old Pagoda, with the New street (being two streets) are allotted to the Left Hand Caste.

"The Market street opposite to the Choultry as far as the Committee's shops, is appointed to the Right Hand Caste; and as far as the Chitties shops in the same street to the Left Hand Caste; where either Caste may pass with their Weddings or Burials; and if either of the Castes act contrary to this Agreement shall pay one thousand dollars.

"The Pattnawars and Carialwars are to pass with their Weddings and Burials from the back side of Mr. Porter's house to the middle of the Quarter Porter's house, and so to proceed to the Portuguese Church; they may likewise go through the Great street.

"Before the Fort is free for all.

"Sheshadree Chitty is mediator to each Caste. His servants, nor the Company's servants and painters, cannot pass these streets. Dated November 5th, 1652.

"Signed by
Aaron Baker.   Cannaree Chetty.
Henry Greenhill.   Sheshadree Naik."
William Gurney.

We have thus reproduced in full the more interesting papers connected with this remarkable dispute between the Right and Left Hands. There are however other entries, far too lengthy to be extracted here, from which we gather that the dispute was aggravated by other circumstances, which were not permitted to rise to the surface. In the first instance there had undoubtedly been a fierce quarrel between the two Hands about the streets in which each Hand might celebrate its Weddings and Burials. But about this time a commercial rivalry arose. The Merchants belonging to the Right Hand had generally purchased the Company's goods exported from England; but now the Merchants of the Left Hand contrived to outbid them. As the Right Hand was said to be favoured by Mr. Fraser, so the Left Hand was evidently favoured by Governor Pitt. The virulence of the hatred between Governor Pitt and Mr. Fraser seems to imply something more than a mere difference of opinion as regards the mode of mediating between the two Hands. That Mr. Fraser was the champion of the Right Hand is sufficiently proved by what has gone before. That Governor Pitt was the champion of the Left Hand seems also proved by a Petition presented by the Left Hand after the return of their enemies to Madras. We are sorry that this Petition should be far too long to be reproduced in these columns; but a careful perusal of it has strongly impressed us with the idea that though it may have been presented by he Left Hand it was originally from the pen of Mr. Pitt. It recapitulates at very great length the whole history of the disputes, and employs exactly the language and style which Mr. Pitt would himself have used to clear himself before the Court of Directors; and it contains a petition that the Left Hand might be permitted to leave Madras peaceably at the end of six months, and seek for employment elsewhere; and that a notice of their intention of doing so might be made public, so that they might have the opportunity of paying up every debt they owed before leaving the town!

In December matters were restored to tranquillity; and during the following year a final arrangement was made between the two Hands for removing into separate streets. But the quarrel between Governor Pitt and Mr. Fraser continued to be as virulent as ever. Mr. Pitt drew up eight charges against the latter, with which however the reader is generally acquainted; but we make the following extract for the sake of its style. "That it is well known by most upon the place, as also by what appears upon the Consultation Books, that he (Mr. Fraser) has ever been found a person of a factious and turbulent temper; and though weak in contriving, yet industrious in promoting mischief and confusion; of a capacity unfit for any business or advice; impatient of peace, and only pleased when factions run high; wherein he has always made one to the great prejudice of the Company's affairs; during the time of our present Governor always herding and siding with such persons as are under the frowns of the Government let their crimes be ever so black ; and at the beginning of these troubles it was observed he was very intimate with his old acquaintance Timapa, a profligate and wicked wretch, but a bird of the same feather, notorious for mischief, and one of the chief contrivers of the rebellion."

Mr. Fraser was promised a copy of the whole of the charges, but notwithstanding his repeated applications, he could not get one till just before the ships were about to sail for England, and then it was only signed by the Chief Secretary. Accordingly he wrote a short protest couched in tolerably decent terms, but which led to the following entry in the Consultation Book.

"Saturday, 6th December. Fraser this morning sending an impudent and saucy paper to the Governor and Council, it was agreed that it should be delivered to the Marshall to be burned under Gallows, which was accordingly done."

In our last chapter we recorded the opinion of the Court of Directors upon the conduct of Mr. Fraser; and we here extract from the same General Letter, a copy of their judgment upon the quarrel between the two Hands. After some remarks on the investments, the Court wrote as follows:

"This naturally leads us to the many and long paragraphs in your letters relating to the differences between the Right and Left Hand Castes; because the heads of them are the men by whom you make your investments; and without entering into a particular detail of the matter, we say in general, that the generality of men in all countries are naturally disposed to be at ease and live peaceably, if they have a quiet possession of liberty and property; and the most turbulent spirits will in a good measure lie still unless they have a specious handle given them on account of hardships done or offered to be done them. Nor does it appear probable to us that either of the two Castes would have ventured to fly in the face of Government, which is or should be power, without a real or apprehended great provocation; nor can we think that the Right Hand Caste would have carried things to that extremity on the single quarrel of the Left Hand Caste making a wedding in their own streets. It seems to us that the seeds of discord lay deeper, and that things growing ripe for a rupture, this handle was taken to begin the quarrel and set fire to the fuel that was before preparing for it. We should have esteemed it a praiseworthy management in our President and Council to have foreseen and prevented this mutinous disposition before it broke out, or at least to have quenched it when it first began to flame.

"Nothing more does better bespeak the ability and diligence of Governors than keeping their subjects and dependents in quiet; and they can never do that without an impartial administration of justice to all under them; for whether they themselves, or others by their authority or connivance, oppress or injure the subject, it comes to all one in the upshot; that is to say, first the people secretly murmur and complain, then they break out into more open reproaches, and at last into down right mutinies and rebellions ; and this seems to us to be the true reason why those scurrilous papers were fastened upon the Stones set up, and afterwards on the walls of the town ; whereas the Wise Man's remark will be found to be eternally true, " That the Throne can only be established in righteousness."

" It was very surprising to us to read that so many of the handicrafts, and other useful hands, went away on this quarrel ; and gave us but ordinary apprehensions of the conduct of the then administration. Surely they were too valuable to be parted with without the last extremity. All nations and times have agreed in this, that useful people are the riches as well as the strength of a city or country ; and although we readily agree that neither the one or the other Caste are over honest, or will scruple laying hold of any handle for their own benefit ; yet it seems plain to us there must be something more than ordinary at the bottom, that should make the Right Hand Castes go away in general in a body, and the heads of them consent to be at the charge of maintaining the handicrafts people at St. Thomé.

" On the whole matter we heartily recopmmen to you all to endeavour in your stations to reventd such like quarrels in future ; and to that ned to take care the established ancient privileges of both Castes be preserved to them, and the like to all other the inhabitants ; and that all of them have the free possession of their liberty and property ; that justice be administered equally and impartially, and no real cause given of discontent ; and then if you find any makebates that would be putting the people in a ferment, make them public examples as their faults deserve, and remember in such cases " too much pity spoils a city."

CHAPTER XXII.

GOVERNORSHIP OF MR. THOMAS PITT.

1708—9.

The Governorship of Mr. Pitt, which extended over the unusually long period of eleven years, was suddenly brought to a close in 1709. The later years of his government are distinguished by events which emphatically belong to the history of the British rule in India. Hitherto the English Governors had only carried on their communications with the Nabobs in their neighbourhood, but circumstances now brought them into more immediate communication with the Great Mogul. During the later years of the reign of Aurungzebe the Governor of Madras had been brought into communication with the Grand Vizier Assad Khan, and with his son Zulfikar Khan. After the death of Aurungzebe, circumstances, as we shall presently see, brought Mr. Pitt into direct communication with the new Emperor himself, Shah Aulum, known in Mahomedan history under the title of Bahadur Shah.

Before however noticing these events, we lay before our readers the following extracts illustrative of the internal state of Madras. The first is a copy of agreement between the Right and Left Hand Castes, dated 14th January, 1708, which appears to have settled for awhile the dispute between the two.

"Whereas there has lately been differences in the Streets between both parties occasioned by a wedding going in procession in the Pedda Naik's Pettah; and it being brought before your Honour, who ordered us to chose out twelve Heads of each Caste to meet in the Gentoo Pagoda, and make matters up, and then report what done to your Honour. (Names of the twelve Heads of each Caste omitted). These twenty-four agreed and confirmed as follows.

"The Left Hand Caste co-habiting in several streets that belong to the Right Hand in the Pedda Naik's Pettah, so that they cannot safely make their weddings; therefore from this day all the Left Hand that live in the Pedda Naik's Pettah, shall have the following streets to live and make their weddings, viz. Eastward of Eccombre Sheraloo Pagoda, as you go in the back side corner street of Vencata Narnapa's stone Choultry, and go from that place along the Southward Street as far as the well before Gulla Annitches house, where besides the South Street there is another North Street as you come from Brahmin Appelia's Garden which joins to the Well; and from the well westward as far as Dubash Ruggana's house; thence as you go northward of Nautowary Pillary Pagoda as far as Mr. Empson's Garden; in which streets the Left Hand Castes shall live and make their weddings. But if the aforesaid streets are not enough to hold them all, some of those houses that lie to the westward which belong to the Right Hand, we will supply them with; and in case those are not enough too, we will find some houses out either of the east, north, or south; and Eccombre Sheraloo's Pagoda, and Vencata Narnapa's Choultry, shall belong to both Castes. And the Left Hand shall carry their dead towards the westward of Bangana Rama's Garden Street. Those of the Right Hand that were living in the above said streets shall now change with the Left Hand that did inhabit the Right Hand street, and henceforward live there. Both parties having thus agreed, we shall keep our Customs and weddings in our own streets. The Left Hand shall not buy those gardens to the westward of the street that fronts Mr. Empson's garden, without the owner's consent, nor shall the Right Hand build any houses there. If any of the Castes act contrary to this agreement, shall be fined twelve thousand Pagodas to the Hon'ble Company, and receive punishment according to the custom of their Caste. To this we both agree and confirm. All the eastward from Nautowarry Pillary Pagoda shall belong to the Right Hand : all the westward to the Left Hand."*

The following curious account of the knaveries of the Madras boatmen, and the strong measures taken in consequence, will be found very illustrative of the character of the times.

"Tuesday, 20th. The Governor this morning summoned this Council to acquaint them, that just then the Pedda Naik informed him that he discovered a villainy in the Boatmen, in opening the Company's bales sent on board the Duchess ; which he hearing of in the night immediately secured the head Boatmen and two Peons, at the watching places by the sea side, on whom he found two pieces of middling longcloth. The Governor immediately sent for the Conicopoly of the Godown to enquire what peons were sent off in the boats, that day they loaded fifteen boats ; which to his great surprise he told him no Peons at all ; though often at the Council Board he ordered that no goods of the Company's should go off or come

---

* This agreement was recapitulated and confirmed on the 23rd June, 1708.

ashore without Peons in the boats; and the same he had often ordered the Conicopoly when with him, and twice or thrice thrashed him himself when that he found he neglected it.*

"The Chief of the boatmen were before us when the Pedda Naik charged them with the knowledge of this villainy, and brought one of their servants to their face to prove it; who did not only do that, but sent some of his people with their servant to one of the Chief's houses, and found four pieces of Bettelees buried underground. Upon which orders were given to apprehend all the Boatmen that were ashore, and those that were gone off in boats when they returned; and as soon as the Governor was informed of it, and knowing four boats were gone off this morning with bales, he sent for Captain Raymond, whom he desired to write to his Mate to search the four boats as soon as come on board, to see whether they had not played the same tricks with those bales. When some of those boats off returned near the surf, their associates in this villany made them some private sign, so that they returned again as far as the Paddy boats, and there consulted one another; from which we apprehended they would run away to the northward or southward. So presently sent two boats with the Vizagapatam boatmen with soldiers to prevent it; which as soon as they discovered, ten boats run away

---

* We wonder what would be said now if a Governor of Madras gravely recorded in the Consultation Book, that he had more than once thrashed a Conicopoly with his own hand for neglect of duty.

to the southward; upon which the Governor ordered the Gunner to fire shot from the Battery and sink them if possible; several of which fell very near, but had not the good luck to do execution†; and the ship observing it sent their Pinnace, who cut off the flight of four and brought them back, but the other six got to St. Thomé, whither the Government sent Peons with our Brahmin to secure them as they came ashore and bring them hitherto; which, if the Governor refused, to charge them with them; both which they (the St. Thomé authorities) refused; upon which it was thought fit to fetch them with a Company of soldiers; but upon consideration, we then heard the Nabob was at Conjeveram and expected every day at St. Thomé, we desisted, believing the consequence would be embroiling the Company's affairs for the present. Upon which it was agreed to write the Nabob a letter, and another to the Governor of St. Thomé, who is now at Poonamallee; and if we have not immediate redress, then to apply ourselves to other courses to procure it.

"Wednesday, 21st. This morning the Governor severely punished all the sea side Peons, and we ordered the two Peons that were taken with the pieces of cloth to be whipped round the town, and to-morrow morning to be put in the Pillory with ears nailed thereto, and at twelve o'clock at noon to be cut off.

"Though we are apprehensive that these vil-

---

† From this and other allusions, Governor Pitt does not seem to have been very fond of the natives.

lains have stole out of the bales on board the Duchess to a great amount, and that we cannot come at the certainty without unloading the ship, which will not only augment the demurrage, but lose so much time as may endanger her passage. Upon which consideration we have resolved to dispatch the ship, and to take an obligation from the Warehouse and Sea gate Concopolies, sea side Peons, and Boatmen, to pay what shall be found wanting when opened in the Company's Warehouses in England."

The following little piece of horsedealing on the part of Governor Pitt, appears to be rather a doubtful transaction. The Nabob was at this time at St. Thomé.

"Tuesday, 16th February. The Nabob being very pressing for a Persia horse of the Governor's for which he has been often offered 450 Pagodas ; but the Nabob being willing to give no more than 400, it is agreed the Company allows the 50 Pagodas."

Mr. Pitt's quarrels were about this time very much on the increase. Mr. Frederick, member of Council, incurred his wrath, from the following circumstance. Captain Seaton had been cashiered for marching his troops over some cloths. Mr. Pitt subsequently nominated a Mr. Roach to the vacant commission. Mr. Frederick, who had married a daughter-in-law of Captain Seaton, objected to the appointment on the ground that Mr. Roach had been in France without leave, and was subject to certain penalties. Thereupon Mr. Pitt made a rather warm entry in the consultation book, in which he upheld the character of Mr. Roach, and thus commented on the objection of Mr. Frederick. " We cannot but think it a severe reflection on us, the Governor and Council here, that we should not be thought by Mr. Frederick to be better judges of those matters than himself; and that he should be the only person amongst us that is fit to judge of men and their capacity, when it is notoriously known by all in this place, that profound ignorance and pride are his only qualifications."

We have now to narrate the progress of events which brought Mr. Pitt into more immediate communication with the Great Mogul. Aurungzebe expired in the camp at Ahmednuggar on the 21st of February, 1707. He left behind him three sons, viz. Moazzim, better known as Shah Aulum, who was Governor of Cabul; Azim Shah, who was Subahdar of Guzerat; and Kam Buksh, who was Governor of Bijapoor. By his will he recommended that Shah Aulum should be recognised as Emperor, but that he and Azim Shah should divide the empire; Shah Aulum taking the northern and eastern provinces, with Delhi for his capital; and Azim Shah taking all the country to the south and south-west, including all the Dekkan excepting Golconda and Bijapoor. These last mentioned kingdoms were assigned to Kam Buksh.

The decease of Aurungzebe was followed by a war between his sons. The moment the second son Azim Shah heard the news of his father's death, he had hurried to the camp at Ahmednuggar, and was immediately proclaimed Emperor of all India in perfect disregard to the will of Aurungzebe. Meantime Shah Aulum had assumed the imperial crown at Cabul. Azim Shah marched against him, and a bloody battle ensued in the neighbourhood of Agra, in which Azim was slain.*

Shah Aulum was now joined by Zulfikar Khan, and Assad Khan; both of whom, as we have seen, are frequently mentioned in the records connected with the later years of Aurungzebe; Zulfikar Khan as commander-in-chief of the army against the Mahrattas, and as predecessor of Dawood Khan in the Nabobship of the Carnatic; and Assad Khan, as father of Zulfikar Khan, and Grand Vizier of Aurungzebe. Another contest still remained. Kam Buksh was not contented with Golconda and Bijapoor, but aspired after the imperial throne. Shah Aulum attempted to win him over by concessions but in vain. At last Shah Aulum marched an army into the Dekkan to oppose him. After a considerable delay a battle took place near Hyderabad in February, 1709,† at which Kam Buksh was mortally wounded.

In 1703, when Shah Aulum was anticipating a conflict with his younger brother Kam Buksh in the

---

* Elphinstone dates this battle in June 1707.

† Elphinstone says the battle took place in February 1708, but it must have taken place in January 1709, or rather in January 1708-9. The exact date we are enabled to give from the records. It is very probable that the previous date of the defeat of Azim Shah, is fixed a year too early; and indeed Mr. Elphinstone appears from the records to have confounded the old and new styles. In the present publication we have invariably given the new style for the sake of clearness.

Dekkan, the Steward of his household dispatched a letter to the Governor of Fort St. George, " professing great kindness and tendering his service in any affair." The reason for this advance is obvious. Kam Buksh was then in command of the Dekkan, and the continued allegiance of the English might prove of importance to Shah Aulum. Governor Pitt determined to take every advantage of the crisis to secure a better understanding with the Mogul's Government. Accordingly he wrote an answer to the Royal Steward, requesting that Shah Aulum would be pleased to confirm the privileges granted the English by his father Aurungzebe. The progress of affairs can now be best explained by the following extracts from the Consultations.

"Saturday, 31st July, 1708. This evening at four o'clock the Governor summoned the Council, and most of the Company's servants, with the chiefest of the European inhabitants, to accompany him to the garden, where he was met by all the Armenians, Persians, Moguls, Patans, and Head Merchant Gentoo inhabitants of this place, there to receive a Husbulhookum from King Shah Aulum to the Government here, procured by Zoodee Khan, Lord High Steward of said King's household, which was received with all ceremonies usual on such an occasion, by firing of great guns, etc.

"Saturday, 7th August. The purport of the Husbulhookum from Shah Aulum seems to invite us to make our addresses to the King for a confirmation of our privileges; which opportunity we resolving to take hold of, believing we shall accomplish it for a much less to the Company, than if we defer it till the contests between the brothers are over; wherefore it is agreed that the Governor draws out a petition to the King, a letter to the Grand Vizier, and another to Zoodee Khan, and lay them before the Council for their advice therein.

"Zoodee Khan's Lady (by whose Husband's means the Husbulhookum was sent us) living still at St. Thomé, to whom it is agreed to send a present of Persia fruit, rosewater, etc. and some fillagree work of Manilla, with a piece of Persia cloth of gold, all to the value of 120 or 130 Pagodas, or thereabouts."

The Husbulhookum was said to be from Khan Khanan Bahadur the Grand Vizier; but the real Vizier at this time was Monaim Khan. Khan Khanan merely signifies "Khan of Khans."

"From Khan Khanan, Bahadur Zephir Jung, Grand Vizier.

"The Governor of Chinnapatanam may depend upon his Majesty's Royal Favour.

"The good and faithful services you have done his Majesty's subjects has been represented to him by some of his Chief Ministers of State, upon whose recommendation of your merits, a mark of his favour to you, he has ordered this Hosbulhookum to be sent you to certify the same; not doubting but your deportment will continue to be such as to increase in fame and reputation; and according as you observe this Husbulhookum you may expect further marks of his Majesty's grace and countenance. Dated June 1st. Received July 31st, 1703.

"Friday, 13th August. The Governor lays before the Council this day for their opinion and advice, a Petition he had drawn up to King Shah Aulum, a Letter to the Grand Vizier, a letter to Zulfikar Khan, and another to Zoodec Khan; which were all read, and agreed to be put in the Persian language, and to be dispatched with all expedition, that so they may arrive before the King comes to Golconda."

Petition to the King Shah Aulum.

"God grant the great King Shah Aulum may live for ever, is the hearty Prayers of the Governor of Chinnapatam, and of all the English Nation in your Majesty's Dominion, who have been here lately blessed with your Majesty's most Gracious and Royal Husbulhookum; and for your Majesty's commands therein, they shall always be kept as sacred as they were in the time of your Majesty's Royal Predecessors, who were pleased to bestow their Royal favours on us in granting us several Privileges to encourage us in our trade; for a confirmation of which we humbly Petition your Majesty to grant us your royal Firmaun, with what additional favours your Majesty in your Royal Wisdom shall think fit; which we shall not only record in our books but in our hearts also; and as in duty bound shall ever pray for your Majesty's long and prosperous reign, and that you may be always so victorious as to lay your feet on the neck of your enemies."

"To his Highness Khan Khanan, Bahawdee Zephir Jung Grand Vizier.

"Your Highnesses noble qualifications and

virtues being known to all the world, which increase by your daily giving instances of your justice and mercy, and particularly your favours and protection which you so liberally bestow on all strangers in your King's dominions; of which we here have a late instance in receiving the blessing of his Majesty's royal Hosbulhookum; which we must attribute to your Highness's favour and great care of us; for which we return our most humble thanks; and humbly request that as we now send our Petition to the great King Shah Aulum, humbly desiring his royal Firmaun for a confirmation of our privileges according to Sallabad throughout his dominions; that your Highness would be pleased to countenance and assist us in procuring the same; for which you shall not only find us grateful but dutiful; and shall always pray for your Highness's health and prosperity, and for ever to be blessed with the favour of your great king."

"To Zulfikar Khan, etc.

"The many obligations we lie under to your Highness are never to be forgotten, being rivetted in our memories as well as recorded in our books; which we should have often acknowledged, but prevented by the great distance and troubles of the country; yet nevertheless we never failed to enquire after your Highness's health, which God continue.

"Your Highness is well acquainted with the privileges our nation enjoyed in the reign of the great Aurungzebe of blessed memory; which we are endeavouring to get confirmed by a royal Firmaun from the great King Shah

Aulum; that we and our trade may go on in
all parts according to Sallabad; to effect which
we humbly petition that your Highness will continue
your constant favours to us in speaking in our
behalves as an opportunity presents, for which we
shall be always grateful, and pray for your Highness's
health and prosperity."

" To his Excellency Zoodee Khan Lord High
Steward of the King's Household.

" It is your noble and generous mind that have
drawn this trouble of our application to you; and
as I wrote you in my last Letter, which I delivered
Aga Makeem, I now send our humble Petition to
the King, and Address to the Grand Vizier; copies
of which I here enclose to Your Excellency; humbly
requesting that you will favour us with the
management thereof.

" We are not ignorant of what should accompany
such Petitions and Addresses; but the hazards
and troubles in the way prevent us from performing
that part at present; in which I humbly
desire your Excellency's advice and direction as to
what would be acceptable to his Majesty, the Grand
Vizier, and such others where you think it is
necessary; and we shall endeavour to procure it
if possible.

" Your Excellency will see that we desire a
Firmaun to confirm our privileges according to
Sallabad in all his dominions; unless his Majesty
shall, out of his Royal bounty, bestow some new
favours on us. Your Excellency cannot but know
that Miliapore (St. Thomé) is a troublesome neighbourhood
to us, creating always disputes and quar-

rels, of little advantage to the king nor will it ever be more; which could we obtain, and the town of Trivatore on the other side of us, it would make us easy, and increase the riches of the king's country.

"And whereas the goods we import are generally carried to the capital cities of Golconda and Bijapoor, etc., which trade we should much increase if there was no custom paid upon them between this place and those cities; and that the Mettas about us, which of late years have been increased to the plague and ruin of trade, were laid aside; which only find employs for some little people, who destroy trade by their vexation and extortion, and in the main very much lessen the King's revenue.

"And we humbly desire that you would get it inserted in a Firmaun, that whenever we are so unfortunate as to lose any ship in any part of his Majesty's dominions, we shall have the liberty to preserve what we can of the wreck, without any molestation from the Government; which is not only practised throughout the world, but the inhabitants are generally commanded to assist therein. For it is a great hardship that, after the great risk that our people have run of their lives, they shall not be at liberty to save what they can of their estates. We must own with great thankfulness that this justice have been granted us by former purwannas from Khan Bahadur and the present Nabob; but as it has been formerly disputed it may again, which nothing but the King's gracious grant can prevent.

"We extremely want the King's blessing and favours to give new life to our trade; for since your Excellency went hence this place has lost nearly three lakhs of Pagodas by misfortunes and most by pirates; so that it is become poor; and nothing can contribute to the retrieving our losses but God's blessing, the King's favour, and Your Excellency's continuance in assisting of us.

"Here are ships in a few days that will depart for Pegu, when we shall write the King what you advised in your former letter, that an Ambassador was coming to him. Khan Bahadur always showed himself a friend to our nation; whose favours we cannot but retain with great thankfulness; so have wrote him a letter which comes herewith, and a copy of it for your Excellency; we leave it to your pleasure whether it shall be delivered him.

"If please God we are so fortunate as to be blessed with the King's favour, as to obtain his Royal Firmaun, we humbly entreat Your Excellency to appoint some able person to see it so fully penned as that it may not admit of any dispute from Nabob's and Governors, where the same is to be executed. Our dependance is entirely on Your Excellency's friendship, for which we shall be always full of our acknowledgments, and heartily wish Your Excellency and all your family health and prosperity."

The following extracts will explain themselves.

"Thursday, 19th August. There having come some people belonging to Zoodee Khan, our great friend at the King's Court, to acquaint the Governor that his Lady at St. Thomé extremely wanted money for her charges; not being able to get bills upon her husband, nor could he remit any, by reason of the great troubles in the way; so desired of the Governor to lend 500 Pagodas for his account; who answered them that it was the Company's positive orders to lend none of their money to any people whatever; nor that their Governors nor any in their service should lend any money to any in the country Government, upon the penalty of being discarded their service; but considering our dependence to procure a Firmaun is upon the friendship of the aforesaid Lady's husband, the Government acquaints the Council that he promised to procure a merchant to lend that money, if Aga Makeem, a merchant of this place, would give his bond for it, which he had done for 500 Pagodas to be repaid in four months without interest; which bond being now produced, it was agreed that the 500 Pagodas be on the Company's account and repaid the Government out of the cash; being a thing absolutely necessary at this time, though not to be drawn into a precedent for the future."

The following entries are in the Consultations of the same day; and are worth preserving though they do not illustrate the current history.

"The Company having a sorrel Persian horse good for little, and there being some people about to buy him, it is agreed the Governor sells him for what he can get."

"We having lately more thefts and robberies committed in this city than usual, and finding they daily increase, to prevent which it is agreed that all persons as soon as convicted shall be punished by being whipt at a cart through all the streets in Black Town, and afterwards lie in prison till an opportunity presents to send them to the West Coast, where they are to be the Company's slaves for ninety-nine years; and this order to be published by setting it up on every Gate of the Black town.

"The Governor being advised from Pegu that a Conicopoly, one Ansapal, that went hence on one of the ships hither, had the impudence to counterfeit a letter to the king of that country, as if it came from the Governor here, and with it sent a present; for which he had an advantageous return in Elephants as usual; so to prevent the pernicious consequences which attend such vile practices, the Governor seized him as soon as he returned, and put him in prison, and intended to have punished him severely; but having been there a Factor for several Merchants of this place, to whom he had not yet rendered any account, and it is thought he never would if he is disgraced by a punishment; it is therefore agreed that he be fined for his crime 200 Pagodas, to be paid into the Company's cash, and give security he never more goes to Pegu."

In September this year, the Government of Fort St. George was informed that the Nabob was about to proceed to join the King Shah Aulum at Golconda, and accordingly a member of Council and the Secretary were sent to him with a present of about 200 Pagodas. In return the Nabob presented the Company with a Perwanna for the five following towns, the names of which are spelt as follows.

> "Trivetore town itself.
> Vasalawada under Perumbore.
> Santunganda under Trivetore.
> Lungumbaca (? Nungumbaukum) under Egmore.
> Cutteewauca under Trivetore."

These Towns were valued at fifteen hundred Pagodas. Subsequently the King's Officers at St. Thomé raised a clamour against this present of the King's towns, and declared that their real value was as much as three thousand Pagodas; upon which the Nabob ordered the King's books to be searched, and the real value to be laid before him. From the following entry it will be seen that the dispute was hushed up in the Oriental fashion :—
"It is agreed that our Moolla and Brahmin return again to St. Thomé with about two hundred Pagodas, which is ordered to be distributed amongst the King's Officers who keep the Records in order to settle this matter."

The next extract is also interesting.

"Saturday, 16th October. We having large experience that it is impossible for us to manage the income of villages, so as not to be imposed upon, and lose at least half the produce; to prevent which it is agreed this day to let or to rent the five villages, lately given the Company by the Nabob, for twelve years to Colloway and Vinketty Chetties, at 1200 Pagodas per annum, to commence from this day; who are obliged to repair all tanks belonging thereto, which have been let run to ruin, as customary, by those who have been lately the renters of them; and the Secretary is ordered to draw out a lease for them."

Towards the end of the year another Husbulhookum arrived from the King Shah Aulum, with answers penned in the usual oriental style from the Royal Officers to the letters sent them by Governor Pitt. It would be wearisome in the extreme to reproduce these compositions here. In return Governor Pitt engaged to forward the necessary presents to the King Shah Aulum and his principal Officers; and sent numerous fulsome letters to the various Ministers of State, all of which are recorded at full length in the Consultation. The following extracts from a letter to the Royal Steward will sufficiently illustrate the tone of the whole.

"To Zoodee Khan, Lord High Steward of the King Shah Aulum's household, January 5th, 1709.

"By your faithful Chobdar Cossae, by whom Your Excellency sent the Royal Husbulhookum, and Vest, and Purwannas, I now send this humble address, which doubtless you expected sooner, and had been sent but for the two following reasons. Your Excellency enjoining secresy, I was obliged to commit the translating of them to some particular friends, which took up fourteen days. When fully apprised of the purport thereof, I could not but be surprised at your unparalleled expressions of friendship and invaluable honours you have done us; which so confounded my thoughts for some days that I almost despaired of being able to acknowledge them by my pen or otherwise; but then considering what a generous friend I had met with, who had been so lavish of his favours to one who had as little power as merit to oblige you; I could no longer refrain from blessing my stars, who were so propitious to me as to give me the honour of your first acquaintance; which I esteem the happiest fate that has attended me through the whole course of my life; which I shall ever remember, and that posterity may do the same, I humbly request that when you come to Golconda you will honour me with sending me your picture; which I will send to England and have copied by the most exquisite limner in the world, and order it to be sent me hither; beside I will erect your effigy finely cut in marble, with such an inscription on it that the world may know the author of our happiness in these parts. . . . . . Your Excellency writes that there must be presents for all the princes and some of the great men. If you mean such as are suitable to their birth and quality, it is impossible for us to purchase them with our Company's estate; who you know are merchants who run great risk to get a little, and who often meet with loss instead of gain. We hope as the presents we intend are suitable to our circumstances, that they will meet with a gracious acceptance from the great king and princes; which puts us in mind of what we read in history that upon many persons making very rich presents to a king, there happened a poor man to come with a drop of water, which was acceptable as any of their presents, being according to his ability."

Shortly afterwards the following Firmaun arrived from King Shah Aulum, by which it will be seen distinctly that the conflict with Kam Buksh was the cause of such demonstrations of friendship.

"Let the chosen of his Caste and Nation, the Governor of Chinnapatam, know that he may be in hopes of the King's favour. Seeing that Kam Buksh doth purpose to fly from the powerful arms of our victorious army; for that reason the command of the sovereign of the world, worthy of all submission and obedience is due, is issued forth; that in case he, Kam Buksh, should come wandering, not knowing where to go, into those parts, and desire to embark himself on some ship in order to get away; that the chosen of his nation shall use his utmost endeavours to procure that he be either killed or made a prisoner; and to effect this let him know that the command from the Royal Throne is strict in the strictest manner. Written the 17th of the moon Ramazan the Blessed in the second year of the King's Reign."

In reply Governor Pitt's promised obedience in general terms, but on the 18th January, 1709, intelligence was brought to Madras that Shah Aulum had obtained a complete victory over his brother, and that Kam Buksh had died of the wounds he had received during the battle.

CHAPTER XXIII.

GOVERNORSHIPS OF PITT, ADDISON, MONTAGUE AND FRASER.

1709—10.

The period upon which we are now about to enter will be interesting to all who are fond of historical coincidences. The rapid succession of Governors, in the years 1709, 1710, and 1711, bears a curious resemblance to the similar changes which took place in 1859, 1860, and 1861 after the exact interval of a century and a half. Within two years Fort St. George saw five successive Governors, viz. Mr. Pitt, Mr. Addison, Mr. Montague, Mr. Fraser, and Mr. Harrison; and now within the last two years of our history we have seen the same event repeated in the rapid succession of Lord Harris, Sir Charles Trevelyan, Mr. Morehead, Sir Henry Ward, and Sir William Denison.

In the middle of the year 1709, Mr. Pitt's government was fast drawing to a close; but though it is apparent from the records that he had some suspicions of the probability of his being recalled, yet he evidently had no idea of the sudden way in which the recall would be carried out. Before however noticing this event, we make the following curious extracts which seem to have some reference to the great Pitt diamond to which allusion has already been made.

"Wednesday, 3rd August, 1709. The Governor this day acquainted the Council, that he having lately heard of some villainous and scandalous reflections that had been made upon him by the late Lieutenant Seaton, who he yesterday sent for from the Mount, and examined thereon; who with his usual impudence averred to him the most notorious falsities that ever could be thought or imagined. Upon which he (the Governor) said, he had confined him, Seaton, to the Ensign's room; and he desired that he might be sent for up, and examined thereto. Which accordingly was done, and when he came into the Consultation Room before us, without first hearing what the Governor had to charge him with, and the reasons of his confinement,— he immediately addressed himself to the Council, saying, "I am come here to accuse the Governor for buying a great diamond to the Company's prejudice." When the Governor answered and told him, "we would discourse of that by and by;" and demanded of him whether he had said, that he had received of Paupia to make him Chief Dubash, five hundred Pagodas; and that Ramapa offered seven hundred to be continued, which was refused. This he acknowledged to have said, but being commanded to prove the same, he answered he had it from a black fellow, but could not remember who he was. After which the two Dubashes before mentioned declared they never gave the Governor a Pagoda, or that ever he asked or hinted to them of any such thing ; and to this they took the most solemnest oath in the Pagoda. Then the Governor demanded what he knew of his buying a diamond. He answered in general terms, that he knew every particular of it ; when he was commanded to acquaint the Council with it, which he said he would then do, knowing that there would be a change of Government this month, and therefore for what this Governor said to him did not signify a farthing, with many such insolent and villainous expressions. He further said that to his knowledge the Governor was betrayed by all the Black servants about him ; insomuch that he knew every thing that was done and said, nay as much as in his Counting house ; and to give an instance thereof, said, that the great diamond he had bought was entered in his books folio 64. He further told us that one Rogers, who went hence in October last for Bombay, had carried papers along with him, signed by Black people, that would do the Governor's business ; which Sir Nicholas Wait had got translated and carried home with him.

"The Governor also acquainted the Council that he had very good reason to suspect that this Seaton was turned Informer to the Government, and held a correspondence with them, and promised in a few days to prove the same ; in expectation of which, and what the Governor charged him with, and he confessed before us,—we now unanimously confirm his confinement till other means can be considered of ; and for what discourse passed between the Governor and him yesterday in the Consultation Room after his coming from the Mount, is as entered as follows, the truth of which we shall always be ready to justify by oath or otherwise."

Copy of what passed between the Governor and Lieutenant Seaton in the Consultation Room on the day before.

"This evening being the 2nd of August about five o'clock, I discoursed Captain Seaton in the Consultation Room, when charged him with his having said that I had 500 Pagodas given me to make Paupia Chief Dubash; which he owned, and he told me that I was betrayed in whatever I did or spoke by all my servants about me; and that I had not a friend upon the place, whatever I thought.

"Then I asked how he durst presume to talk up and down of what I bought or sold, and how it was possible for him to know anything of it; to which he answered that he had so good intelligence that there was not the least thing said or done by me, but that he knew; and to convince me desired leave to ask me some questions, which I permitted him to do and were as follows. "Whether Mr. Roberts did not write to me, requesting that he might be concerned in a great diamond I had bought?" Answered: "False." "Whether a person did not come and wish me joy of its being sold for 500,000 dollars?" False. "Whether two persons did not come from the Dekkan to demand a great diamond, and that I gave one of them at coming eleven rupees, and the other at going away, a hundred and fifty." All false, only that one man came. Upon which I told him that I found him (Seaton) a villain; and as I found him endeavouring to betray me, doubtless he would do the same to the Government; so ordered the Captain of the Guard to confine him to the Ensign's room, none to come to him but the Council.

"Thursday, 11th August. It is unanimously agreed that Lieutenant Seaton be confined till the first ship goes for England, and on her to be sent home a prisoner to the Company."

In the following month Governor Pitt was suddenly recalled, as will be seen by the following entry.

"Sunday, 18th September. Yesterday evening appeared a ship to the northward of this Port, and about nine at night came ashore Captain Tolson, who acquainted the Governor that he was commander of the Ship "Heathcote" come directly from England; and that he had brought the Company's packet which he produced directed as follows:—

"To the Hon'ble Gulstone Addison, President, Messrs. Fraser, Montague, Martin, Raworth, Frederick, Hunt, Bulkley, and Jennings, Fort St. George."

And withal told him there was great alterations here, and that he was dismissed the service; therefore pressed that the Council might be immediately called. The Governor told him that it was impossible to be done, not only from the lateness of the night, but that several of them were at the Mount; so desired the Captain to strictly observe in what condition he delivered the packet, and be here to-morrow morning at eight o'clock, against when the Council should be summoned, that so he might see it in the like condition he delivered it. This morning accordingly all the late Council met, when the Governor refused to surrender the Government by virtue of the superscription on the packet, but demanded a supercedent to his Commission, by virtue of which he had been Governor of this place upwards of eleven years. So after some hesitation the packet was opened, wherein there was a Commission which superceded his. He also demanded the reading of the General Letter, which was refused him; but in the packet there being a Letter from the Managers to him, wherein it was fully expressed his dismission from their service, the constituting Gulstone Addison, Esquire in his room, so he immediately read the cash and tendered the balance thereof; but the new Governor desired the payment for that time be deferred, for that he was very much indisposed. So the Governor just as he left the Chair, challenged the whole Board, or any upon the place, to charge him with an unjust action during the whole time of his Government, or that he had ever refused a kindness to any one that asked it, and that it lay in his power; or that ever he acted arbitrary in any one matter, notwithstanding some villains of this place have had the impudence to represent him otherwise; so rose out of the chair and placed the new Governor in it."

The recall of Mr. Pitt, at the moment he had succeeded in establishing friendly relations between the Company and the court at Delhi, proved anything but advantageous to the English; and the Directors on more than one occasion had cause to regret their precipitancy, and quoted the government of Mr. Pitt as an example to his less politic and less energetic successors. The following extract from a general letter of this period will alone warrant this inference.

"We read with pleasure that when Messrs. Raworth and Davenport visited the Nabob at St. Thomé with a present of two hundred pagodas, he gave you for us the grants of five towns adjoining to ours, worth about fifteen hundred pagodas a year, which you are now in possession of; and that you preserve a good understanding with the government, notwithstanding some little jangling. This we take to be the effect of your good conduct and President Pitt's interest with the great men; and shall be glad you, our present President and Council, will follow in the same steps, which is now so much the easier because the path is ready trodden."

The administration of Mr. Gulston Addison, who was brother to the greatest of English essayists, did not extend over a month. On the Sunday morning that he succeeded to the government, he was too much indisposed to receive the balance of the cash from Mr. Pitt; and his signature is wanting to the proceedings. On the Monday he made his appearance and stated that he had "laboured under most severe pains, which almost rendered his limbs in a manner useless to him;" and the trembling signature which appears in the consultation book seems to indicate that he was still suffering from the attack. He only attended five consultations afterwards; and at the last one to which his signature is appended, he signed the instructions to the Captain of the "Heathcote" to receive Mr. Pitt on board, and to treat him with all the respect due to an ex-Governor during the voyage to England. Mr. Addison died at noon on Monday, the 17th of October, 1709. The event is interesting from its connection with the fortunes of his more celebrated brother. Whilst Gulston had been toiling away in the Company's service at Fort St. George, the fame and fortune of Joseph had been rapidly rising in England. Literature in those days was on a different footing to what it is now. The Battle of Blenheim in 1704, had been celebrated with a chorus of such wretched poems, that the government had actually routed out Joseph Addison from his little garret in the Haymarket, to write "The Campaign." The poem met with vast applause, and the subsequent promotion of its author was rapid. In 1708 he was chief secretary to the Lord Lieutenant of Ireland on two thousand a year, and keeper of the Irish records on four hundred a year. About the very time that Gulston died, Joseph furnished his first contribution to the Tatler. But shortly afterwards the Whigs went out and Joseph lost his chief secretaryship. This was unfortunate as he had deemed it expedient to fall in love with the dowager Countess of Warwick; a lady of mature charms, who considered Mr. Addison as the chief secretary and Mr. Addison as the mere literary man, to be two totally distinct individuals. Accordingly though she had smiled on the secretary she now frowned upon the author. It was at this juncture that Joseph inherited his brother's fortune, and the inheritance seems to have won back the heart of Chloe. In due time the pair were married; but poor Gulston's wealth had better have been left at Fort St. George. Henceforth, as the story goes, Mr. Joseph Addison was far happier over a bottle of claret at a tavern, than in the company of his magnificent countess dowager at Holland House.

But to return to Madras. The succession to the Governorship belonged to Mr. William Fraser, the enemy of Pitt and Higginson; but as Fraser was at that time Deputy Governor of Fort St. David, Mr. Edward Montague took the post of provisional governor until his return. The administration of Mr. Montague only lasted a fortnight, and was distinguished by only one incident worthy of notice. The government had at last resolved to send Captain Seaton to England on board the "Heathcote." The Captain however refused to leave his house, and the Governor was obliged to send Ensign Dixon with a file of soldiers to carry him on board. What transpired is best described in Ensign Dixon's own narrative of the proceedings, addressed to the Governor and Council on the 25th of October, 1709, which was follows:—

"HONOURABLE SIRS,

According to orders, I carried your prisoner Captain Seaton alongside of the Ship "Heathcote," and laying there some time I found no person appear to hand us a rope or any to assist us. Then I went on board and delivered your Honor's and Council's order to Captain Tolson, desiring him to receive the prisoner. I informed him that the said prisoner was carried from the Sea Gate, and that he refused to come on board, unless he were hoisted in. Captain Tolson replied that all his passengers came on board willingly, and would not hoist him in, nor suffer anybody else to do it, nor would he overhale the least tackle in his ship; and that he would not suffer any gentleman lying alongside of his ship to be forced on board or ill used. Captain Tolson asked the prisoner, if he would come on board, which the said prisoner refused. Then the prisoner demanded of Captain Tolson, whether he had any further commands for him. Captain Tolson answered no. I waited for a note, but at last he told me I might go, for he would give none." Subsequently Captain Seaton appears to have left the Presidency of his own accord.

On the 2nd of November the new Governor, Mr. Fraser, reached Madras from Fort St. David; the members of Council and other English Gentlemen, together with the chief inhabitants of the place, going out as far as St. Thomas' little Mount to receive him. The next day a council was held, as will be seen by the following extract.

"Thursday, 3rd November, 1709. The Council being duly summoned met in Consultation, and having taken their places, the President, rising up from the chair, exhorted the Gentlemen of the

Council to forget and forgive whatever hitherto had given cause and occasion to the difference that had formerly happened amongst them ; and that all such piques might for ever be buried in oblivion, and that they might henceforward agree amongst themselves, in the Unity of Love and firm Friendship, with all reciprocal respect to each other ; in testimony of which they were desired to shake hands all of them ; which was accordingly done with all promises of sincerity to the performance of the promises."

The Governorship of Mr. Fraser lasted little more than eighteen months, being brought to a conclusion on the 11th of July, 1711, when Mr. Harrison came out as President of Fort St. George. The records connected with the administration of both Mr. Fraser and his successor are much occupied with two or three discussions which it is impossible to treat in detail. In the first place there was an interminable correspondence with Zoodee Khan, concerning the present intended for the Court at Delhi, and which was detained for years on its way. It seems that Governor Pitt had intended to forward it to the King whilst the latter was staying at Golconda after the victory over Prince Kham Buksh ; but part only was sent by sea to Masulipatam, and there got no farther ; the King having by that time been called back to Delhi and the North-west in consequence of the rising of the Sikhs.

Many consultations were held, not only with the members of Council, but with also the chief merchants and inhabitants of the place, as to how the present was to be conveyed. To send it overland to Delhi was declared to be a Herculean labour, the imperial city " being little less than 2000 miles off," which would occasion " an immense charge to the Company." Subsequently it was determined to send the portion that was at Masulipatam to the Subah at Golconda, there to remain until the King's pleasure could be known ; whilst the remaining portion was to be sent on to Bengal, thence to be forwarded to Delhi. Very many months however after this decision was recorded, we still find Zoodee Khan applying for the present, and the Governor of Fort St. George sending every kind of excuse and apology for the delay.

Another subject of endless correspondence between the Governor and the Nabob of the surrounding country, was the five new villages which had been granted to the Company by the Nabob Dawood Khan. Notwithstanding the present to Dawood Khan, and the judicious bribe administered to the keepers of the records, the Mogul government determined to recall the villages, on the ground that they belonged to a jaghire which had been granted to Zulfikar Khan, now styled Khan Bahadur. There were also troubles both at Vizagapatam, and Fort St. David ; but these subjects will be sufficiently explained as we proceed. We shall now produce our extracts in chronological order.

The first refers to a severe storm which broke out about a fortnight after Mr. Fraser's accession, and is thus described in the consultation book.

" Saturday, 19th November 1709. Saturday

in the evening, it rained very much, and about 8 at night began to thunder and lighten, which was very violent (for about an hour), by which the Flag Staff was rent and shattered from the top to the ground. Some pieces flew near 600 feet, and thousands of small pieces strewed the curtains and other places. A large iron hoop was burst from the mast, and flew near 200 feet, and two holes struck through the truck as though it had been with a shot.

"The Company's house at the Garden was likewise damaged at the Southernmost end, one leaf of a window being shattered to pieces and one side of the Frame much rent; the door pierced through in several places, and the upper part of the Frame much scorched, whereby it was rendered unserviceable. The wall was pierced through in two places; one hole just above the Terrace, being about 5 inches diameter; and the other, which went beneath the beams that bear up the Terrace, was about 7 inches diameter, and the beam next the wall was likewise pierced through in two places, and all this with little or no wind."

We may here add that the season of 1709-10 proved in other respects a remarkable one. The monsoon rains returned in January with considerable violence, a circumstance which we believe is of very rare occurrence on the Coast of Coromandel.

The next extract will be interesting to our Armenian readers, for notwithstanding the complaints recorded against one of their community, the following story plainly indicates that the Armenians had gained considerable wealth and were aiming at independent power.

"Thursday, 13th January, 1710. Lewis Melique, an inhabitant of this place, presents a petition setting forth the abuses and insolencies of Cojah Saffur, an Armenian, also an inhabitant here, who hath for some years past lived at St. Thomas' Great Mount, where he hath impudently assumed a power to himself, as if he was Havildar there; insomuch that in a controversy between the said Lewis Melique and Antonio Soares about a piece of ground, the said Saffur concerned himself so far, though not belonging to him, that he threatened to beat the said Lewis Melique, and send him a prisoner to the Catwall of St. Thomé; which he had certainly done, had not the said Lewis Melique made his escape.

"On which the Governor sent for the said Saffur yesterday, who appeared before us this day, and the matter being put close to him did stiffly deny every thing, notwithstanding the evidence that was brought against him; and it being well known that the said Saffur has been an insolent troublesome fellow to all the English in general, who have resorted to the Mount for their health; of which there has been several instances, too many to be enumerated here.

"And that there is cause to believe, that the said Cojah Saffur, with others of his nation, intend to associate and form themselves into a Factory at the Mount, and make St. Thomé their port, as appears by their having in the late Governor Pitt's time bought and built several houses there, which they ought not to have done without leave of the Governor and Council; and that they intended to build a Gate at the end of the lane to stop up all avenues, and prevent all others having any entrance there but themselves; to prevent which growing evil, it is thought expedient to pull up their insolent weed of ill humour by the root.

"Agreed and ordered that the said Cojah Saffur be confined to the Fort, until he give security of Pagodas 5000, for his forthcoming and good behaviour for the future; for which none of his own nation would engage for him, and therefore was committed."

The following entry illustrates the war between Great Britain and France which had extended to the Bay of Bengal. The false intelligence by which Governor Fraser proposed to deceive the French will be found creditable to that gentleman's invention. It will be seen that Mr. Montague, the late provisional governor of Fort St. George, was now Deputy Governor of Fort St. David; and that he and his Council were anxious to dispatch the ship "Somers" to Europe, but were afraid to do so whilst the French ships were at Pondicherry. Accordingly the design of Governor Fraser was to induce the French ships to leave Pondicherry, so as to leave the coast clear for the "Somers."

"Tuesday, 31st January. This morning received a general letter from the Deputy Governor and Council at Fort St. David, dated 28th instant, and the President found matter enough contained therein to summon the Council to meet immediately. They, at Fort St. David, advise the Ship "Somers" to have been full laden that day. They likewise advise of their great fears and apprehensions they have of the St. Malo's ships at Pondicherry, of their having some ill design in agitation against the "Somers." For which reason they think it not adviseable to despatch her though full laden, and therefore do earnestly desire our orders and directions in that matter.

"The President propounding to the Council what they thought might be the best ways and means to be used to prevent the "Somers" being in danger of the French. Upon the whole we come to this following resolution, that a letter should be devised as from Bengal, advising the great troubles the English were in there, by reason of the country Government stopping their goods from coming down the river; which occasioned a warm skirmish, in which a great many Moors were killed and some English; and that the Council there thought the Company's affairs in great danger, and forthwith desired our utmost assistance. As also to write the Deputy Governor and Council (and send them copy of said devised letter) for to send for Captain Peacock and endeavour to agree with him on further time according to a New Charter party, that he might be unladen and sent to Bengal; with the intent that the same might be industriously diffused and spread abroad, in hopes it might occasion the French Ships departure the sooner thence, who had lain full laden for some days. It was also agreed, we should write our joint letter to Deputy Governor Montague, Mr. Raworth, and Captain Peacock to unravel and explain to them the mystery of our general letter to the Deputy Governor and Council, and that it was only feigned with a design in hopes, it might hasten the despatch of the French."

By subsequent entries we learn that this device proved unnecessary, but it nevertheless received the warm approval at the Court of Directors.

The following petition will explain itself.

" To the Honorable William Fraser, Esq. etc.

" The petition of the Ministers and Churchwardens of the Parish of St. Mary's in Fort St. George.

" Humbly representeth,

That whereas the monuments of the dead, and the ground where they are interred are held by most people in some measure sacred, and not lightly applied to any common or profane use, yet it is our misfortune that the English burying place in Fort St. George (where so many of our relations, friends and acquaintants lie buried) is not kept in that decent and due manner it ought to be, but every day profaned and applied to the most vile and undecent uses; for since the year 1701, when an old building that stood in the burying place (and in which the Buffaloes used to be shut up) was taken down to build lodgings for the soldiers at the Gate adjoining, the Tombs have been made use of for stables for the Buffaloes; which is not only a thing very undecent, but also a very great damage to those buildings, by having so many stakes drove into the pavement and with the walls to fasten the Buffaloes to.

"Another occasion of our complaint on this subject is the Cocoa-nut trees standing in the burying place; the profit arising from them, we know is inconsiderable, but the nuisance accruing to the place thereby, we are sure is very great. For the Toddy men have people employed there all the day and almost all the night in drawing and selling of Toddy, so that we are obliged on their account to keep the Gates always open, both by day and by night. And there about eight o'clock at night after work is done, is such a resort of basket makers, Scavengers, people that look after the Buffaloes, and other Parriars, to drink Toddy, that all the Punch houses in Madras have not half the noise in them; and by reason of the gates lying open, beggars and other vagabonds (who know not where to go) make use of the tombs to lie in, and what unclean uses the neighbours thereabout do make of that place we forbear to tell. We hope, what is here urged, together with the reflection it must cast on our Church and nation to have so little regard to the repositories of our dead, when all other nations who live among us have so just a regard to theirs, will prevail with your Honor &c. to take this matter into your consideration, and to find out some method to redress these abuses. And your petitioners as in duty bound shall &c.

    GEORGE LEWIS. } *Ministers.*
    ROBERT JONES. }

    EDWARD BARKHAM. } *Church Wardens.*"
    FRANCIS COOKE. }

FORT ST. GEORGE,
February 19*th* 1710.

We are glad to inform our readers that the matter was taken up by Governor Fraser, and the profanation removed. The Rev. George Lewis, who has signed his name to the above petition, appears to have been an active Chaplain, and we shall have occasion to mention him in a future issue in connection with some Missionary proceedings.

The following letter from Zoodee Khan to the Governor of Fort Saint George, is not only interesting as illustrative of the new relations which at this time began to spring up between the Mogul's government and the English, but it seems to indicate the commencement of a new commercial policy on the part of Shah Aulum.

"From Zoodee Khan, Ameny and Phoujdar of Hooghly and other seaports under the Subah of Bengal, as also of Orissa, Masulipatam, Peddipolle, Chinnapatam, St. Thomé, Pulicat, Chicacole, &c., under the Subah of Golcondah, received May 16th 1710.

"I lately wrote your Honor by your peons that the King had granted me the above mentioned Ameny and Phoujdarship, and therefore I have appointed Mirza Mahomud Zaman, son-in-law of Aloudabeeg, and Mahomed Salaubeeg, Deputies under me for Masulipatam and Peddepolle and my friend Aga Mookeem, Deputy at Chinnapatam, St. Thomé, Pulicat and Chicacole, and have sent them their commissions with a copy of mine attested by the Codjee at Court.

"As there is a great friendship between us, and you have often informed me that it was your opinion that if all the seaports under the King's dominions were under the Admiral (as a Company) he might settle the sea affairs, destroy the pirates, enrich the seaports and encourage the sea Merchants to come and depart, which will increase their profit ; and you desired me to use my utmost endeavours to obtain this ; which I have done ; and on account of our friendship have undertaken this great business myself, and if it happens otherwise, the discredit will be the same to us both. For I have no other hopes than the safety of all subjects, the security of ships and merchants going or coming by sea, extirpation of pirates and the enrichment of the King's seaports. So your honor must use your endeavours in this matter likewise, and advise all your Gomastas and merchants every where to trade freely, without suspicion of any danger, and augment their trade.

"I want your advice if you think it proper to send some of the King's ships to bring Elephants from the other coast."

"The King has ordered me to build a Fort at Ballasore and enrich your Factory."

"After I arrive at Hooghly I will observe how affairs are managed and advice your honor."

"And now I must desire you to think of means, how things may best be carried on for the King's advantage and your Company's ; that so all persons may live happy and serve their Maker. For I have neglected other business, and undertaken this on your account, in hopes to get a great name by it ; and within 5, 6, or 12 months' time, if it is your request that I should take in the other sea ports, as also Surat, I can procure it; and we must endeavour to promote both our fames. For if we agree we can conquer the whole world, and clear the seas of all dangers for the merchants.

"As to the present, I have wrote you lately to send it to Bengal, according to the king's order, which be sure you do. For it is very necessary that you send a present, and when I come to Hooghly, I will advise you of all other matters; and you should send a Vakeel to be with me; which if you approve of, you may send such a one as Cojah Hamud, or Surapa, or write your people at Calcutta to send one. For I shall want him on several occasions. I heartily wish you all health and prosperity."

We are sorry to add that this arrangement proved to be only a temporary one, and that after a few months the seaports on the coast of Coromandel were again placed under the ordinary jurisdiction of the Subah of Golconda.

We now return to the subject of the five new villages which had been obtained by Governor Pitt. It must here be remarked that the purwanna for the out towns had been received from the Nabob Dawood Khan, and subsequently confirmed. The Nabob had also given to the Company a piece of ground of about forty acres at the Mount, in order that a house with a garden attached, might be built there as a sanatarium for the Company's servants. In April 1710 the Nabob recalled the villages, and ordered them to be delivered to Zulfikar Khan's* officers, on the ground that they belonged to his Jaghire. About the same time Dawood Khan was himself recalled to Delhi, in consequence probably of the rise of the Sikhs. The Government of Fort St. George suspected that the Nabob had been persuaded to this action by Yeavellappa, the Manager of Poonamallee, otherwise the Renter of the country surrounding the English dominions; and for a long time they deferred giving them up. In May the same year, a letter arrived from Dewan Sadatulla Khan at Arcot, who is described as the new Nabob, demanding not only the five villages recently granted, but also the three old towns of Egmore, Tandore and Pursewaukum, which had been granted some years previously by the Nabob Zulfikar Khan. The following letter from President Fraser to the Dewan Sadattulla Khan, puts the whole matter in a clear light.

"To Dewan Sadatulla Khan, Health.
Fort St. George, May 25*th*, 1710.

"About some three days ago a servant of yours by name Muzzadeen brought me a letter, said to be from you, which I gave my Brahmin to be translated, at which I desired your servant to go and rest himself after his journey, until I had given answer to said letter; when he insolently and very pertly, as void of all manners and respect, insisted on the delivering up the villages. Else he would carry back your letter; which he did. I told him

---

* We continue the old name to prevent confusion; but henceforth Zulfikar Khan is styled Khan Bahadur in the records.

my business was not with him but with his master yourself.

"But, supposing the purport of said letter was to demand back the new villages, because they belong to Zulfikar Khan's Jaghire, which may be true. But you cannot but at the same time know that my noble great friend, the late Dawood Khan, gave an equivalent out of his own Jaghire to the great Zulfikar Khan which makes that matter even, and thus far I am in the right; and you likewise know that I gave away more than those villages brought in, so that the English here lived in all friendly tranquility with the late Nabob, until Yeavellapa, that plague of the poor and Cockatrice of all venom, when at Cudapa, never let the Nabob be quiet till he had gained his point to revoke the several former as well as late Perwannas, which confirmed those villages to our Company. So that one Perwanna is not sufficient to take away the force and power of all our former grants under the Nabob's signature and great chop; by which you would make the promise, faith, and truth of a great man of no more value than that of an ordinary man; which is a great derogation to the honor of a great personage.

"Yeavellappa deals treacherously with Madras, a place he is so much beholden to, where he stores up so much paddy and grain to await a scarce and dear season to increase the misery of the poor; and borrows large sums of money at the same time to enable him to pay his rent at the time due, else he must have been necessitated to sell at the market price which would be cheap.

"As for the four old villages, they were granted and confirmed to us about twenty years ago by the then Prince Khan Buksh, the great Assad Khan, and the then Zulfikar Khan, now Khan Bahadur, under their several and respective larger seals.

"My friendly council and advice to you is that you would consider and value the English as being the king's friend and in his favour, as may appear by his Royal Hosbullhookum from the throne to my late predecessor; and that you would keep the king's peace, by not committing any manner of hostility. I hope you will do nothing misbecoming, so wise a man as yourself, in so great a post and place of trust; and then you and I may come to have a better understanding at least till I hear from the Great Zulfikar Khan to whom I am now going to write, and have his answer; till when I shall be awake I need say no more."

About the same time Governor Fraser wrote another letter to Zulfikar Khan reminding him that the old villages had been granted to the English in consequence of the services rendered to the army of Aurungzebe by President Yale during the siege of Ginjee, and that the grant in question had been signed by his Zulfikar Khan's father, namely Assad Khan, the grand vizier. The remonstrance however was of no avail. Zulfikar Khan merely sent a short purwanna ordering that the villages granted by the Nabob Dawood Khan out of his jaghire should be delivered up to the Manager of the Poonamallee district.

CHAPTER XXIV.

GOVERNORSHIP OF MR. WILLIAM FRASER.

1710—11.

The administration of Mr. William Fraser was short and unhappy. It only lasted from November 1709 to July 1711, and was distinguished by circumstances which excited much animadversion from the Directors or Managers at home. It was through Mr. Fraser's intrigues and inveterate opposition, that Mr. Nathaniel Higginson had resigned and Mr. Thomas Pitt had been recalled; and now that he had obtained what appeared to be the object of his ambition, disorders arose at the Presidency and out-stations; and whilst quarrels broke out between the subordinate chiefs and the country authorities, the accounts were neglected, the consultation books were badly kept, and the advantages obtained by Mr. Pitt as regarded the out-villages were wholly lost, and the latter were retained for a while by the Renter of Poonamallee.

In the first place we must notice the troubles at Vizagapatam, which had their origin in circumstances that took place twelve years previously, but which reached a climax during the Governorship of Mr. Fraser. It seems that about the year 1698, two neighbouring Rajahs, Ananterauz and Pycrow, had borrowed large sums of money from Mr. Holcombe, the Deputy Governor of Vizagapatam.

Mr. Holcombe had been induced to enter into these transactions by a Brahmin named Juggapa, who had been largely bribed by the Rajahs to exert his influence in this direction. Unfortunately Mr. Holcombe had not lent his own money, but had borrowed for the purpose 44,000 pagodas of Fuckerla Khan, Nabob of Calinga. Seven years elapsed, but Mr. Holcombe had only repaid 37,500 pagodas, leaving a balance of 6,500 pagodas of the principal; and thus the debt due to the Nabob, inclusive of arrears of interest, amounted to some sixty or seventy thousand rupees. The following letter, written to Mr. Holcombe by Fuckerla Khan as far back as 1705, exhibits the then state of affairs.

"From Fuckerla Khan to Mr. Holcombe chief at Vizagapatam dated the 10th May 1705.

"You wrote me that you have received Pagodas 44000 principal of me.

"An account of what paid.

To a merchant upon my bill and order for a Jewel I bought of him Rs. 16,000 is Pagodas...	4600
Sent me to Vellore.............................	28000
To a bill payable to Govindaus and Veresedaus	4100
To Sundry bills amounting to..................	800
The total amount of what paid is...	37,500
The balance is Pagodas...............	6500
Together is...	44000

"It is true you have receipts under my seal for all the above mentioned accounts, excepting the balance 6,500 Pagodas out of the principal money lent, which amounts to Rs. 23,000.

"Other people in the world allow 3 or 2½ per cent., but you gave me a bond allowing me but one per cent (? per mensem); notwithstanding that being pretty tolerable interest, I agreed to it, and now it is above six or seven years past; for which time there is due to me 60 or 70 thousand rupees with principal and interest. Likewise 10 or 15 thousand rupees more or less, which together amounts to a hundred thousand rupees.

"I have showed a great esteem for you, and had that confidence in you as to intrust my estate into your hands. Therefore I am satisfied that no person of any other religion would have dealt so uncivilly and unrespectfully by me as you have acted. Likewise now you unreasonably defer the payment in telling me you will discharge the debt as soon as you receive money, and at my arrival in your place; but in the meantime you have traded with the money, and make at least 25 or 50 per cent. profit. Besides is it proper or handsome you should occasion me so much trouble in perpetually writing to you, and sending my people up and down, who always return without satisfactory answer? My money is like bread as hard as iron, so not easily digested. Perhaps you may imagine I cannot come to your place, so intend to wrong me of my money. But if I live I will certainly come into that part within the space of 4, 6, or 12 months, if I meet with any convenient opportunity; and then how can you hope or expect to have my favour, having rendered yourself so unjust and uncivil. Perhaps you may intend to give me the slip, and go for Madras or some other sea port town; but go where you will, you are still in king Aurungzebe's country. So I can procure order-sent by the Gusbadars to the Subah of that country, and seize upon your house and goods, and therewith clear my money or debt. Then afterwards take no further notice of you, which you will not digest, or well approve of. For according to any law I can demand my money, and will have it by fair means or foul. Therefore fear God and consider I must have my money. So draw bills upon Masulipatam, or else you shall repent it as long as you live. I write you this, as likewise I wrote you before by Phauntee Mahomed, which pray peruse and consider well of it. You must not think I only threaten you. For God knows, I am very impatient so expect a full and satisfactory answer; or else you shall find I will send orders with Gusbadars to Meida Khan and will wait no longer."

Shortly after this Mr. Holcombe died without paying the remainder of the debt; and Fuckerla Khan claimed the amount from the Company, as Mr. Holcombe had actually affixed the Company's seal to the obligation. The question was still unsettled when Mr. Fraser succeeded to the Governorship of Fort St. George. Meantime there had been a competition between Fuckerla Khan and another chief named Habib Khan for the Nabobship; and the successor to Mr. Holcombe had been imprudent enough to acknowledge the latter, and thus to increase the exasperation of Fuckerla Khan. The following extracts from the consultation books shortly after Mr. Fraser's accession will exhibit the progress of affairs.

" Monday, 27th March 1710. From the

chief and Council at Vizagapatam dated the 2nd and 7th instant, advising the great troubles they have had with Fuckerla Khan, by their having been so closely besieged by his people stopping up all avenues of their bounds. For remedy of which they advise us that they resolved to make proposals to accommodate matters in a friendly way with him, intending him a present of 5000 rupees in Europe goods; in order to which they sent a Portuguese Padre and a Dubash, in hopes thereby to appease him, or obtain his patience for some days. But he refused their offer, and sent back the messengers in a very angry manner, and wrote the chief that he must immediately pay the money (due from Mr. Holcombe), or leave the place or prepare to fight."

"Tuesday, 15th August. General letter from the Chief and Council at Vizagapatam read: wherein we observe that their troubles are rather suspended than any way accommodated, by Fuckerla Khan's being gone up to the Dasheroon's country to adjust accounts, and agree with Habib Khan for the Government of those countries; and they still continue to urge their arguments for the Company's paying that debt of Mr. Holcombe's. They advised that they have supplied Habib Khan with ten candy of country gunpowder and five candy of lead, and that the said Nabob desires a further supply of thirty candy of powder and twenty of lead, which they desire may be sent them down."

"Monday, 11th December. Received general letter from the Deputy Governor and Council at Vizagapatam assuring us that they had sent the Moollah and a Brahmin to Fuckerla Khan's camp, to have a sight of the seal affixed to Mr. Holcombe's obligation. But after waiting for some days they returned with answer that Fuckerla Khan was enraged to the last degree, and would not hear any more proposals about his money without prompt payment, but was coming himself within a day or two with guns, ammunition &c. to besiege their town; and had placed guards on the roads to prevent their sending or receiving any letters and provisions coming to them; and that Fuckerla Khan refusing to show the obligation, they are of opinion and believe that Mr. Holcombe's seal is affixed thereto and not the Honorable Company's.

"That on the 8th past the said Nabob with his army, consisting of about 7000 foot and 800 horse, encamped behind a great sand hill near the Town, and the 9th at night fired on their out guards; which being returned again by the English, made the enemy retire further and turn their siege into a blockade by stopping all provisions of which they were in great want; that they have made a Brigantine of the "Rising Sun" smack, and fitted her up in order to secure what may be put aboard in time of extremity."

"The foregoing being a recital of their said general letter almost verbatim.

"First. We observe that the Chief has strangely erred in his politics (not to say worse); that he having by his former frequent letters advised us, what he had then foreseen, as what might be the result and issue of not paying Mr. Holcombe's old debt to Fuckerla Khan, as the event now proves,—that the Chief in that case should not sooner and earlier get sufficiency of provisions for the use of their Garrison, at least until the monsoon should serve for our sending them supplies hence.

"Secondly. That the Chief should supply Nabob Habib Khan and Fuckerla Khan with so large a quantity of gunpowder and lead, when the said Nabobs and the Chief were on so precarious terms; and not only so but by their general letter of the 27th July last write us to send them 30 Candy of powder and 20 Candy of lead for a further supply to the said Nabob; notwithstanding the frequent cautions we gave them, or without ever considering they were strengthening the hands of said Nabob, who were then contriving of the means and ways of laying that siege, they have since formed against that Factory.

"Thirdly. It being now the Northerly monsoon, it is strange that the Chief should not have wrote to Bengal to the President and Council there to be supplied thence with whatever they wanted.

"Fourthly. That Juggapa the Brahmin, that arch knave and villain, who was the chief cause and instrument by the powerful bribes he received from time to time from the Rajahs Ananterauz and Pycrow, by whose means and persuasions he prevailed so far with Mr. Holcombe, as to induce him to lend those large sums of money at high interest to those said Rajahs; which is still a debt, which we may reasonably suppose to have been most or all Fuckerla Khan's money, and has been the original cause and first spring, whence all these troubles are derived and devolved upon us ; and notwithstanding our having so often or frequently wrote to Mr. Hastings, the Chief there, to send us up the said Juggapa either by sea or by land, which has never been complied with ; and being credibly informed Fuckerla Khan does demand of the Chief the said Brahmin, and that on the delivery up of him all the causes of their troubles shall cease.

"And now upon the whole, it is unanimously agreed that we write the Chief and Council, that upon the reading the said intended letter to them, that they had that instant seized the said Juggapa, and put him in irons, and secure all his books, papers and accounts ; which if the Chief should oppose or hinder the same, it is our positive and peremptory order that the Council, or any one of them, do execute this our order, and that the military and peons be assisting to him or them in this matter.

"It is likewise agreed that the President write his letter to Fuckerla Khan relating to the premises, and desire him to send us up a person fitly qualified to accommodate all matters and that in the meantime to withdraw his forces from the Factory."

Next year this troublesome business was brought to a close through the mediation of Habib Khan ; the money demanded being paid to Fuckerla Khan, and the obligation which was found to have the Company's seal affixed, being forwarded to Fort St. George. The record is chiefly remarkable as exposing the evils which arose at this early period from pecuniary dealings between the Company's servants and Native authorities ; and it is worthy of note as being the origin of a standing order which strictly prohibited all such dealings for the future.

We now turn to a curious entry which is very suggestive.

"Monday, 4th December. They having wrote us from Fort St. David that it has been usual for us at the festival times of the year to send them one of the ministers of this place, and Christmas being now approaching they request that one may be sent. It is, therefore, agreed and ordered that Mr. Jones do proceed thither, as soon as conveniently he can ; and that the paymaster do take care to fit him out for his journey accordingly."

Cases of breach of promise of marriage are always interesting, but we are rather inclined to regard the one we are now about to place before our readers as somewhat unique in its character. The matchmaking tendencies of the mamma and daughter, and the "interested" nature of the gentleman's affection, are plainly evident throughout the papers. Moreover the record is valuable as illustrating social life as it actually was at the commencement of the last century. The extracts will explain themselves.

"To the Honorable William Fraser, Esq. Governor of Fort St. George and to the Gentlemen of the Council.

"The petition of Anne Foquet and Elizabeth Brown doth humbly set forth the unworthy treatment your Petitioners have met with from Captain Henry Cornwall, Commander of the "Sherborne." Your Honor is no stranger to this story, nor the rest of the Gentlemen at this Honorable Board; therefore shall be as brief in relating it as we can. In the year 1707 and before he went last for England, Henry Cornwall aforesaid, and your Petitioner Elizabeth Brown, did enter into a contract of marriage, and that in as solemn a manner as such contracts usually are, or can be done; for we plighted our faith either to other in the most binding terms, and changed rings in the presence of competent witnesses; Anne Foquet your petitioner, Mr. James Wendey, then one of the ministers of this place, and Mr. Bernard Benyon, merchant being present. And for the due performing of the aforesaid contract, the said Henry Cornwall and Elizabeth Brown did enter into articles in writing, and did both of them sign and seal the same in the presence of the Rev. Mr. James Wendey and Mr. Bernard Benyon aforesaid, who hath been sworn in Court. And moreover, the said Captain Henry Cornwall did bind himself in a bond of one thousand pounds sterling for the due performance of those articles; and further to confirm us in the reality of his intentions, he made a gift to your petitioner Elizabeth Brown of what estate he had in India and left a will in her hands; wherein he bequeaths her his whole estate and makes her sole Executrix. But notwithstanding all the vows, ties, and obligations he had brought himself under, Captain Henry Cornwall in a short time after his arrival in England marries himself to another woman ; and after all this injurious and unfair dealing towards your petitioner, the said Henry Cornwall, to prove himself the same man throughout, would have his bonds and obligations under his hand and seal to go for nothing, and to be of as little force and validity as his words and vows. We, therefore, your petitioners humbly apply ourselves to your Honors for redress, hoping you will oblige him to satisfy his bond for one thousand pounds, which he hath forfeited ; a poor reparation for all the injustice he hath done us. There hath been a suit commenced upon this Bond, for some time depending in the Mayor's Court, but deferred to be brought to a judgment upon advice that Captain Henry Cornwall was designed for this place ; presuming, as may be supposed, he would either comply with his bond, or offer such terms as would be accepted of ; and the Revd. Padre Lewis did before and since the arrival of the "Sherborne," speak to your petitioners to accommodate matters amicably with Captain Cornwall (if it might be done) and not drive things to extremity. To which your petitioners did not seem averse. But instead of offering to come to an accommodation, Captain Henry Cornwall, the second day after his arrival, sent a letter to your Petitioner Elizabeth Brown, of which she cannot better, nor more modestly give you the contents, than by saying, it was made up of all the ill nature and ill language he is master of ; and after so much unworthy and base treatment as we have met with from this man, for him to think at last to run us down, and to carry his point by calumny and slander is so vile a thing, that no man who hath the least sense of honor or the least grain of honesty would be guilty of. We shall not be further troublesome to your Honors, but only beg leave to observe, that if such principles and such practices be connived at, no man's honour, person, or estate can be any longer safe. We hope your Honors will take things into your serious consideration, and do us that justice which to your wisdom shall appear our due. The reason of our addressing your Honors at this time is, that Mr. Mayor hath refused his warrant to arrest Captain Cornwall in an action of one thousand pounds, at the suit of your Petitioner Elizabeth Brown, and we as in duty bound shall ever pray. Fort St. George, February 12th, 1711."

Captain Cornwall's answer to these charges is still more interesting.

" Monday, 19th February. To the Honorable William Fraser, Esq. Governor of Fort St. George and Council.

" Gentlemen—" You were pleased on Thursday last to summon me to answer to a petition, preferred by Mrs. Elizabeth Brown and Anne Foquet of this place, touching a designed marriage between the said Elizabeth Brown and self, a perfect account of which I gave at that time, and comes inserted in this narrative.

" The motive that induced me to enter into an obligation of that nature was the assurances Mrs. Anne Foquet gave me of preferment from England by her and her friends' recommendations home ; which proved no ways serviceable, but rather the contrary. I often repeated to her and daughters, if I could not better myself by post or fortune, I would by no means think of complying with that obligation. When Mrs. Foquet's friends proved of no use, I solicited my own relations, that entirely refused all merchandize, being strangers to trade. Then the time drawing near for the India Shipping to depart that year, I petitioned the Honorable United Company to come abroad a passenger on Captain Phrip, which they granted and he refused, being full and my circumstances not able to permit me to pay for my passage. I then solicited both the Captain Hudsons who refused the same. I then advised with my friends what method to take that might be of service to Mrs. Elizabeth Brown, and a sufficient acquittance to me. First, I declared my circumstances, so miserable when in England, I was forced to run in debt and that considerably. Secondly, I had no interest in the Company then governing to serve me by recommendation abroad. Thirdly, I presume the most of this place knows Mrs. Foquet not able to better any one's circumstances by interest or fortune. Notwithstanding her present encouragement in this affair, these circumstances considered on both sides, if any one gentleman can see the least appearance of any thing but complete misery, in case of that marriage, I should willingly submit to the several sentiments. I cannot perceive that, Mrs. Anne Foquet ever designed a marriage, because she declared to Robert Raworth Esq., Mayor of this place, that she refused me marriage before I went home, because she was assured I would marry in England, when she would have the opportunity of prosecuting this obligation. Further, why did Mrs. Anne Foquet and Brown give me an obligation of Captain Lee's, now Commander of the " Litchfield," to prosecute him for not complying with the marriage according to his obligation, not out of date at the commencing of mine, if she designed her daughter my wife. I can give several instances wherein Mrs. Foquet has showed herself a designing woman of no sincerity. She and her daughter are pleased to term the penalty of the obligation, a poor reparation for injuries I have done them. If they were as just in their aspersions as I have been in this proceeding, they would not have troubled your Honor and Council with their petition on this occasion.

" I think, since I could not procure a passage out occasioned by my miserable circumstances, Mrs. Foquet and daughter are under obligations to me, that I advised them of it in order to Mrs. Elizabeth Brown's not refusing any offer to her advantage. I did at my first arrival at the West coast, order my attorney here to make Mrs. Elizabeth Brown a considerable present for the favours received when last here. But since my arrival at this Port, I found so many malicious reports from her, that it has entirely removed the thoughts of any such thing. My circumstances are miserable enough, having lost all I was worth, by my misfortune in Ceylon ; and the balance of my accounts for four years' service in this place amounts to so small a sum that I fear

I shall go off a debtor from this place. I am
ready to make oath in every particular here inserted ; hoping your Honor and the Council will
take it into your serious consideration ; then doubt
not but you will perceive my actions on my side
justifiable ; otherwise I must refer myself to the
Courts at home, by whose verdict I must rest
satisfied. I am, with due respect,

Your Honor's and Council's most humble Servant,
HENRY CORNWALL."

The Judgment of the Governor and Council
upon this case is worthy of record.

"Monday, 19th February 1711. Pursuant to
the order of last Consultation, Mrs. Foquet, and
her daughter Elizabeth Brown, as likewise Captain
Cornwall appear now before us ; where after all
parties were fully heard, more especially Captain
Cornwall, all persons being desired to withdraw :—
it is the unanimous opinion of the Board (Mr.
Raworth excepted), that Captain Henry Cornwall,
having married a wife in England notwithstanding
his preengagement with Mrs. Brown, he has forfeited his obligation and thereby become liable
to the penalty therein expressed ; but in regard
we ought to weigh matters in the scales of Equity
and right reason, and considering the present
circumstances of Captain Cornwall which are but
moderate, having met with great losses, and
he generously offering a moiety of what he has in
the world, and he having cleared the reputation of
said Mrs. Brown ; both parties being called in,

were reconciled and made friends, and the said Captain Cornwall's proposal accepted of."

About this time the King of Pegu appears to have been very anxious to obtain some articles, of European workmanship, particularly clocks, as appears from the following letter to the Governor of Fort St. George, dated 24th February, 1711.

" In the jurisdiction of Sunapranda and Thamadiha, the precious kingdom of Ava and Golden Court, Rajah of Ni and king of twenty and three kingdoms and Monarchies, Lord of Silver, Gold, Amber, Ruby mines, and red and gold Palaces 12 in number made of Gold, Lord of the Elephant of great value, Lord of many horses of great price, Lord of all nations, Lord of all manner of arms, Lord of many armies, Lord of this world, the excellent High and Mighty Lord,

" His order to the Governor of Madras, being informed, that amongst the English nation, there are many able men, and that without much trouble a clock may be had. I desire that it may be thus, viz. that it strikes the hours distinctly, beginning in the morning by one and so on till twelve ; having two images to strike the hours on the bell or clock. This and another clock of Malta, with a woman's image pouring oil in a vessel which runs all the hour ; and when it is out the said image fills it again and so every hour. The king having heard of these things will have much to be done to get them ; and if not to be got, to send a man here to make them and shall then return to his country. I have sent by the Captain of my Ship, Cojah Simon, to the Governor of Madras two Ruby rings ; if amongst the English or Portuguese there is any curiosity to be got, let it be sent. If my desire is accomplished there shall be great rewards according to my piety, &c."

The governorship of Mr. Fraser was, as already indicated, brought to a sudden close by the arrival of a successor, as appears from the following entry.

"Wednesday, 11th July. This morning about 8 o'clock, came ashore the Honorable Edward Harrison Esq., who produced hisCommission, dated the 22nd December 1710, appointing him President for the Right Honorable United East India Company's affairs on the coast of Coromandel and Orissa, and of the Ginjee and Mahratta country, and Governor of Fort St. George, Fort St. David, and the Island of Sumatra. Which being read, the late President William Fraser Esq. did resign the chair, and deliver the keys of the Fort to the said Edward Harrison Esq."

CHAPTER XXV.

GOVERNORSHIP OF MR. EDWARD HARRISON.

1711—12.

The commencement of the Governorship of Mr. Harrison is a fitting moment for reviewing the contemporary state of Southern India and the Dekkan. The declining condition of the Mogul power had led to the establishment of new relations between the English and the Native authorities; and at the same time we are approaching the period when our historians generally have commenced what they have been pleased to term the history of the British empire in India. Henceforth therefore the new facts we shall bring forward from the official records will rapidly increase in value. They will serve to throw a clearer light upon one of the most obscure portions of the history of the Mogul rule; and thus they will form a connecting link between the dry Native annals of Southern India, and the delightful and picturesque history of Robert Orme.

The death of the great Aurungzebe in 1707, and the subsequent struggle between his three sons which led to the establishment of Shah Aulum on the throne of Delhi, have already been noticed; and it will be remembered that a large portion of the Mahomedan conquests in the Carnatic, including the country round Madras, had been granted as a jaghire to the celebrated general Zulfikar Khan. The rising of the Sikhs to the west of Delhi had called away Zulfikar Khan to the assistance of his royal master Shah Aulum. For a brief period Dawood Khan had acted as Soubah of Golconda, in behalf of Zulfikar Khan; but in his turn was called away by the troubles in the North West.*

In 1710 the Dewan Sadatulla Khan was appointed Nabob of the Carnatic, and appears to have retained the government until his death in 1732. He is briefly mentioned by Orme as having been a regular and acknowledged Nabob of the Carnatic; and appears to have been noticed by that historian in consequence of his being the first Nabob who attempted to render the office hereditary. Orme says that Sadatulla Khan, " having no issue, adopted the two sons of his brother; appointing the elder, Dost Ali, to succeed in the Nabobship; and conferring on the younger, Boker Ali, the government of Vellore." This Sadatulla Khan has already been mentioned as having required Governor Fraser to deliver up the five out-villages to the Renter of Poonamallee; and his further intercourse with the English will be fully illustrated in future chapters.

As regards the general state of the Mogul em-

---

* From entries in the Consultation Books, respectively dated 2nd of October and 24th of November, 1710, we learn that Isuph Khan held the post of Subah of Golconda at this time, but that in consequence of some troubles caused by the Mahrattas in the neighbourhood of Golconda, Dawood Khan was again appointed Subah in his room.

pire during the reign of King Shah Aulum, but little need be said. Shah Aulum sacrificed the prestige of his sovereignty for the sake of a hollow peace. He effected a compromise with the Rajpoots and Mahrattas, but though he thus appeared to secure his throne from their attacks, he was wholly unable to repress the growing disorders, which in the end produced the downfal of the Mogul dynasty. He died in 1712, after a short reign of five years.

The great event in the governorship of Mr. Harrison, namely the rupture between the English at Fort St. David and the Mussulman Governor of Ginjee, is strikingly illustrative of the contemporary state of Southern India. Sixteen miles south of Pondicherry and a hundred miles south of Madras, was the English settlement of Fort St. David, to which we have already had frequent occasion to allude. In 1691 the English had bought the settlement, previously named Tegnapatam, of Ram Raja, the Mahratta sovereign who was at that time in possession of Ginjee. The plot of Dr. Blackwell to deliver up Fort St. David to Zulfikar Khan in 1693 has been mentioned in its proper place. The celebrated fortress of Ginjee is worthy of a passing notice. It is seated on the declivities of three detached rocky mountains, of very difficult ascent and from four to 600 feet in height, which were connected by lines of works enclosing an extensive triangle in the plains between them; and for centuries this place had been regarded by the natives of Southern India as the strongest Fort in the Carnatic. Its origin dates far back in immemorial antiquity. Somewhere about the time of the wars of the white and red Roses, it appears to have been the great stronghold of the kings of Chola (Tanjore) against the famous old Hindoo sovereigns of Bijanugur. At length about D. 1500,—about the time of the battle of Bosworth Field and the accession of the house of Tudor,—the kingdom of Chola, and with it the fortress of Ginjee, was transferred to the possession of the Rajahs of Bijanugur; and long after the kingdom of Bijanugur had been overthrown by the Mussulman sovereigns of the Dekkan, the Hindoos still retained possession of Ginjee. About 1669 the Fort was captured by the Mussulman king of Bijapore; but in 1677 it was taken by Sevajee the great Mahratta. For four or five years it held out under Ram Raja against the whole force of the army of Aurungzebe; but was finally captured by Zulfikar Khan in 1698. A series of Rajpoot governors were then appointed by the Mogul, and ruled the surrounding country in his name; but during the anarchy which followed the death of Aurungzebe, these Rajpoots affected independence and assumed the rank of Rajahs.

At the time of Mr. Harrison's accession to the Government of Fort St. George, Serope Singh was Governor or Rajah of Ginjee. It is difficult to assign the exact limits of the country under the jurisdiction of Serope Singh; but it was probably bounded on the north by the territory under the Nabobs of Arcot, and on the south by the Hindoo principalities of Trichinopoly and Tanjore. Fort

St. David was thus included in the country under Serope Singh, in the same way that Fort St. George was included in the country of Sadatulla Khan. It appears that a former Deputy Governor of Fort St. David, Mr. Roberts by name, had in some sort of way, not sufficiently explained in the records, become security to Serope Singh for the sums collected by the Renters. Subsequently the Renters had run away with the money, and Serope Singh held the English Company responsible for the amount. By way of expediting a settlement, Serope Singh had carried away two European Officers of the garrison of Fort St. David, and confined them and treated them with the greatest barbarity at Ginjee. In February 1711, an attempt was made by the Government of Fort St. David to seize some Chief men of the Ginjee government, who happened to be in the neighbourhood of Fort St. David. No prisoners were taken, but three Moormen, and one of the Fort St. David Garrison were killed on the spot. Great troubles were therefore to be anticipated from this direct act of hostility on the part of the English; and as it appears that the Government of Fort St. David had acted in many cases most injudiciously, and that the utmost disorder prevailed in the Garrison, Mr. Raworth, a member of the Council of Fort St. George was dispatched to the scene of action, accompanied by five European ships whose presence it was hoped would bring the enemy to terms. Mr. Raworth set off in July 1711. The following extracts will illustrate the state of affairs. The enemy's force from Ginjee had blockaded Fort St. David by land, so that ammunition and provisions could only be forwarded by sea. The first extract is entered in the consultation on Sunday evening 19th August, 1711, and is entitled " A true narrative of an action that happened between Captain Roach's party and our enemy this day, being the 11th of August, 1711." It is related in Captain Roach's own words, and describes a desperate encounter in which he was engaged with the forces of Ginjee. The narrative is as follows :—

"I was ordered to possess myself of a part of the bounds, where the enemy were seen to be firing very briskly from last night; which I did this morning by break of day. I ordered about 200 peons that belonged to the outguards to attend me. The coolies began to work about the demolishing the walls by six in the morning, and continued till 12 at noon; but could not hear of any of the enemy's to be near our bounds, only a few peons about a mile off. But about 12 o'clock, intelligence was brought that Mahobat Khan, with all the force of Ghinjee, was within a mile of our bounds. Upon which I despatched immediately a peon to the Governor and Council, who was not arrived in two hours. In the interim, before I had any relief from the rest of the bounds, they attacked me with about 400 horses and 1000 foot. It was a great misfortune to me their attacking the party Captain Coventry had the command of, and Ensign Somervile; the latter proved such a coward, that he was the occasion of the ruin of the whole party, in showing them an example by running away first, which cost him his life, and abundance more of the same party. But I must do Captain Coventry that justice, that he behaved himself extraordinarily well, and would have made a very good officer, if please God he had lived. He received several wounds before he dropt. I had my horse shot under me, and was charged several times by the whole party of horse upon both flanks and rear, and kept them in play till they were glad to leave me master of the field with less than forty men. There was not one of the 200 peons I carried with me, would stand, neither officers, nor peons ; but when the horse charged me, they presently ran away. If they had but stood by me, I would have mounted as many horses of the enemies as would have made a good troop for the Company. For there was not less than seventy or eighty of them running about the field, without riders, their masters being dismounted. We compute that the enemy could have lost not less than 140 and 150 men killed and wounded, besides horses. I have buried the dead all in the field of battle, excepting Captain Coventry and Ensign Somervile whom I sent to the fort. I leave any impartial person to judge what the loss of the enemy must be, when they were at the push of the pike for two hours together, and applied with our bullets and swan shot as fast as possibly we could. This is the true narrative of what happened."

The next extract, dated 10th September, 1711, will show the disorders which prevailed at this time amongst the soldiers of the garrison. It is entitled

"An account of the murder of Thomas Parsons, Serjeant, by Jacob Vanbashayson, Centinel, one of the Bengal men, but at present belonging to Captain Roach's party."

"Thomas Kirk, John Buck, and Abraham Clark, belonging to Captain Viver's company at Cuddalore, by his permission came to the Fort to visit some of their comrades, particularly Thomas Parsons who had the command of the party at Tevenapatam Gate. On meeting him they went in company to a punch house near the said gate, where they found several more of their vocation drinking; but being none of their acquaintance, they passed by them, saluting them with their usual ceremony, " Good morrow to ye brothers," and so went into another yard, where they stayed no longer than to drink a dram each man. Then they were returning, when Jacob Vanbashayson, a Dutchman, without any manner of provocation given, attacked the said Serjeant Thomas Parsons with his naked sword, and struck him several blows over his head. Secondly, without giving him time to defend himself, he gave him a thrust into his body, on which he immediately fell. John Kirk abovementioned was the person next to the Serjeant, who the said Jacob Vanbashayson attacked in the same manner he did Parsons. But seeing the fate intended him, he defended himself so well with his sword (which was not drawn), that though he cut his scabbard in six places and made several thrusts at him, yet he received no harm; but had certainly been murdered, had not John Buck stept into his assistance. John Buck immediately called Jacob Vanbashayson, and seized his sword, which—notwithstanding he drew through his hand and gave him some strokes over the head, and at last made a stab at him which just touching his thigh,—for safety of his life he was obliged to quit his hold; when the said Jacob Vanbashayson still pursued him, and to save his life, having no weapon, he was forced to dodge him round some pillars which were in the yard, till he found an opportunity to go out of the door; which he immediately embraced, but as he was going over the threshhold was prevented by Derrick Johnson, who pulled him back by the coat and likewise knocked down John Kirk. By this time the guard from Tevenapatam came, and made the two Dutchmen prisoners. Though they resisted some time with sword in hand, before they would surrender, and the murderer was so very desperate for fear of condign punishment, that had he not been bound he would open breasted have run upon the bayonets on the muzzle of the guard's pieces.

"Jacob Vanbashayson says nothing more in his defence than that he was drunk and knew not what he did, that he had no malice at all against the Serjeant, and repented sincerely of the fact. Notwithstanding, as he had imbrued his hands in a fellow soldier's blood, he thought he deserved to die; but begged if we could not be merciful, as he had good relations (though he now was no more than a Centinel) that he might not die the death of a rogue, but a soldier, and be shot to death by a file or two of men of the party he belonged to.

"Derrick Johnson who was with him, is a fellow that has been publicly scourged at Batavia, and wears the cross on his back. He denies he was accessory to the murder, and that he only interfered when he knocked Kirk down, to part the persons engaged. But all circumstances make the contrary appear, and shows his inclinations as good. But it was not in his power to commit as heinous a crime as his companion.

"Thomas Parsons was brought speechless into the fort; but at that juncture more occasioned by liquor than his wound. The Doctor had some hopes at first; but in six hours they ended with the fellow's life. Upon opening his body we found the wound, very near direct down, and that the sword had penetrated his midriff and wounded several of his intestines.

"'This is what the three persons first named have declared upon oath before the Deputy Governor and Council.*   THO. GRAY. Secretary."

"Fort St. David, September 11th 1711.

About this time a Lieutenant and Ensign were found drunk and incapable whilst on guard at Cuddalore, at a time of imminent danger. Accordingly they were sent to Madras, and the following remarks upon their case, as well as upon the murder of Parsons, are entered in the consultation book as follows:—

"Thursday, 20th September, 1711. Lieutenant Viver and Ensign Williams being sent for up, and

---

* The murderer appears to have been subsequently executed.

the charge against them being read by the Secretary, they were asked by the President, what they had to say in their vindication; who making many frivolous excuses, but at last confessing their crime and begging pardon, were ordered to withdraw, and the President offered to the board as follows. That the military in general under this Presidency are, by slack discipline for the past two years, become so intolerably sottish and disorderly that it is high time a reformation should be made for the security of our settlements, and the Honorable Company's estate committed to our charge.

"The barbarous murder lately committed on Serjeant Parsons by a drunken Dutchman at Fort St. David, is testimony sufficient to what a height of insolence matters are grown; and it is well known that Mr. Farmer when Deputy Governor of Fort St. David durst not go out of the Fort for fear the Guard should shoot him as he passed the gate.

"Add to these instances the daily disorders of drunkenness in this garrison, which though severely punished, yet the seeds still remain, and the cure is not thoroughly perfected.

"If the officers themselves, whose business it is by strictness of discipline and good examples to preserve their command and keep their people within the bounds of their duty; if they shall be found dead drunk upon their posts in a time of service when surrounded by the enemy, what can be expected but ruin and destruction to the affairs of those that employ them.

"Offered further that the crime in our European Armies is punished in a capital manner; and then the question was put and unanimously agreed that Lieutenant Viver and Ensign Williams be cashiered, and that Lieutenant Viver do prepare to go for England by the Halifax."

Whilst Fort St. David was thus in danger of falling into the hands of Serope Singh, Mr. Harrison thought it advisable to lay the whole matter before Zulfikar Khan, in the hope that the interference of so great a man might have its effect upon the Rajah of Ginjee. The letter to Zulfikar Khan is dated 11th October, 1711 and is as follows:—

"To His Excellency Zulfikar Khan Bahadur, Nurzerat Sing, Backshee of the whole Empire, &c.

"Sir,—Understanding how great a share your Excellency bears in the Government of this mighty Empire, I thought it my duty to acquaint you of my arrival here to preside over the English affairs in these parts; and I think myself obliged more especially so to do, in regard that my predecessor in this Government (Mr. Pitt) have informed me, before I left England; that as your Excellency was one of the Chief pillars of the Empire, so you had upon sundry occasions manifested your good inclinations to the English in these parts; and that it was under your shadow and by your good countenance that they enjoy those privileges and security in their trade, which now they do. While Your Excellency lay with your army at Ginjee, I understand you were pleased to issue out your Purwanna for securing to us our privileges at Tevenapatam (Fort St. David). Upon my arrival here I found that place in trouble; Serope Singh having seized some of the English there and carried them prisoners to Ginjee, on occasion of some disgust given him by a former Governor. We are but a small handful of people, and our business is trade ; and, therefore, all quarrels with the Government is extremely prejudicial to us, and distroys the end for which we settle in these parts. Since my coming I have laboured all I could to compose this difference, but to my great trouble, it hath hitherto proved ineffectual. If this affair comes to be represented at Court, no doubt but Serope Singh's agents will do it as much to our disadvantage as they can. I, therefore, humbly beg of your Excellency, that if any complaint be made against us on this subject that you will be pleased to excuse the matter, and that we desire nothing more than to live in tranquility and peace in our small Factories. And if Your Excellency would be pleased to procure us his Majesty's Hoosbullhookum to Serope Singh, to let us live in quiet and mend on trade, it will be a singular service to your petitioner, and which he shall always retain a grateful sense of."

To this letter no reply appears to have been received. Zulfikar Khan, now the great Bahadur Khan, was far too much engaged to trouble himself about the affairs of a small Factory of foreign merchants, like those at Fort St. David and Fort St. George.

Our next extract is a still more curious one.

Mr. Raworth on arriving at Fort St. David to take up the duties of Deputy Governor, discovered that his immediate predecessor Mr. Farmer had ordered the destruction of a great quantity of grain and a large number of villages belonging to the Ginjee government, simply because he had heard that Mohabat Khan, the commander of the beseiging force, had boasted that the English " dared not make another attempt by marching out into the country belonging to Serope Singh." This needless act of destruction and ravage naturally increased both the exasperation and the demands of the Rajah of Ginjee, who at that time had sent ambassadors to Fort St. David with the terms on which he was prepared to conclude a peace. When these terms were communicated to Fort St. George, together with the cause of their being so much in excess of the Renters debt, the matter was warmly commented on by Governor Harrison and Council as follows :—

" Monday, 29th October. A general letter from Fort St. David was read ; in which to our great surprise, we find that Mr. Farmer and the Council in his time have set their hands to the following paragraph.

" It is most certainly true that Serope Singh could not before in justice demand more of us than the Renters debt, and not that neither because Mr. Roberts was their security when they run away, not the Company ; but the destruction of fifty or sixty thousand pagodas worth of grain, about fifty two villages and towns, among which was his favorite town Yembollum, and killing the

Pandarrum: these are things which really make his demands carry too much justice with them; and we heartily wish the differences may be composed, and so happily settled as before the commencement of this war. Without your permission though to disburse something considerable out of the Company's cash, we shall not ask it till we find an absolute necessity."

"We (the Governor and Council of Fort St. George) cannot but observe with a great deal of concern the unaccountable folly and ill-management of these gentlemen through the whole course of this affair; but most particularly in this article. For after they had sent out all their forces, without any orders from hence, to burn and destroy all the country and grain round about them, empowered by a single order signed by Mr. Farmer only,—they now as good as tell us in so many words, that the unlawful depredations they have committed really make Serope Singh's demands carry too much justice with them; and shamefully confess that they are afraid they shall be necessitated to ask us to disburse something considerable out of the Company's cash. Mr. Farmer and his then Council would have done very well to have considered this inconvenience before they proceeded so rashly on their own heads."

A few days afterwards some further progress was made in effecting a settlement with the ambassadors of Serope Singh, as will be seen by the following extracts.

"Tuesday, 6th November. The President

communicates to the Board a letter from the Deputy Governor of Fort St. David; the substance of which is as follows :—

"That the enemy cannot be brought to more moderate demands than thirty thousand Chuckrums, which is sixteen thousand six hundred pagodas. In consideration of which they will give us three towns, Trevandrum, Padre Copang and Coronuttum, besides their half of all the towns that lay part within and part without our bounds. They likewise agree for ever to renounce all claim to our bounds, and all pretensions upon us whatsoever, with the usual presents of horses and vests upon the like occasion. To all which the Deputy Governor desires a speedy answer; this being their last result, and that he keeps the ambassadors with very much difficulty from returning to Ginjee."

"Then the state of the Fort St. David war was taken into consideration and fully debated.

"Agreed that our Honorable Masters are at four thousand pagodas charge more or less per month for maintaining the war, besides several stores and provisions sent from hence; and no rent was received for the villages in our bounds since the beginning of the war, which is an intolerable charge; and no hopes of any ease as long as the war continues, amounting to forty-eight thousand pagodas per annum.

"Agreed that if the war continues, our people will be shut up in their bounds, and we must supply them with grain from hence and all other necessaries. Most of their inhabitants out of fear would desert them; and our merchants, though they have made a large contract, will never be able to bring in their goods; and consequently we shall have our broad cloth left upon our hands when the next year's shipping arrives.

"Agreed likewise unanimously that let us continue the war never so long, we can never hope to be reimbursed one farthing of our vast expenses. It would indeed have been well, if all these things had been duly considered before our predecessors were so far engaged in it. But it is never too late to repent of wrong measures, and now we must make the best of a bad market; wherefore we have agreed that a letter be wrote to the Deputy Governor and Council of Fort St. David as follows :—

"To Robert Raworth, Esq., Deputy Governor of Fort St. David and Council.

"Sirs,—This morning the Governor has laid before us Mr. Raworth's letter of the 3rd instant, wherein he writes that the enemy will not come to any agreement unless we consent to pay thirty thousand Chuckrums, which we take to be sixteen thousand six hundred and odd pagodas. In consideration of which they will give the villages of Trevandrum, Padre Copang and Coronuttum, besides their half of all the towns which lie part within our hedge and part without, and that they will entirely renounce all claim to our bounds on any pretence whatsoever.

"We have very seriously considered the first article and find it to be so unreasonable a sum of money that we can never consent to pay it on our Honorable Masters' account.

"We cannot judge if it be worth while to buy the three villages before mentioned, and the half of the towns that lie part within our bounds and part without, till you send us a computation of what revenue they will annually yield, and what security we can have we shall continue in quiet possession of them hereafter. For we must be of opinion we have too much ground already at your settlement to defend against an enemy. If Serope Singh dares dispute a grant confirmed to us by Zulfikar Khan Bahadur, what value ought we to put upon his grant, (or what else he will call it) who is no more in comparison with the other than his Buckshi is to him, and may be not so much. Pray let this point be urged home, and let us have a speedy answer.

"An entire renounciation of claim to all things within our bounds is a tender point to be handled; for his pretending to a claim, after Zulfikar Khan Bahadur's grant, is an undeniable reason why we should buy no grants of him; since by the same rule the next Governor of Ginjee may dispute our title to all we possess, and, by the same forcible means may compel us to pay what sum he pleases, so that our title will always be precarious.

"We should consent to paying off the Renter's debt; and if we could have good security that even he himself and the rogues about him would not molest us in the possession of these grants he offers, we might though unwillingly consent to pay a sum of money for them, but never the sum they insist upon. Since upon the best account we can get of the villages here, the rent will be but inconsiderable.

"We shall wait your answer to these material points, and in the mean time desire that the treaty may go on in the manner we have mentioned; that is to say that the Renter's debt be kept apart and made up by itself; and if we give any thing more that it may be for some thing that you are satisfied will bring in an equivalent in a few years, or otherwise we can never consent to buy till we have orders from England.

"We leave this management as we did formerly to the Deputy Governor, with the same directions that he lay the treaty before the Board, ere the agreement is perfected."

Immediately afterwards further intelligence was received from Fort St. David to the effect that the Company's merchants and all the chief inhabitants, were determined to leave the bounds if the treaty should break through; also that the towns offered by Serope Singh were worth six thousand chuckrums per annum; and that if the ambassadors were once suffered to return to Ginjee there would be no hopes of getting them down a second time; and if the English should be forced to send their own ambassadors to Ginjee for a peace, it would cost at least double the money. Accordingly another letter was dispatched to Mr. Raworth, from which we make the following extracts.

"We are still of the same opinion for a speedy and honorable peace. We agree that Serope Singh ought to have satisfaction for the Renter's debt, and we should as readily agree to make Mr. Roberts pay it, if it was in our power. But since it is not, we must by the necessity of affairs submit to pay it for him; because he was the Company's Governor, and it being always customary for the Governors to treat singly with the great men of these parts, that whatever is transacted between them, they look upon it as firm as if done with the Company themselves. We shall apply the money we have attached belonging to Mr. Roberts, for the payment of this matter as far as it will go, and shall take care to debit him for the remainder.

"We think this article of our treaty ought to be first settled; and as to the remaining part of the sum demanded, we had much rather let his precarious villages alone than have any thing to do with them; though we must confess six thousand chuckrums per annum is a sufficient rent for the sum we are to pay.

"If you can make good what you write in your letter, and can have good security that we shall enjoy the villages peaceably, and be unmolested in our affairs, we are content that you make a peace upon the terms that you mention; though we hope you will show your dexterity in procuring an abatement.

"It will behove you to be very circumspect in the Articles of the treaty, and to part with no money till you have some security. For there is not a more faithless wretch upon earth than the man you have to deal with. We desire that there may be an article inserted for the ease and security of passengers at Tanapollum, which we think is the place where Mr. Raworth formerly met with so much trouble in going to Fort St. David.

"You will do well to lay these matters now before your Council; and before you conclude the treaty, it will be proper that you protest in form jointly against Mr. Roberts as the author of all these troubles, and the person that ought to be accountable for all the damages sustained thereby.

"As for your merchants offering to leave the bounds, we cannot but think it a great piece of insolence at such a juncture; and since they would seem thereby to necessitate you to a compliance, it was a very proper time to ask them how much they could contribute to a peace. When they made their contract, they knew the war was a afoot; and though you have not yet sent us a copy of your contract, we do not remember you ever mentioned that you had obliged yourselves to buy a peace.

"It is a great sum of money we now consent to, and should never have done it upon any terms but the equivalent to re-imburse us. We shall impatiently expect your answers."

We gather from the following graphic account of an attack on the enemy's entrenchments, that the negociations were for a while broken off.

"Friday, 25th January, 1712. A general letter from the Deputy Governor and Council of Fort St. David, dated the 20th instant, was read; acquainting us that they had made an attack upon an entrenchment of the enemy's at a place called Crimumbaukum, about half way between that place and Pondicherry, in the following manner.

"Mr. Raworth being advised that a party of about three hundred Moorish foot detached from their entrenchment at Crimumbaukum, used in their rounds to pass between Coniquile and our hedge. Ordered Captain Courtney and Captain Howson, with sixty Grenadiers, to lay ambuscade for them on the 19th, in a place that was thought the most convenient, and if possible cut them off. Accordingly at nine they went to the place appointed, where they waited till one o'clock, when perceiving none of the enemy appeared they marched directly to their entrenchment, which was immediately alarmed, about forty of them being without the door, who repairing in with a great deal of precipitation on their approach, excluded about twenty-two of their comrades. All which were immediately put to the sword, and then they (Captains Courtney and Howson) ordered Serjeant Aulin with two file of men, to mount the wall on the opposite side; which he did with a great deal of bravery, and forced them to retreat where the two captains were with the main body of the party; who immediately upon it ordered forty grenadoes to be flung in, which did wonderful execution. And while they were in this consternation, the grenadoes flying in pieces amongst them, and the serjeant on the other side firing upon them with swan shot, they forced open the door and entered sword in hand; where they met with a good stout repulse. But the execution done upon them before had so dispirited them, that in the end every man began to shift for himself; some making for the door, and others flinging themselves over the wall into the ditch, in order to make their escape; till what with those that got away, and those that fell, they had in a short time free possession of the place without any molestation; when they had an opportunity to view the slain which amounted to more than one hundred. Besides which they say the ground was all strewed with pieces of skulls, hands, and legs, which to be sure was the effect of the grenadoe shells."

The disorderly state of the garrison of Fort St. David has already been illustrated, but still we cannot avoid bringing forward the following particulars as giving us an insight not only into the affairs of Fort St. David, but into military life in general as it was a hundred and fifty years ago.

" Wednesday, 28th January. The President acquaints the Board that the Deputy Governor and Council of Fort St. David have sent up Lieutenant Courtney, Ensign Brooks, and Serjeant Peterson prisoners in two Mussulars, for several crimes set forth as follows in their general letter.

" On Tuesday last Captain Courtney having dined with the Deputy Governor (Mr. Raworth) went as he was accustomed into Mr. Weld's room, where was sitting Ensign Paddle. He walked backwards and forwards for sometime without speaking a word. But at last attacked him in a very odd sort of a manner, telling him he was an impudent fellow, son of a Skip Jack, and used abundance of other epithets, very improper for a man that carries a commission, to utter or take; but Paddle it seems, regarding the place he was in, and not caring to make any disturbance under

Mr. Raworth's roof, bore it very patiently, till Courtney at last drew and assaulted him; and before the guard could come in to quiet the disturbance, had wounded Paddle about an inch and a half deep in the belly and stabbed him in the left temple. The Deputy Governor immediately secured them both under guards in different appartments, and yesterday acquainted us with it in consultation; when they were both sent for up, and heard what they could say for themselves, and the declarations of Messrs. Matthew Weld and Henry Cottrel taken. The one of which was present when some words past between them on Sunday last; and the others not only there but likewise the greatest part of the time they were scuffling together. The copies of which we enclose for your Honor's perusal."

"*The Declaration of Mr. Matthew Weld.*

" Sunday the 20th in the Afternoon. Captain Hercules Courtney and Ensign Joseph Paddle being at my lodgings, where also was Mr. Henry Cottrel, when Captain Courtney asked Ensign Paddle to give one Richard Pain, a Centinel on the main guard and a drunken abusive fellow, liberty to go out of the Fort for two or three hours in a day about some business he had for him. To which Ensign Paddle replied, he could not. Thereat Captain Courtney paused a little, and then flew into a passion, saying, " What do you mean Ensign Paddle, D— me, I will have him without asking you." To that Ensign Paddle said, " If he is a man belonging to your Company you may have him, but as he is upon this guard, I must have another in his room to do his duty." Hereat Captain Courtney grew very abusive to Mr. Paddle the Ensign of the guard, giving him the lie, calling him an impudent saucy fellow, and threatened to beat him and thrust his cane down his throat, which he shook at him in a menacing manner, uttering many other abusive expressions. To all which said Ensign Joseph Paddle made civil replies and mild, and gave his reason, why he could not permit said Pain to go out of the Fort; he being so frequently guilty of misdemeaners when at his liberty, that he feared, he should be blamed if he suffered him abroad; desiring Captain Courtney not to treat him so scurvily, and that he would not strike him, for he would not suffer it. When their difference grew to this height I desired them both to forbear quarrelling in my house. Whereat, they then gave over, and I thought all would have been past by.

"But Tuesday the 22nd of January 1712, about three in the afternoon, Captain Hercules Courtney came into my lodgings, where Mr. Joseph Paddle was with me at a table smoking a pipe of tobacco; and after taking some few turns in my room seemingly in a passion, stood by me and demanded of Ensign Paddle, how he came to write so saucy and impudently to him in the parole note; telling him that his superiors used him with more respect than barely to conclude after the word with his name only. To this Ensign Paddle replied he wrote it in haste and designed no affront by it, and hoped he would not make this omission occasion of quarelling with him, on account of their late difference about said Richard Pain; adding that Captain Courtney had then very grossly abused him, who answered he had not, but he very much deserved it; and immediately flew into a passion, and said he was a saucy impudent fellow and would make him know his distance, and let him see he did not make such as him his companion, with several such like scornful expressions. To which Mr. Paddle replied in a very calm manner, "Sir, I bear a Commission so well as you;" and then desired he would curb his passion, for he could not bear such abuses.

"Upon that Captain Courtney flew into a more violent passion, and stepping back into the middle of the room immediately drew his sword. Whereat Ensign Paddle (whose sword lay with the belt and scabbard about two steps on one side of him upon two chairs) got up and took hold of it. But before he had completely drawn, and putting himself into a posture of defence, whilst the point of his sword was scarcely out of the sheath and pointing downward, Captain Courtney who drew first and was in a readiness, advanced on him and struck a forcible blow on Ensign Paddle's sword, which beat it up backward and so struck it out of his hand, pushed Ensign Paddle into the belly who notwithstanding readily got hold of his sword again. But in the very instant as he stooped to recover it, Captain Courtney closed in with him, and shuffled him down into the window; where Captain Courtney had him under, with his left hand on Ensign Paddle's sword arm, and his own sword pointed at Ensign Paddle's breast, bidding him deliver his sword and beg his life. Upon this I left them, and made what haste I could to call a guard ; and on my return found Captain Courtney with both swords in his hands and Ensign Paddle asking for his sword, which Captain Courtney returned. After this a dispute arose about the difference, when Ensign Paddle told Captain Courtney that he used him very scurvily in drawing on him in the Fort and unawares ; but that now he was so good a man as himself. With that Captain Courtney said "D—— me Sirrah, what after I have given you your life and sword, you have the impudence to prate :" and immediately run furiously upon him, and catching hold of Ensign Paddle's sword, broke it in two pieces ; and then they fell to cutting, but were parted by Serjeant Wanton. Soon after came the Captain of the Guard, in whose presence Captain Courtney continued to abuse Ensign Paddle in very scurrilous language, calling him " skipkennel," " sorry fellow," " just come from waiting at a table ;" and treated him with abundance of such like insufferable expressions ; though at the same time Ensign Paddle desired him to shake hands and be friends. To which Captain Courtney replied, he would not concern himself with any such fellow as he is."

MATTHEW WELD."*

---

* The other deposition is little more than a repetition of the above. Captain Courtney was subsequently recalled.

The troubles at Fort St. David were at last brought to a conclusion in April 1712, through the mediation of M. Hebert, French Governor of Pondicherry; but the peace appears to have cost the Company a sum of 12,000 pagodas in direct payment to the Rajah Serope Singh and his officers, in addition to the other charges and losses attending the war. This mediation of the French was only accepted after some deliberation, as the war with France was not brought to a final close until the treaty of Utrecht in 1713. It may be mentioned here that the fortress of Ginjee was captured in 1715 by the Dewan Sadatulla Khan.

CHAPTER XXVI.

GOVERNORSHIP OF MR. EDWARD HARRISON.
(Continued.)
1712—13.

During the troubles at Fort St. David recorded in the last chapter, but few incidents of importance appear to have taken place at Fort St. George. In 1711 the celebrated Danish Protestant Missionary, Bartholomew Ziegenbalgh appears to have arrived from the Danish settlement at Tranquebar on a visit to Madras; and in the consultation book of the 13th August, 1711, we find the following entry.

" The Danes Padre, Bartholomew Ziegenbalgh, requests leave to go for Europe on the first ship; and in consideration that he is the head of a Protestant Mission espoused by the Right Reverend the Lord Arch-Bishop of Canterbury, and the rest of our Episcopal Clergy, and that our Masters were pleased to send out their money freight free, we have presumed to grant him his passage without paying permission money."

A few days afterwards a member of the Danish Council at Tranquebar arrived at Madras on his way to Bengal, and requested that this permission might be rescinded, as a dispute between Ziegenbalgh and the Danish commandant which had been referred home to the king of Denmark. Accordingly the passage was refused until the said

Missionary had obtained the consent of the Governor of Tranquebar.

The following extract from a General Letter, dated February 2nd, 1712, and addressed by the Board of Directors to the Governor and Council of Fort St. George, containing some further information respecting any Missionary proceedings in Northern India.

"It is proper here to tell you that since the entire union of the two Companies, we act on the foot of the new Company's Charter, which directs, that the Company shall constantly maintain, in every of their garrisons and superior factories, one Minister; and that all such Ministers as shall be sent to reside in India shall be obliged to learn, within one year after their arrival, the Portuguese language; and that they shall apply themselves to learn the native language of the country where they shall reside, the better to enable them to instruct the Gentoos that shall be servants or slaves of the Company or of their agents in the Protestant religion. That in case of the death of any of the said Ministers residing in the East Indies, his place shall be supplied by one of the Chaplains out of the next ships that shall arrive at or near the place where such Minister shall happen to die; and that the Company shall from time to time provide School Masters in all their Garrisons and superior Factories, where they shall be found necessary.

"We are further to acquaint you that the Society for Promoting Christian Knowledge, which is composed of many of the Reverend Bishops and other Clergy, together with divers well disposed Gentlemen have addressed to us in behalf of the Protestant Missionaries (at Tranquebar), to give them our protection and encouragement, and to permit them a Charity School or Schools at Madras. They find it difficult to get any English to undertake this service, but hope to be able to do it in another season. We have consented to their sending three persons by this shipping, viz. Mr. Berlin to be a School Master, Mr. Adler a printer, and his brother. They are not certain whether he will reside at Madras, but wherever it is, he is to instruct children there gratis. They have printed some small Tracts in Portuguese of prayers, the Catechism, and other pious collections, for the use of the scholars. We recommend to you to give your countenance and protection to the said persons, and other Protestant Missionaries; and to supply them with a few of the Portuguese Liturgies as you find it necessary, and do whatever you think proper for the strengthening their hands in this difficult but honourable work of spreading the Gospel among the heathens. Some other requests they have made us, among the rest, that you should be empowered to prefer such as they shall instruct, preferable to other natives; which will be time enough to pronounce upon, when we hear the success of their endeavours, and whether you have any and what objections thereto."

About a year after receiving the above, Governor Harrison and Council replied as follows in a General Letter, dated 16th September, 1713.

" The design of erecting a Charity School or

Schools at this place is a very noble one, and worthy that Honorable Society for Promoting Christian Knowledge. We will not only be ready to adjust them with the power you have given us, but also with our purses; and do not doubt but many of your inhabitants will do the same, if the persons they send out are of tempers and qualifications fit for the undertaking. But we hope they will be English and not foreigners. The Danish missionaries have not wanted for our assistance on all occasions, though we must still continue of opinion that they spend a great deal of the Society's money to little or no purpose; and though there may be some good men among them there is one very turbulent person, of whose principles you may please to judge, by his contriving the escape of Mr. Abendana's widow from her creditors here to Tranquebar, and marrying her though a Jew to a Christian by the way." To this letter the Directors replied by the next ships as follows. "The Society for Promoting Christian Knowledge have presented to us, that they have not as yet been able to prevail with any of the British nation to undertake the Service of the Protestant Mission to the East Indies. But are advised to make an experiment of two Malabar Christians, educated at Tranquebar under the Danish Missionaries, to be employed as masters of two Charity Schools, one to be kept at Fort St. George and the other at Fort St. David, subject to the inspection of yourselves and direction of our Chaplain at Madras, and of the Deputy Governor and Council at Fort St. David; and desiring we would approve thereof.

and protect the persons that shall be employed
therein. We have promised to recommend this,
as we hereby do, to your consideration ; and to
give them all proper assistances for propagating
the Protestant religion in the way they propose.
We have also allowed the Society to send the Missionaries three hundred pounds' value in pieces 8-8,
and fifty-five reams of paper, with a chest of Books,
a chest of Beer and a cheese, Freight free."

We must add that the Charity School was not
founded in Madras until the Governorship of
Mr. Collett, the successor of Governor Harrison.

From the two following extracts from the consultation books, it would seem that at this time
the morals and manners of the Company's servants themselves were very far from what they
ought to have been.

"Thursday, 2nd August, 1711. The Right
Honorable Company's Servants, Factors, and Writers
being summoned, according to an order last Consultation do now attend, and being called in,
were severally checked by the President, for not
giving their attendance at Divine Service ; and told
that for the future, whosoever shall be absent on
Sundays from morning and evening service shall
not only be fined nine fanams to the poor but
be under the displeasure of this board and be
treated accordingly."

"Monday, 30th June, 1712. Several disorders
having been committed at the General Table,
which we find to be partly occasioned by the absence
of those persons in the service, that are of a superior standing and might awe the young ones

into better behaviour;—we have thought fit to appoint Joseph Smart head searcher, and five others, to take their turns, either weekly, or monthly, or as they shall agree among themselves, to be present at the Table, and to take care that no indecencies or disorders are committed."

We must now turn to the history of the Presidency. Whilst Fort St. David was warring against the Mussulman chief of Ginjee, Fort St. George seems to have maintained tolerably peaceful relations with the Dewan Sadatulla Khan, now Nabob of Arcot. The Dewan sent Governor Harrison the customary vest, turban, and purwanna, all of which were received in public with the usual solemnities. It is a noticeable fact that at this time the authority of the Mogul was declining, whilst the distant authorities were become more independent in the exercise of their power. The following story of the arbitrary conduct of the Foujdar at St. Thomé fully illustrates this state of things.

"Monday, 21st January, 1712. Pier Zudda, Foujdar of St. Thomé, is a Moollah of the Serad Caste, which is the chief of all the Moor's castes in these parts. He is likewise chief priest to the Dewan Sadatulla Khan; and has such an influence over him that whatever he says is a law, and the Dewan does nothing without his advice. When Pier Zudda visits him, he rises from his seat, and meets him at the door; and when the Dewan goes to him he receives him sitting, and frequently suffers him to kiss his feet.

"This priest has his Jaghire in and about St. Thomé to the yearly amount of nine thousand pagodas; and has by his cruelty to the Portuguese inhabitants of that place forced most of them to quit it and retire hither, the Bishop among the rest. They found means by a Christian woman in Shah Aulum's Seraglio to lay their complaints before him; who ordered Zulfikar Khan to send down a Perwanna immediately to the Dewan, commanding him to restore the Portuguese to their habitations and privileges, and to see restitution made them. A copy of the said Perwanna was sent by the Christian woman to the Bishop of St. Thomé, who sent several persons with the same to the Dewan at Arcot. But he received them very roughly; charging them with accusing him falsely to the King, put them in prison, and threatened them till they paid a sum of money for their release; withal obliging them to sign a paper in the Persian language without reading it, wherein it is said they own all their former complaints to be false and scandalous. This is a piece of roguery that we cannot forbear taking notice of, to show the weakness of the present Government under Shah Aulum, and the great power of Zulfikar Khan, whose creatures the Dewan and Pier Zudda are; and undoubtedly he has directed them what to do in this affair. However the Portuguese are preparing for a second complaint by the same hand, by which we shall see if the King will exert his authority or no."

In April the news of Shah Aulum's death had reached the Presidency, as will be seen from the following extract.

"Monday, 7th April, 1712. The news of King

Shah Aulum's death being duly confirmed, we find the neighbouring countries round about us under a great apprehension; all the Poligars having long waited this opportunity to set up for themselves, and assert their ancient rights and privileges; and our Dewan, who is at present Soobah (Nabob) of these parts, being marched away towards the Tanjore country to raise money, which is what he chiefly minds, and neglects the welfare and security of the Government committed to his charge. We have just reason to fear advantages will be taken of his absence by the petty Governors, to the prejudice of trade and our investment; and several considerable persons and inhabitants of Arcot, and other neighbouring places inland, have within these few days past sent considerable sums of money to be lodged here for security against the expected troubles. Wherefore it behoves us to put ourselves into as good a posture of defence as we can, for the security of our Master's Estates, our own inhabitants, and all such as shall have recourse to our protection."

It will here be necessary to glance at the events which immediately followed the death of Shah Aulum; and we cannot do so better than by extracting the account sent home by the Governor and Council of Fort St. George, in their General Letter to the Court of Directors. It records some circumstances which have not yet been published in reference to the accession first of Jehander Shah, and secondly of Feroksere; together with the first appointment of the Nizam of the Dekkan.

The first extract is dated October 14th, 1712, and is as follows.

"On the 3rd of April 1712, we received advices by way of Golcondah that king Shah Aulum died at Lahore on the 17th February, after very few days sickness, and most people are of opinion that he was poisoned. All his four sons being present when he died, immediately put themselves at the head of their friends to dispute the Empire. Azim-oos-Shaun, the second of the four who had the Government of Bengal many years, where he amassed vast treasures, was much more powerful both in men and money than any of the other three. For which reason Zulfikar Khan the Vizier, who was entirely in the interest of Moiz-ad-deen, the eldest brother, found means by fair promises to unite the elder with the two younger brothers against Azim-oos-Shaun; a verbal agreement being made between them, that Ruffeh-oos-Shaun the third brother should have the kingdom of Cabul, and Kojesta Acktar, the fourth, the kingdom of the Dekkan. Upon these terms they joined their armies and fought a bloody battle with their second brother; in which after a stout resistance, he and his eldest son were slain. Moiz-ad-deen, having gained so complete a victory, and being proclaimed king, the two younger brothers sent to him to make good their agreement by a firmaun, that they might depart to their several kingdoms. To which Moiz-ad-deen returned answer (as it is said by the advice of Zulfikar Khan) that he was ready to put them in possession of their several Governments; but that he would reserve to himself the stamp of all money coined in his reign, and the Duroy,—for which we have no word in English, but the sense of it is that he would retain a Supreme power and command over them. These new terms enraged the two younger brothers to such a degree that they immediately joined their forces and invited the elder to a battle; declaring that they would be either real kings or die in the dispute. In this second battle fell the two younger brothers and their sons after a very sharp engagement; and it is said that of the youngest brother, who was a very valiant prince, had not been killed by a chance shot just as he had surrounded the eldest, he had taken him prisoner and won the battle. Zulfikar khan having been the main instrument in promoting the interest of Moiz-ad-deen, and behaved himself with wonderful courage in both battles, he was immediately confirmed Prime Vizier and received other unusual Honors, one of which was permitting him to have a seat in the king's presence. As soon as he had established the Government he slew several great Omrahs, who had been in his brother's interest, and imprisoned them. After this he marched with his camp away to Delhi, having disgusted most of the great Omrahs, by the honors done to Zulfikar Khan.

"Azim-oos-Shaun, upon leaving Bengal to go to his father Shah Aulum's court, left the Government of that kingdom in the hands of his second son Feroksere; who no sooner heard the death of his father, but he immediately set up for himself, raising forces and coining money in his own name, and endeavoured to seize upon the king's treasure in possession of the Dewan, but we do not hear he has yet effected it. The last advices we had from Bengal were dated the 26th July, and give us an account that he was then at Patna with a considerable army ; where he waits for Moiz-addeen's son, who is marching against him ; and they were in hopes the affair would be decided before the rains were set in, but that we believe is impossible."

The next extracts are taken from a General Letter to England, dated 18th September, 1713.

"We wrote your Honors by the last year's shipping the great Revolution that had happened in this Empire upon the death of Shah Aulum. We added that Prince Feroksere, son to Azim-oos-Shaun that governed Bengal, had passed Agra with his army and defeated the king his uncle Jehandar Shah,* which has been since confirmed as follows.

"This young prince, hearing the sad fate of his father, by advice of an old Seiad called Abdulla Khan, whom Aurungzebe had given him for a Tutor, immediately caused himself to be proclaimed king ; and with his father's treasure, and what he raised in Patna among the merchants of all nations, he got a pretty good army altogether ; and hearing his uncle had disobliged most of the great Omrahs, by his barbarous cruelties and vicious course of life, he marched directly for Agra, near which city the king's army gave him battle and was entirely defeated, many great men going over

---

* Jehandar Shah was the title assumed by Moiz-addeen on ascending the throne.

to Feroksere's side. The king with Zulfikar Khan fled to Delhi; but Feroksere with his victorious army followed them close at their heel and surrounded the city that immediately surrendered and took them prisoners. Few days after they were both murdered, and Feroksere now remains the peaceable possessor of the Empire. He has made Seiad Abdulla Khan his prime Vizier and Gousdeen Khan, who came over to him in the battle, Nabob of all the Dekkan country, which includes this Carnata, Bijapoor, and Goleonda; he has the character of a brave generous man, and a friend to the Europeans.* We have news of his (the Nizam-ul-Mulk's) arrival at Aurungabad, and expect him to take his residence near Bijapoor, at a place called Burhampoor, where when arrived it will be absolutely necessary for us to address to him, because he has a very great interest with the present king and indeed throughout the Empire. Whatever we are obliged to do shall be managed with the greatest frugality. Your Honors will have heard from Bengal that our old friend Zoodee Khan came early into this new king's interest, and made a very brave defence in Hooghly against

---

* The father is here apparently confounded with the son. Gousdeen Khan (more properly Ghazee-ud-din Khan) was the father of Cheen Kulich Khan (Chicklis Khan in the records); and it was the latter who was appointed Viceroy of the Dekkan under the title of "Nizam-ul-Mulk, or "Regulator of the State." Cheen Kulich Khan, the "Nizam," was the founder of the great independent kingdom of the Dekkan, whose sovereigns still bare the name of their illustrious ancestor.

a much superior force on the side of the former king. He is now rewarded by being made Dewan of all the Dekkan country under Gousdeen Khan (i. e. the Nizam); which is a very great employment. The gentlemen in Bengal, who were very assisting to him under hand at Hooghly, seem to have their chief dependance upon him for introducing our present to the new king.

"Zulfikar Khan being cut off, there came immediate orders from Court to re-assume all the lands and villages that were granted him in these parts by Aurungzebe, in consideration of his good services in the conquest of the Gingee country. Accordingly the Dewan Sadatulla Khan sent us a summons to deliver up Egmore &c., villages granted us by Zulfikar Khan on account of the assistance we gave him with ammunition, and what else he wanted to carry on his designs. We have hitherto staved this business off with good words and pleading our rights; and when the new Nabob (Nizam) comes nearer, we will endeavor to get our grant confirmed. In the mean time, if any force is used to take them from us we resolve to defend them as well as we can. We are in daily expectation that our Dewan Sadatulla Khan will be turned out, as having been a Creature and Vassal of Zulfikar Khan. For which reason, we avoid purchasing his friendship in this matter by presents.

"The new king Feroksere is a young man of about twenty-six years of age. He has the character of being brave, prudent and generous; and is the last of the race of Aurungzebe except some young children imprisoned in the fortress of

Gwalior, where when once they have entered they never came out, and have potions given them to destroy their senses. This seems to be the King for whom Providence has designed your present, which leads us to touch upon that affair."

The following extract from a General Letter to England dated 14th October 1712 is curious as showing the changes in the trade which attended these revolutions in the Government, as well as the nature of the Native demand for the more important articles of English manufacture.

"In obedience to your commands we shall lay before your Honours, the best account we can get concerning the consumption of Broad Cloth and other manufactures in the Mogul's dominions. The coarse red and green broad cloth is chiefly used among the soldiers and ordinary Moormen for saddles, saddle cloths, sumpture cloth, covers, beds and cushions, for palankeens, carpets to sit upon, mantles to cover them from the rain and sometimes covering for their tents of pleasure. The fine broad cloth as scarlet, aurora, some blue and yellow is used for the inside of tents for vests or mantles in the rainy season among the great men; covering cloths for the Elephants and hackarys cloths to hang round their drums; for shoulder and waist Belts, scabbards to their swords and Jimdars or daggers; for slippers and for covers, beds and pillows, and for palankeens. The embossed cloth is used to hang round the bottom on the inside of the great men's tents three feet high; for spreadings to sit upon, and cushions to lean against; and for cloths to cover the Elephants and horses. Perpetuanos are only used among the meaner sort of people for caps, coats, and covering cloths to sleep in during the rains.

"And now we are upon this subject, we must inform your Honors that at least nine-tenths of the Woollen manufactures vended in these parts is among the Moors; the Gentoos making very little or no use of them. The greatest consumption is in the Mogul's camp, which when at Lahore or Delhi is supplied wholly from Surat and Persia; but when at Agra, partly from Surat and partly from Bengal by way of Patna, from which ports the conveyance to the camp is easy and safe. But what is disposed of hereabouts is dispersed among the Nabob's flying armies in the Carnatta country, Bijapore and Golcondah, seldom reaching so far as Aurungabad, because the carriage is very chargeable, and the roads are difficult and dangerous to pass. When king Shah Aulum came down to Golcondah with his army in the year 1708 to destroy his brother Kam Buksh, we immediately found a quicker vent than ordinary for our broad cloth; and indeed for all other sorts of goods consumed among them. And when Dawood Khan was formerly Nabob of these parts, he always kept a good body of horse in pay, which obliged the neighbouring Governors to do the same, being always jealous of each other. And among these horsemen by much the greatest quantity of our broad cloth then imported was consumed; the trade from this place to their camps being very considerable. But now our Dewan, who is Subah of all this country, seldom keeps above five hundred horse with him; and the Government in general being grown much weaker than in Aurungzebe's time, none of the great men keep up the number of horse allowed by the king, but apply the money to their own use; and this has brought a considerable damp to our trade in general, but more especially upon the sale of your manufactures. For we have not only lost the camp trade, but the roads are become impassable for want of these horsemen to scour them as usual; so that the merchants are discouraged from coming down with their money and diamonds to buy up and carry away our Europe and other goods as formerly; and we cannot see any likelihood of better times till the Government is well settled and some active man employed on the Government of these parts."

We now proceed with the general current of events at the Presidency. The troubles which accompanied the death of Shah Aulum and Jehandar Shah, and the accession of Feroksere, had induced a number of wealthy persons to take refuge in Fort St. George. Amongst others came the Nauvajee, or Collector General of the revenues of Zulfikar Khan, with treasure estimated at five or six hundred thousand pagodas. The following extract respecting this individual will explain itself.

"Thursday, 26th March, 1713. The President produces a Purwanna from the Subah Sadatulla Khan, wherein he demands by virtue of an order from Court, that the Nauvajee Collector of Zulfikar Khan's revenues in this Carnata country (who came down hither upon the beginning of the late troubles for the security of the treasure under his charge) be delivered up with the said treasure into the hands of Fire Khan his Deputy Governor at Arcot.

"The reason of this demand, we take to be, because the new King Feroksere has cut off Zulfikar Khan and his father Assid Khan, and would now seize upon all their treasure.

"The President further acquaints the Board that immediately upon receipt of the Perwanna, he sent it to the Nauvajee, with the slight intimation that we could not think of engaging ourselves in any disputes with the Country Government, by protecting persons employed under the King, contrary to his positive commands. To which he returned answer that he was ready to go directly to the Subah with the treasure, acknowledging the many civilities received during his residence here.

"Agreed that a proper answer be returned the Subah, acquainting him that as the Nauvajee came here a stranger upon his master's business, we were under an obligation to receive him with civility and distinction, but know nothing of the treasure he brought with him, it not being our custom to search strangers. But finding him very willing to return upon the first summons, we had no occasion to use any compulsion; and whatever he might bring with him he carries back under charge of the person that brought the Perwanna."

Our next extract is a further illustration of the disorderly character of the times.

"Wednesday, 16th September, 1713. The President acquaints the Board that Fleet Aynsworth writer did, on the 14th instant in the evening upon rising from supper at the General table, draw his sword and made several passes at Thomas Wilford writer, one of which entered his body, just under the left pap about three inches. Dr. Robson being sent for and examined, declares he has hopes the said Wilford may do well but that he is not yet out of danger. Ordered that Fleet Aynsworth writer be kept under strict confinement till further order." A few days afterwards it was agreed " that the said Aynsworth always behaved himself in a very disorderly manner, continually drinking, quarrelling with one or other, for which he has frequently been reprimanded to no purpose, as appears by this last bloody action;" and he was therefore dismissed the Company's service and sent to England by the first ship.

The following Will, which is entered in the consultation book of this period, furnishes a curious picture of social life.

" In the name of God, Amen, this thirteenth day of May in the year of our Lord one thousand, seven hundred and twelve, I, Thomas Saunders of Bengal, mariner, make this my last Will and Testament, in manner and form following. First, I commit my soul into the hands of God that gave it, and my body to be decently buried as my Executors shall think convenient. As for those worldly goods it has pleased Almighty God to bestow upon me, I give and bequeath in manner and form following; viz.

" To my Uncle Richard Saunder's Children, on

account of an adventure which was lost in the ship that I came to India, valued at one hundred and ten pounds sterling or thereabouts, sixteen hundred rupees, if they give no further trouble to my estate. Otherwise no more than the Law will give them.

"To a slave girl, named Clara, her liberty, with all her jewels and five hundred rupees; and if brought to bed within eight months and a half after my leaving Bengal, being the twenty-third day of January one thousand seven hundred eleven twelve, I bequeath unto the said child four thousand rupees and to be under the care of my Executors. A slave boy named Pompey 1 give his liberty, and five rupees per month during his life. A slave boy named Anthony, his freedom. If the said child that I bequeathed four thousand rupees dies afore it comes to age or married, then the said four thousand rupees shall go to my son John Saunders.

"The remainder part of my estate I bequeath unto my son John Saunders, after my debts are paid. If my son should die I give my wife, that was now Mrs. Martha Bingley, four thousand rupees, and each Executor four thousand rupees; the remainder part of my estate after the said Legacies above and my debts are paid unto my loving brothers John and Richard Saunders.

"I appoint executors to see this my last will and Testament executed, my esteemed friends Mr. James Williamson of Bengal and Mr. Charles Boone of Madras; and to manage my estate to the best advantage till my son comes of age. I allow my said Executors the power of remitting money to England for the use of my son, if there, and employing my estate to sea, if they shall think convenient for my son's best advantage; I put my son wholly under the care of my said Executors till of age. In witness whereof I have hereunto put my hand and seal in Gombroone the day and year above mentioned."

THOMAS SAUNDERS.

Our next extract will explain itself.

"Thursday, 8th October, 1713. The present Nabob Sadatulla Khan, having received a firmann from the new King Feroksere, confirming him in the Government of these parts; upon which the French and Dutch have presented him each to the amount of a thousand pagodas or thereabouts; and having lately received a message by a horseman from him, that if we do not forthwith deliver up the villages he intends to come and take possession of them."

"Agreed that a present be sent to the amount of about five hundred pagodas, and lodged in the hands of Sunka Rama at Arcot, to be presented the Nabob by way of congratulation on account of his new dignity; but that it be a clause in the instructions to Sunka Rama, not to part with it before he gets assurances that we shall have no further troubles about the villages; and this to be done as from himself, because we will insist upon the goodness of our title and reserve a right to defend them upon occasion."

The year 1713 closed with a singular rebellion at Fort St. David. Our readers will remember that Mr. Raworth, the Deputy Governor, had gallantly conducted the defence of the place against Serope Singh, Rajah of Ginjee. They will now be surprised to hear that this same Mr. Raworth, openly rebelled against the authority of Governor Harrison. The story is best told in the following extracts from the consultations.

" Monday, 5th October. The President offers to the Board that the Method established by the Right Honorable Company for carrying on their mercantile affairs, and for the Government of their Garrisons and Factories, has been entirely neglected and despised by the Deputy Governor of Fort St. David, who has assumed to himself a liberty of acting as if he was independant of this Board. Consultations are neglected ; Paymaster's and Cash accounts are fictitious and irregularly passed ; and our strictest orders have been contemned. He has promoted and commissioned officers of the Garrison unknown to this Board. He has considerably increased the pay and allowances of several persons, particularly in Diet money to the Gentlemen of Council, three pagodas per month each, and almost all other expences in general. He has laid out considerable sums in building, and has let out the Company's bounds to rent without our knowledge or consent. He has used the Company's merchants very barbarously, whereby they have been necessitated to seek protection and redress from this Board. He returns no answers to such persons as have large and just demands upon him ; with many other irregularities, which this Board ought not to bear with any longer, lest the Honorable Company's affairs should be brought into irrecoverable confusion.

"The President further offers to the Board several paragraphs of their general letters, as also a copy of a paper or protest signed by Mr. Raworth and Council, which were read and considered; and the Board came to the following Resolution.

"That whereas the Deputy Governor in his name, declares our proceedings (in sending for the Company's merchants up hither at their repeated request) to be highly prejudicial to the Company's interest, and that of this place; we are obliged to justify ourselves in as plain and public a manner as possible to our Right Honorable Employers; though we cannot but think it an inexcusable piece of presumption in Mr. Raworth to send us such a charge in a general letter from a subordinate Factory, which is giving encouragement to those under him by his example to dispute and disobey our orders hereafter.

"Agreed that a charge be brought in against Robert Raworth Esq. Deputy Governor of Fort St. David, containing such articles as can be fully proved without any room for dispute.

"Monday, 5th October. All the foregoing premises having been fully considered and debated the following question was put:

"Q. Whether this Board is not obliged upon the charge now read, and other circumstances concurring, to remove Robert Raworth Esq from the Government of Fort St. David?

"Agreed in the affirmative nemine contradicente.

"Q. Whether he shall be suspended or dismissed?

"Agreed unanimously that he be suspended, that his commission be revoked and superseded, the same to be signified in a general letter to him with orders for him to repair hither when his charge shall be delivered him."

"Agreed and ordered that Mr. Henry Davenport be commissioned as commissary and Provissional Deputy Governor of Fort St. David, to set out this evening, in order to receive the Government from Mr. Robert Raworth.

"Sunday, 11th October. The President communicates to the Board a letter from Henry Davenport Esq., advising us, that, upon his arrival at the edge of the bounds of Fort St. David, he dispatched Lieutenant Porrier before with our letter to Mr. Raworth, and a short one from himself. To which Mr. Raworth in a short time returned answer, that he would not allow him any authority to rule there by whatever commission he could receive from us. All the outworks were alarmed with the usual signals for enemies when Mr. Davenport entered the bounds; and when he came to Tevenapatam gate, he was denied entrance by shutting it upon him, and the officer's declaring he had an order not to let him in. All the Council came in to Mr. Davenport, except Mr. Richard Harrison. Ensign Hobbs being posted at the Garden with a hundred men, Mr. Davenport sent to him for admittance there; but he sent word that he would obey no orders but Mr. Raworth's, and that if he offered to come into the Garden with any peons or soldiers, he would fire upon him. Upon which, finding the whole Garrison debauched from their duty (except old Captain Hugonin and some other of the officers which were confined before hand), he was forced to retire out of the bounds to a choultry about five miles distance, for the security of his life and the treasure he has with him ; Mr. Raworth having given out several unaccountable orders to some of the officers, and publicly threatened to cut him off.

" This affair being debated, with the greatest concern to see a whole Garrison of five hundred men and upwards, seduced by some false persuasions from their duty to our Right Honorable Employers, and commanded openly to resist our orders which may be of very ill consequence hereafter.

" Agreed that it is not safe for Mr. Davenport to remain where he is, considering the small guard he has with him and the threatening expressions Mr. Raworth has used.

" Ordered that he do forthwith return hither and bring with him the Gentlemen of the Fort St. David Council (that cannot safely return into the Bounds), to inform us of several necessary points before we can come to any further resolution."

" Monday, 12th October. A general letter from Henry Davenport Esq. and Council dated the 10th instant from Monapa's choultry ; read also a private letter from Mr. Davenport to the President ; advising that Mr. Richard Harrison is as active in this rebellion as any officer in the Garrison ; that the council now with him (Mr. Davenport) affirm that by the promotion of several officers and increasing their pay, Mr. Raworth has the majority entirely at command, and that he openly declares he will stick at nothing to be revenged. They add further that he has held no consultation, since August; transacting the Company's affairs wholly by himself.

"The President's private letter being wrote after the General advices, that Ensigns Paddle and Handlon were come over to Mr. Davenport, and acquainted him that the Garrison was in great confusion and most of them would follow, if they were sure of a place to resort to; that they had received no pay for two months past, which is very surprising to us considering that we know they are in cash, though they have kept the account so long from us.

"Agreed that orders be immediately sent to Mr. Davenport to remain where he is, and see what the Garrison will do; that a party of sixty chosen men be forthwith sent away to be landed at Pondicherry for a guard to Mr. Davenport and the others, against any sudden attempt of the desparadoes; and that a protest be drawn up against Mr. Raworth for this unwarrantable way of proceeding."

"Thursday, 15th October. A general letter from Henry Davenport Esq., dated the 13th instant read, advising that he has dropped declarations and copies of his commission at the several guards, which has had a very good effect and occasioned many men coming in; that whole Garrison seem inclinable to return to their duty, and that he has now so many men with him that he is forced to draw towards Pondicherry for assistance to maintain them.

"Agreed that it be an instruction to Henry Davenport Esq., and Council to avoid as much as possible coming to blows; and not to attack any party or post, unless obliged to it for their own safety; but to use all peaceable methods of recovering the men to their duty, promising them full pardon and their arrears.

"Agreed that Mr. William Warre and the Revd. Mr. George Lewis be immediately sent down with proper instructions to persuade Mr. Raworth to reason, by representing the ill consequences that are likely to attend his rash way of proceeding."

"Monday, 19th October. The President lays before the Board several letters from Henry Davenport Esq., advising that finding himself strong enough he marched into the bounds on the 17th very peaceably, finding all the out guards deserted; and that he put a serjeant with twenty men into one of the most considerable to protect it from the country enemy. After which he marched to the Garden, where he found Ensign Hobbs posted with about fifty men, whom he summoned to their duty. But they absolutely refused to surrender, and he would not force them, though it was very practicable, for fear of shedding blood. But while they were parleying, they were saluted with a twenty-four pounder from the Fort that fell within twenty yards of Mr. Davenport. After which he marched away and took possession of Cuddalore, that was also entirely deserted; in their way being open to the Fort, they were again saluted with a twenty-four pounder, which fell among them, but by God's good providence did no harm.

"Agreed that Henry Davenport Esq. and Council remain at Cuddalore, endeavouring to save our bounds without committing any acts of hostility, whilst Mr. Warre and Mr. Lewis are endeavouring to terminate this unhappy affair; and that they do set the merchants to work as fast as possible to procure Long Cloth and Sallampores."

"Wednesday, 21st October. The President communicates a letter from Henry Davenport Esq., advising that he has put men into as many of the out guards as he can spare from Cuddalore. But that on the 18th instant Mr. Raworth sent a party of horse to beat the men out of Condapah Choultry, who dismounted and summoned them within to surrender; which being refused they fired upon them and threw in several Granadoes, which wounded some of the men and killed one outright. The Serjeant that commanded immediately fired a field piece with partridge shot, which killed two and wounded three more of the attackers. Upon which the rest fled, leaving five of their horses behind them. The Serjeant being so near the Fort, and at least six miles distance from Cuddalore, dreading a more dangerous attack in the night, when he could not be supported, withdrew in time to Cuddalore and the five horses with him. Mr. Raworth just before the attack was made, fired three great shots at the Choultry from Tevenapatam, which fell very near them."

Friday, 23rd October. "A general letter from Henry Davenport, Esq., and Council, dated the 19th instant read, advising that those who remain in the Fort and at the Garden with Mr. Raworth, are already reduced to such necessities that many of them would get away if they could.

"A letter from Messrs. Warre and Lewis, dated the 20th instant, read, advising their reception by Mr. Raworth; that they had fairly laid all matters before him as recommended in our instructions. Upon which he desired sometime to consider thereon, and he would give them an answer in the evening, seeming in very good temper; that they went to Cuddalore and returned to him about five o'clock, when he very briefly answered that provided the Governor would come in person, he would immediately resign, upon condition that those who had been faithful to him (as he calls it) should be treated with superior respect to such as deserted. Upon which they desired time to receive our answer, and got his consent to forbear all acts of hostility till then. This matter being debated,

"Agreed that as matters now stand here with the Nabob, and considering the necessary preparations to load our shipping that are expected early from Bengal, it is no way convenient for the President to leave this place; especially when Mr. Raworth insists on such terms as are impossible for us to consent to; since it is no better than confessing ourselves in the wrong, and encouraging others hereafter to follow this wicked and pernicious example.

"It was also considered that if the Nabob should come to St. Thomé, as is credibly reported, the President cannot come back hither till February by sea; nor can he come by land without passing through his camp at his mercy, since he can have no body of men with him fit to force his way.

"Agreed that a letter be wrote to Mr. William Warre and the Rev. Mr. George Lewis, requiring them to see Mr. Raworth once more, and offer him every thing that is in our power to grant, provided he will surrender quietly without any further troubles or mischief.

"Agreed that a short commission be given Mr. William Warre to receive the Government at Mr. Raworth's hands, if he should consent, and to make all easy, insisting only upon not seeing Mr. Davenport before he comes away hither.

"Agreed that if Mr. Raworth does not accept the terms offered him in our letter of this date, Mr. Warre and the Rev. Mr. Lewis be permitted to return."

"Wednesday, 28th October. General letter from Messrs. Davenport: Warre and Lewis, dated 24th instant read, advising that the two latter having been with Mr. Raworth that same day, found him in much worse temper than ever peremptorily declaring that he would resign the Fort to none but the President himself.

"A letter from Henry Davenport Esq. singly of the same date read, wherein he says, he is very well assured Mr. Raworth will not deliver up even to the President himself, and that there is no way but to starve him out.

"Sunday, 1st November. The President produces a letter from Mr. William Warre and the Rev. Mr. George Lewis, dated the 27th, wherein they say that though they must acknowledge themselves mistaken as to Mr. Raworth's sincerity, they are still of opinion, the Governor's presence would soon put an end to all disputes. The foregoing words being considered and debated, and the President acquainting the Board that by the last advices from Sunka Rama at Arcot, matters are likely to be fairly accommodated with the Nabob about the villages,

"Agreed that there seems an absolute necessity for the President to set out for Fort St. David, as soon as the rivers will permit, in order to put an end to the present troubles if possible before further mischief is done.

"Agreed that a party of sixty men be despatched away before hand to Pondicherry, for a guard to wait the President's arrival; and that a hundred Pagodas be advanced the ensign to defray their expenses."

"Wednesday, 4th November. This evening the Honorable President attended by the Rev. Mr. Stevenson, Lieutenant Roach, and Messrs. Theobalds, Bulkley, Maubert, Nanney, Langlier, Turner, and Richardson set out overland for Fort St. David.

"Friday, 6th November. A general letter from the Honorable President and Mr. William Warre, dated the 5th November, read, enclosing several letters and papers the Honorable President met upon the Road, and advising that they have fired six shots into Cuddalore from the Fort in one day, but it pleased God they did no damage; that some deserters daily came in, and that Henry Davenport Esq. has possessed himself of Condapa Choultry and Horse tail point, in order to facilitate the Honorable President's entry into the Bounds.

"A general letter from Henry Davenport, Esq. and Council dated the 3rd instant read, wherein they acquaint us that they were in great hopes Mr. Raworth and his adherents, would by this time have been reduced to a very low condition for want of provisions. But that contrary to their expectations, and to the promise made to the Deputy Governor from the Gentlemen at Pondicherry no ways to assist them, of which he reminded Governor Dusivier in his letters dated 29th ultimo and 3rd instant; notwithstanding which there was a chelinga sent them full of provisions. They further advise the sloop, that was sent down with stores for Cuddalore, as she passed by Fort St. David they fired three shots at her; but that she continued her course for the road and that Mussoolas were gone off to bring the stores ashore. They also remit us their account cash for the month of October, balance being six thousand three hundred and ninety-five pagodas.

"Thursday, 12th November. Another of the 10th informs that after the hopes they had of bringing matters to an end that they found Mr. Raworth the same fickle and unfaithful man as veer; that they had sent the same persons in that morning with such terms as they thought he neither could nor would refuse; but were strangely surprized at their return to find he absolutely refused what he gave under his hand the day before; which was that if the Governor insisted he would bring the keys of the Fort where he pleased; that they had offered to venture into the Fort if he would permit Captain Road to go in first with fifty men for the Governor's Guard. For which his answer was under his hand, that he would not suffer the Governor to enter with any guard, and several other extravagancies; so that they can see no hopes of his being brought to better temper whilst he is able to hold out."

" Sunday, 22nd November. General letter from the Honorable Edward Harrison Esq., Messrs. Davenport and Warre dated 20th instant read, wherein they acquaint us that having perused the Fort St. David cash accounts from April 1712, and by what they can learn from the Council &c., Mr. Raworth ought now to have a balance by him of seventeen thousand pagodas, which they took to be one of his chief reasons for acting in this unaccountable manner; that Mr. Raworth and his adherents being cooped up in the Fort and in want of provisions are very uneasy; that some desert him daily, but not without the risk of their lives. They add that on the 18th in the morning Mr. Raworth saluted them in the Garden with a fourteen pounder; but afterwards made an apology that a drunken Dutchman fired the gun, between sleeping and waking, that happened to be pointed that way; that on the 19th at night the President, being accompanied with all the Madras Gentlemen, went into Tevenapatam to visit the men posted there ; and having been for sometime in the streets, they were briskly entertained from the batteries with all the guns they could bring to bear, besides their small shot, in the reach of which they happened to be ; but by Good Providence no mischief was done ; that they returned them a Culverin salute from Patcharee hill, which went through Mr. Raworth's lodgings, as they learn from deserters ; that several of the men sallied from the Fort, but were warmly received, and two very dangerously wounded, which made them return faster than they came out."

"Tuesday, 1st December. General letter from the Honorable Edward Harrison, Esq. and Mr. William Warre, dated 29th ultimo read, wherein they acquaint us that they have not as yet brought Mr. Raworth to an accommodation ; and that they are fearful they must be obliged to consent to his going to Pondicherry to reside there and settle his account; and if so Governor Dusivier is to give his parole that in case satisfaction is not given us in fifteen days he will deliver Mr. Raworth to us at Fort St. George."

"Monday, 7th December. From the Honorable President and Mr. William Warre, dated the 2nd instant, advising but that that morning the Honorable President entered the Fort, according to articles of agreement passed between him and Council and Mr. Raworth ; who received him at the head of his rebellious crew in such a manner as none but Mr. Raworth could be capable of ;

seeming no ways concerned for the many ill actions he has committed in this affair. There was a hundred and thirty men under arms in the Fort, of whom eighty Europeans, who seemed to be as stout men as any in the Company's service. Every thing was found in confusion; which will require the President's longer stay than he expected; as also to settle the Garrison and separate those he found in the Fort, that it may not hereafter be in their power to act the like again."

"Monday, 7th December. Henry Davenport acquaints the Board, that he this afternoon received a private letter from the Honorable President, dated the 5th, advising that Thomas Frederick, Esq. arrived at Fort St. David that night; and that the next day in the evening the Honorable President designed to depart thence for Fort St. George, expecting to reach the Mount to-morrow night, where he desired the Gentlemen of the Council would go and wait upon him.

"Monday, 21st December. The following general letters read. From the Governor of Pondicherry dated 30th instant (new style) advising that Mr. Raworth, having publicly demanded their king's protection and passage upon their ships for France, which they cannot refuse him without exposing themselves to their king's displeasure.

"The President likewise produces a letter from Father Thomas de Poictiers, Capuchin of the Church here, whom he has employed at Pondicherry to solicit the Governor and Council on this affair; wherein the said Father Thomas advises that one of the principal reasons why Mr. Raworth refused to come hither and settle his account with us, was that he had seen a letter from a member of this Board to a person at Fort St. David, mentioning that it was resolved to have him assassinated. Every member now present solemnly declares, and offers to take his oath if required, that he never gave him any such advices, nor ever heard the Governor say any thing tending that way.

" The Governor for himself solemnly protests before God that he abhors the very thought of so barbarous an action; though he can bring sufficient proof that Mr. Raworth, when Deputy Governor of Fort St. David, did more than once threaten the same to him.

" It being debated what measures are most proper for us to take upon this extraordinary proceeding of the Governor and Councils of Pondicherry; agreed that we defer coming to a resolution thereupon till Father Thomas returns from Pondicherry."

" Thursday, 24th December. Mr. Raworth's answer to the proposals made him in the Governor's name by Padre Thome read which is full of notorious falsities and calumny without any manner of ground or proof and of a piece with all the rest of his behaviour, and upon the whole it appears very plain that he will do or suffer anything rather than come to a fair account for what he has had under his charge."

This extraordinary affair ended shortly afterwards in Mr. Raworth's departure to France; and it is a singular circumstance that he died at Paris, just as the Directors of the Company were preparing to prosecute him in England.

CHAPTER XXVII.

GOVERNORSHIP OF MR. EDWARD HARRISON.
(Continued.)

1714—7.

Before proceeding further with our extracts from the records of the Governorship of Mr. Edward Harrison, it will be necessary to glance at the contemporary state of India. Shah Aulum, eldest son of Aurungzebe, had died in 1712; and a struggle ensued between his four sons which terminated in the establishment of Jehandar Shah on the throne of Delhi. Jehandar Shah owed his elevation to the support of Zulfikar Khan, but his vices rapidly lowered him in the eyes of his subjects, and excited the religious hostility of all who respected the precepts of the Prophet. A drunken sovereign, ruled by a concubine who had once been a public dancer, and frequently appearing in the streets of Delhi in a condition which but too plainly indicated his vices, was not the potentate who could long hope to maintain his authority over a distracted empire like that of the Moguls. Two Sciads, or descendants of the Prophet, advocated the cause of Feroksere, a nephew of Jehandar Shah. Forces were raised, the imperial army was defeated, and Jehandar Shah and his minister Zulfikar Khan were both taken and put to death.

Feroksere now ascended the throne at Delhi, and ruled the empire from 1713 to 1720. His reign thus corresponds to about four years of the Governorship of Mr. Harrison, and three years of his successor Mr. Collett. It is remarkable from the fact that a mission was at this time sent to Delhi by the English Governor of Calcutta; and many advantages, including the disputed out villages near Madras, and the Zemindarship of some villages in the neighbourhood of Calcutta, were at that time obtained from the Mogul. Fortunately copies of most of the original dispatches from the English envoys at Delhi to the Governors of Calcutta and Madras, have been preserved in the Madras records; and these documents throw a flood of light upon the intrigues of the period, and enable us to obtain a clear picture of the court of the Great Mogul. This mission arrived in Delhi in 1715 and left it in 1717, and thus extended over a period of two years. As it is a subject of imperial interest rather than of local interest, we shall not incorporate the narrative embodied in the dispatches with the history of Mr. Harrison's administration, but reserve it for a future and separate chapter.

As regards the changes more immediately effecting the Madras Presidency, we may remark that Cheen Kulich Khan, variously spelt in the records, had been appointed Subah of the Dekkan under the title of Nizam-ool-Moolk; an individual who is remarkable in the history of Southern India as the founder of the present kingdom of the Dekkan. Our old friend Dawood Khan obtained the Soubahship of Guzerat in place of Golconda, but was killed in a battle a year or two afterwards. At the same time Sadatulla Khan continued Nabob of the Carnatic, and effected the reduction of the great fortress of Ginjee, which had been defended by the son of that Serope Singh, who has already been introduced to our readers as the Rajah who nearly succeeded in capturing Fort St. David.

We now turn to the local annals of the Presidency. The records of the remaining period of Mr. Harrison's Governorship contain but few matters worthy of interest. The reduction of Ginjee in 1714 is thus noticed in the consultation books.

"Saturday, 9th October 1714. General letter from the Deputy Governor and Council of Fort St. David, dated the 6th instant, advising that our Nabob Sadatulla Khan had drawn all his forces round Ginjee, and summoned Serope Singh's son to surrender, upon pretence of an order from Court to take possession of that place; which he refused to do, and making a desperate sally with about 300 Rajpoots, was very near killing the Nabob, having cut the harness of his Elephant with his own hands. But timely succour coming into the Nabob's rescue, Tejah Sing, Serope Singh's son, with Mohabut Khan and several others of the principal men belonging to Ginjee, were overpowered and cut off, so that it is believed Ginjee will surrender in a few days." On the 15th of November the news arrived that Ginjee was captured by Sadatulla Khan.

The following strange revelation appears in a

petition addressed by one Dr. Thomas to the Governor in Council, dated 9th November, 1714.

"The humble petition of Doctor Thomas.
"Showeth,

"That your petitioner's father-in-law Lewis de Melho in his life time held a converse with one of his slaves named Ignacia near the space of thirty years; living with her in a separate house, and entrusting the greatest part of his estate in her hands, and taking no notice of his wife or daughter. But upon his death bed repenting himself of the ills he had done, he asked pardon of his wife for his ill usage of her; and declared that the said Ignacia had been the cause of it by the power of medicines she had given him, and that he had delivered into her charge 2600 pagodas in money, besides jewels and medicines of value. And he did appoint and constitute his said wife and daughter heiresses to his estate; as appears by a certificate under the hand of the Rev. Padre Paschall Perciva de Cuntra. But now so it is, may it please your Honor that the said Ignacia refuses to deliver up or give any account of the said estate; though it can be proved by witnesses that she has divers things of a large value as well as money in her possession. Wherefore your petitioner, in behalf of his mother-in-law Francisca and his wife Isabella, humbly prays that your Honor will oblige the said slave to make a true discovery and surrender of all those things in her possession, belonging to the estate of the deceased Mr. Lewis de Melho, that so they may have their right, and he as in duty bound shall ever pray."

The Governor and Council ordered that the goods should be secured, but referred the matter to the decision of the heads of their Castes.

On the 1st of August, 1714, died Queen Anne, and the crown of England thus descended to George I. The event passed off quietly and more than eight months passed away before the news reached Madras. It will be seen from the following entry, that the Presidency still kept early hours.

"Friday, 8th April, 1715. The letter read advising the unfortunate death of Her late Majesty Queen Anne, and the happy accession of His most serene Highness the Elector of Hanover and Brunswick to the Imperial crown of Great Britain under the title of King George ; at nine o'clock this morning the Mayor and Aldermen, attended with the proper officers and a company of soldiers belonging to the Garrison, proclaimed his Royal Majesty King George ; and at noon there was an entertainment made for the council and all the chief inhabitants of the place, at which his Royal Majesty, the Prince of Wales, the Royal family and the Honorable Company's healths were drank and guns fired at each."

The following extract concerning the Capuchin Friars, is a curious testimony to their character at this time.

" Monday, the 12th December 1715. "Edward Harrison Esq., President of and for all the Right Honorable United English East India Company's affairs on this coast of Coromandel and Orissa, in the Ginjee and Mahratta countries, Commander in Chief of all the forces, which now are or hereafter may or shall be employed for the Service of the said United Company under this Presidency, and Governor of the Fort St. George, St. David, and Council. To all to whom these presents shall come Greeting.

"Know ye, that the Reverend the Capucin Fathers of the French nation that officiate in the Portuguese Church of this place, and others of the same nation and order at Pondicherry that formerly resided here, having made application to us for our assistance to justify themselves from several aspersions that have lately been cast upon them in France by their inveterate enemies, in order to blast their reputation and render them contemptible in these parts of the world, and having in order thereto humbly proposed the following queries.

"1st. Whether the Capucin Fathers that have dwelt and officiated in this city of Madras from the first settlement to this time, viz. Ephraim de Nevers, Zenon de Bauge, Cosme de Gien, Jacques de Bourges, Esprit de Tours, Laurent d'Engouleme, Michael Ange de Bourges, Rene d'Engouleme, and Thomas de Poitiers; they or any of them ever behaved themselves otherwise than became their sacred function as Missionaries and persons in Religious orders, or whether they have given any cause for scandal by their deportment.

"2nd. Whether they have ever had any quarrels or differences among themselves, which obliged them to have recourse to our Tribunal for an accommodation, and particularly Father Esprit de Tours with Father Michael Ange before mentioned.

"3rd. Whether the Capucin Fathers of Madras or those of Pondicherry, particularly Father Esprit de Tours, either now have or ever had any money at Interest or otherwise in the Cash of the Right Honorable Campany our Masters.

"4th. Whether Father Thomas de Poitiers, now residing and officiating here, ever bought or sold 500 chests of Persia wine, as he is accused of having done in the year 1713, or before or since that time.

"To the first article we are obliged to declare that the Capucin Fathers above named, who have had the care of the mission in this city of Madras from the first establishment thereof to the present time by permission of our Right Honorable Masters, have always demeaned themselves in so handsome a manner, both in spiritual and temporal affairs, as to give no just cause of complaint to us their representatives; their conduct has been regular and agreeable to their profession, nor have we ever heard of or remarked any action of theirs that could occasion the least scandal to their order.

"To the second article, we never heard, nor can we find upon examining our Registers, that any of the said Capucin Fathers, particularly the persons before mentioned in this article, ever had any difference, which obliged them to have recourse to this or any other Tribunal here for a decision.

"To the third article, we must declare it to be a notorious falsity that the Capucin Father of Madras or Pondicherry, or of any other place, ever had any money or effects at Interest or otherwise in the Right Honorable Company's cash that we know of.

"To the fourth article, we know it to be very false that Father Thomas de Poitiers bought or sold 500 chests of wine in 1713, either he or any other of the same order; and we further certify that none of the Capucins before mentioned have ever been known to be concerned in any sort of commerce whatsoever. In witness whereof, we have at their humble request given them this our certificate, which could not in conscience be refused. Done in Fort St. George this 12th day of December 1715, and sealed with the Right Honorable Company's seal."

From this testimony to the character of the Capuchin Fathers we turn to the proceedings of the Protestant inhabitants. The scheme set on foot for a Charity School in Madras has already been noticed; and the following copy of the Rules will be found curious and interesting.

"Rules for the better establishing and management of the Charity School, erected by the unanimous consent of the Vestry of St. Mary's parish in Fort St. George, on the 28th October 1715.

"That in some convenient place within the English town, there be proper accommodation made at first for 30 poor Protestant Children, diet and education gratis.

"That the Scholars be trained up to a practical sense of religion, and be particularly instructed in the doctrines of the Church of England as by law established; and therefore no person shall be capable of being master of the School unless he be qualified according to the acts of Parliament.

"That the children, whether boys or girls, shall be taken into the School house at five years of age or thereabout; and be put out to service or apprenticeships when they are about 12 years old. And while they are entertained in the School, the boys shall be taught to read, write, cast accounts, or what they may be further capable of, and the girls shall be instructed in reading and the necessary parts of house wifery.

"That no scholar shall be taken in, nor any matter of moment transacted, without the previous consent of the Honorable Governor for the time being.

"That besides the Ministers and Church wardens, who shall always be overseers of the Charity School, there be three others chosen yearly by the Vestry for the better management and more careful inspection of the affairs of the School; and in order thereunto, that the said overseers (or at least four of them) meet every week at the Vestry, and keep Minutes of what they agree upon (if it be of any moment) to be laid before the Governor for his approbation.

"That one of the overseers annually chosen by the Vestry shall at the same time be nominated Treasurer to the School, and be obliged to keep exact regular accounts of the School stock and expenses; to be laid before every Vestry, and before the other overseers, or any of the contributors, when they require it at any of their weekly meetings or otherwise.

"That when the Cash belonging to the School stock shall amount to the sum of 1,000 pagodas, it shall be employed at sea, or let out at interest, by the treasurer, with the advice of the rest of the overseers, and the consent of the Governor; and if the money cannot be thus employed, that it be lent to the Church at the usual interest.

"That all Bonds, Deeds of conveyance, and other writs for the use and benefit of the Charity School, shall be drawn and granted in the name of the Treasurer and other overseers for the time being.

"That all Legacies, Gifts, and Benefactions to the School, whether of money or other things, be duly entered by the Treasurer in a Book to be kept for that purpose, which he shall sign at the foot of every page.

"That no part of the School stock shall on any pretence whatsoever be employed to any purpose, or in any manner, but what is agreeable to the original design and institution above expressed.

"That in all difficult cases and disputes about any matter of consequence, the overseers shall make application to the Governor for calling a vestry, wherein all such matters shall be determined by the majority of the contributors.

"That the aforesaid articles shall be the standing rules and fundamental constitutions of the Charity School, according to which the overseers shall always be obliged to act. And therefore that the said rules shall be registered in the beginning of a

Book, wherein the said overseers shall enter all the subsequent orders and regulations which they may have occasion to make hereafter concerning the said school; providing that such subsequent orders shall be first approved by the Governor and Council for the time being."

In connection with this subject we make the following extracts, respecting the library in Fort St. George, from a general letter received from the Board of Directors about this time.

"We understand that the Library in Fort St. George is worthy our notice, as consisting not only of a great number of Books, but of a great many that are choice and valuable. John Dolben Esq., Mr. Richard Elliot, and others having made a present of their Books (which were considerable) to the Library, besides other augmentations it hath lately received from the Society for Promoting Christian Knowledge. We therefore recommend the care of the Library to our President and Ministers; ordering that the said Books (such at least as are of value) be put up in close presses to keep them from dust and vermin; and that none of them be lent or carried out of the Library, without the consent of both Minsters, if two shall be on the place; and the Books so carried out shall be entered in a book kept for that purpose, inserting the day and year when the person to whom it is lent on one side of the folio, and on the other the day and year when returned.

"And we order our Ministers to sort the said Books into proper classes, and to take a catalogue of them to be kept in the Library, of which they shall deliver a copy to our President, and send a copy home to us; and we desire our President to order two of our Servants, together with our Ministers, to examine the Books by the Catalogue once a year; that is to say some few days before the Vestry is held and make their report at the Vestry. It would be very proper also to put our chop on the said Books in the title page or first leaf, to show to whom they belong, if they should any of them happen to be stolen, and to stamp our arms on the cover."

The next extract refers to an incident already recorded, from which it seems that at one time the Mussulman inhabitants contributed to the support of the Hindoo pagodas; an arrangement which was finally abolished during the Governorship of Mr. Harrison.

"Monday, 16th January, 1716. Petition of the Patan Merchants Inhabitants of this place, and several others that trade hither annually from Bengal; wherein they set forth the hardship of being obliged, contrary to the rules of their religion, to contribute to the maintenance of the Gentoo Idols.

"This affair having formerly occasioned great disputes and troubles, particularly once in the time of Governor Pitt, and again since the arrival of the present Governor; at which time it was decided in favour of the Gentoo Pagoda upon account of its having been a custom of long standing, and that our Honorable Masters approved of what was done in the time of Mr. Pitt; but now the Board being sensible it has occasioned a great heart burning among the Patan merchants aforesaid, who annually import great quantities of rich goods from Bengal; insomuch that we find they begin to leave us and land their goods at St. Thomé, where the present Nabob has granted them a Cowle with several valuable privileges, and particularly that they shall pay no more than 2 per cent. custom :—it is thought high time to use all means in our power to make these people easy and prevent their forsaking us to settle at St. Thomé.

"Accordingly agreed that the President make for them a Cowle for collecting that duty themselves, Kanakapillâ, of 25 cash for every pagoda, to be applied to the maintenance of their own Mosque; and to promise them all manner of favourable usage, and encouragement, if they continue to trade hither as usual."

The following extraordinary story of a common soldier, who passed himself off as a Chaplain, and married himself to the daughter of his Captain without her father's consent, is worthy of preservation.

"Tuesday, 12th June, 1716. The worshipful the Mayor acquaints the Board that Captain William, having entered an action against John Mitchel in the Mayor Court for defaming his daughter and deluding her by a pretended marriage, in which he officiated himself as Priest and husband. Upon which a trial ensued, and due proof being made by several sufficient witnesses, as well as from the said Mitchell's original letters; the Court had respited judgment on account of his being in the Military service, till the pleasure of this Board be known, what punishment shall be inflicted in such a case.

"The Board taking this matter into consideration, it appears that the forementioned John Mitchel came out a soldier upon the last year's ships to serve the Honorable Company the usual term of years. But pretending himself a regular clergyman in Holy Orders, and that he had served some years Chaplain of one of her Majesty's ships of war, but was forced to abscond and fly for these parts upon account of a debt contracted by being bound for a brother in England; which circumstances inclining every body to compassionate him (though he brought no Orders with him) he was taken off is duty as a Soldier, and employed as Master to the Charity School lately established in this place, at a handsome salary, with all fitting encouragement, besides a recommendation to the Honorable Company in our last general letter. But since that time he has been guilty of many irregularities and scandalous actions, altogether unbecoming the profession he pretends to; many of which appear under his own hand, and others are proved by undoubted testimony, and particularly his unwarrantable action of marrying himself clandestinely. Wherefore the Board thinks fit to come to the following resolutions concerning him.

"That the said Mitchel, if in holy orders (as he pretends but cannot prove) has basely scandalized the priesthood by an irregular and unheard of way of marrying himself to a woman, and absolutely against her father's consent.

"That the Board is not obliged to regard him otherwise in this case than a soldier, enlisted in the Honorable Company's service upon the usual terms, and that he ought to be punished accordingly.

"That however as he has appeared under the notion of a clergyman, and been entertained as School Master, it will not be proper to expose him to public punishment in the eye of the natives; and not having wherewithal to make just satisfaction to the persons he has injured, it is agreed that the said John Mitchel, Centinel, do give sufficient security for his good behaviour; or else that he be kept under confinement till opportunity offers to send him off the place for Europe."

Mr. Edward Harrison left the Madras Presidency on the 8th January 1717, upon which the governorship fell to Mr. Joseph Collett. The last months of his administration and the opening months of the administration of his successor were occupied by another of those strange disputes between the Right and Left Hands, which furnish such curious illustrations of the character of the people. We have already brought forward the narrative of more than one of these caste riots; but some curious particulars are recorded in connection with the present disturbance which are worth preserving.

It may help the reader somewhat if we mention that in olden times the Chetties and Comatees had separate streets and separate idols; the Chetties belonging to the Left Hand Caste and the Comatees to the Right Hand. A Comatee could never enter a Chetty street except by permission of the Chetties, and then he could not enter it in a carriage, or a palanquin, or even with shoes on his feet. A Chetty was also prohibited in the same manner from entering a street belonging to a Comatee. The present dispute seems to have arisen in consequence of a Comatee having presumed to offer ceremonies to an idol belonging to the Chetties.

"F.iday, 12th October 1716. A dispute having arisen between the Chetty and Comatee or Banian castes, about some ceremonies at their feasts, the former pretending that the latter have usurped several titles belonging to them, and performed some ceremonies before an image that they have no right to do. The heads of the Right and Left Hand castes were called in, and acquainted that the Board is very unwilling to intermeddle in any business of this nature, which they cannot pretend to understand; and therefore they are strictly enjoined to keep the peace among themselves, and by no means to disturb the quiet of the place, upon pain of forfeiting the 12,000 pagodas mentioned in the agreement between the castes in consultation the 21st of June, 1708. They were further required to choose a number of persons out of the neutral caste to decide their differences without further delay by fair arbitration; which the Left Hand side readily agreed to, but the Right Hand insist to choose out of their own caste, and a number of Brahmins* besides ; which the Board judges to be unreasonable and therefore orders them to choose ten Brahmins for each party, and to enter into arbitration bonds without further delay."

" Monday, 15th October. The President acquaints the Board that upon summoning the heads of the Comatee and Chetty castes to sign their arbitration bonds according to order of last consultation, they flew off from their agreement ; the Comatees insisting to choose out of all the Right Hand castes, which are of their own side. Consequently the Left Hand would be over-powered by numbers, and therefore refuse to comply. Whereupon we were obliged to confine them all to the Merchants Godowns till they can come to some agreement among themselves ; the disturbance daily increasing in the Black Town ; and the Painters of Triplicane, that had the Honorable Company's work in hand, having deserted their habitations."

" The Heads were again called in, and the ill consequence of this foolish dispute fairly laid before them ; but all persuasions being to no purpose, they were again remanded to the Godown."

" Thursday, 18th October. Colloway Chetty appears as the Head of the Chetty caste, and makes an offer of having the difference between them and the Comatees decided among the heads of all their castes in the country ; by means of

---

* The Brahmins are the neutral caste; they belonging neither to the Right Hand nor to the Left Hand.

Deputies to be sent from hence; which appearing to be a reasonable expedient, it is agreed to let the parties concerned have their liberty, in hopes they will come to an accomodation in this way."

" Thursday, 25th October. The President acquaints the Board that when all things seemed in a fair way towards an accommodation between the castes, the following accident happened on the 21st instant.

" A young lad of the Left hand caste having done hurt to a Pariah woman of the Right hand castes (big with child), the whole caste got together and came in a tumultuous manner to demand justice. Upon examining the matter, he ordered the offender to close confinement, promising the heads of the caste to do them justice when it should appear whether the woman would die or live. They seemed satisfied, and the crowd was dispersed. But in the night, without any further provocation, they got together again; and all such as serve under the Honorable Company and the English Inhabitants, deserted their Employs; such as Cooks, water bearers, coolies, palankeen boys, roundel men (umbrella carriers) and other useful servants; and arming themselves with pikes, daggers, and long staves, made a grievous uproar in the Black Town; stopping all the water from coming in, and committing many other disorders. The Captain of the Guard, with the Steward and several others, were sent to them to demand their reasons for making such an uproar; and finding they were headed by several peons in the English service, they seized two of the ringleaders and brought them to the Governor, who are secured in irons till further order.

" The Heads of the Right Hand Caste are ordered to go immediately and acquaint them that we will make any shift without them rather than submit to such usage; and not a man of them shall ever be taken into service again, if they do not forthwith disperse and return to their duty; also to let them know that orders are given at all the guards to fall upon them if they commit any disorder, or draw near in a body where the guards are posted."

" Thursday, 1st November. The Painters that deserted Triplicane, as mentioned in consultation the 15th ultimo, on account of the caste disputes, have made some overtures towards returning to their habitations ; but at present insist on such unreasonable terms, that the Board cannot comply with them, considering that they ran away without any just provocation, and on purpose to distress us in our affairs."

" Friday, 16th November. The President acquaints the Board that he has intercepted a vilainous letter or Cojan, wrote by some of the Right hand castes to the Painters that deserted Triplicane and now reside at St. Thomé ; wherein they are encouraged to insist upon unreasonable terms, and promised to be supported with money for their expenses, in hopes of creating further disturbances. Those that write the letter are inconsiderable persons, but he hopes to discover those that set them to work. In the mean time all possible diligence is used to reconcile those unhappy disputes and prevent future trouble."

"Monday, 10th December. The President acquaints the Board that though he hoped all things would have continued quiet between the castes, upon a resolution formerly taken to have the controversy decided by the heads of them that reside in the country; the Chetties have this day shut up all their shops, and called all the coolies from their work that belong to their caste; and that he has employed proper persons to enquire into the meaning of it, which he will lay before the Board in next consultation"

"Thursday, 20th December. The President produces a petition delivered last night by the heads of the Chetty caste, that have for sometime shut up their shops and refused to do any business. The substance of the said petition is, that they have already complained of the Comatees singing their Naggarum before the idol named Chindadry Pillarry (Ganesha, the "Belly God");* and that their caste people in the country have heard of it, and threaten to turn them out if they suffer such abuses. Wherefore they desire the matter may be decided by the Brahmins (who are the fittest persons to do it); otherwise they cannot continue in this place; and that a bond of 12,000 pagodas on

---

* The Naggarum is the verse which is addressed to Ganesha "the remover of hindrances," before undertaking any kind of business or engaging in any affair. Naggarum is properly the name of the language rather than of the verse. The complaint here made was that the Comatees recited their verse before a Chetty Pagoda.

both sides may be signed to stand to the said Brahmin's award.

"Agreed, that since the Comatee and Chetty castes cannot be persuaded to reconcile their differences by the heads of their own or any other castes, the Board will on Monday morning next hear the opinion of all neutral persons among the inhabitants, and endeavour to determine the matter in dispute so as will best secure the peace and quiet of the place.

Monday, the 24th December, 1716. "The heads of the Chetty and Comatee castes being summoned made their appearance, and a great number of witnesses were examined concerning the ceremony in dispute, whether the Comatees have a right to cry out their Naggarum (Sanscrit hymn) before the Chindadry Pillary Pagoda or not. After three hours spent in vain endeavouring to persuade them to come to some agreement among themselves, the Board deferred the affair till next meeting."

"Monday, 7th January 1717. The President (Edward Harrison Esq.) being ready to embark for Great Britain, proposes to the Board the best method that he can think of, after having discoursed with all the principal inhabitants of the place that are not actually engaged in the dispute now afoot between Comatee and Chetty castes, for putting an end to all future trouble; and the Board upon reading them came to the following resolutions.

"That for anything that has yet appeared the Comatees, may cry out their Pennagundoo Naggarum at their houses, feasts, weddings &c. according to Salabad, but not before the Pagoda of Chindry Pillary, till that matter can be decided in the manner hereafter mentioned."

"That whereas the Comatees did agree before this Board to defer the matters in dispute to 20 Brahmins, which are the neutral caste; ten of which to be chosen by the Comatees and ten by the Chetties; though they went from their word next morning, and insisted upon joining some of their own Right Hand caste, when they found the Chetties were willing to comply; the Board think it just for the Company's and their own honour, that the Comatees shall be obliged to make good their promise by referring the ceremonies in dispute to 20 Brahmins as before mentioned.

"That in case of any foul play by the 20 Brahmins that shall be chosen on this occasion, upon full proof thereof being made, the parties aggrieved shall have justice done them.

"That in case the Comatees refuse to comply with their first promise of a reference to the Brahmins, the image of the Chindadry Pillary Pagoda shall be removed to the great Gentoo Pagoda; and to prevent all future disputes the Chindadry Pillary Pagoda shall be shut up for ever.

"That, whereas great numbers of these small Pagodas have been clandestinely built without the knowledge or permission of the Government, and more are daily begun, which tend to raise disputes among the castes, none shall be built henceforward without the permission of the Governor and Council.

"That no colours for the future shall be used at any feast in Madras, but the English, commonly known by the name of St. George's colours, with a white field and a red cross.

"That the Pedda Naik shall be Overseer of the Pariah caste, and take care to keep them in due obedience; and that no other person shall pretend to summon or have any command over them.

"That whoever shall hereafter presume to stir up the castes to mutiny or desert on account of the disputes between the Comatees and Chetties, or any other such frivolous pretence; such person or persons, upon full proof being made before the Board, shall forfeit the Honorable Company's protection, be rendered incapable of any employ in their service, and fined at the discretion of the Board.

"These resolutions will be pursued by the succeeding President and Council, unless any unforeseen difficulty should arise to occasion an alteration in opinion; and there is good reason to hope that all matters will be fairly accommodated by the Brahmins."

"Wednesday, 8th January, 1717. Early this morning the Honorable President, Edward Harrison Esq., embarked upon Ship "King George," for Great Britain; upon which the Government of this place fell to the Honorable Joseph Collett Esq. pursuant to the Honorable Court of Director's appointment in their general letters by the last ships."

"Tuesday, 22d January, 1717. The President reports that he has received an answer from Colloway Chetty and Collastry Chetty to the summons affixed yesterday at the gates to this purpose: that they would not return unless we would oblige the Comatees to refer the differences between them to 20 Brahmins as formerly proposed.

"Agreed that although we had determined, if the Chetties had stayed for our decision, to have referred the matter as they propose, yet that now it is not fit to make such an agreement with them in order for their return for the following reasons.

"First, the immediate consequence would be that all the Comatees, and probably several other tribes of the Right Hand caste, would desert the place upon our making such a condescention to the Chetties, on condition of their returning; by which we should be drove to greater straits that we are or can be by the desertion of the Chetties.

"Secondly, such a condescention would so far enervate and weaken our authority, that we should never after be able to govern the several castes with any steadiness; who would be ready on every occasion to threaten us with a desertion, by which they would govern us at their pleasure.

"For these reasons we think it necessary to assert our authority, and either to force them to a compliance, or take what satisfaction we can get out of their estates."

"Ordered that the Warehouse keeper, assisted by one of the board alternately, remove the most valuable wares belonging to the said Chetties into the Fort godown; and take an exact account of them; there being large quantities to a considerable value. By which means we hope to frighten the Chetties into a submission, and return; or otherwise to obtain some satisfaction out of their estates for the damages that may accrue to the Honorable Company by their desertion.

"Ordered that an attachment of moneys due from any inhabitant of Madras, whether Europeans or others, to any Chetties now deserted, be affixed at the Sea Gate; with a declaration that whoever shall pay any such debts after this publication to any of the said Chetties, or their order, shall be obliged to repay the same to the Honorable Company."

These resolutions appear to have brought matters to a conclusion; and the President accordingly drew up the following agreement.

Thursday, 7th February, 1717. "We, Joseph Collett Esq., President and Council of Fort St. George, in order to determine and put an end to the differences which have been for sometime past between the Comatee and Chetty castes, and also to prevent all public disturbance of the like kind for the future, do hereby appoint and order for determination of the present differences, that the Comatee shall have the liberty of saying the Pennagundoo Naggarum, or any other of their titles, before the pagoda within the Pillarry or any other in the Right Hand streets; and that the Chetties shall have liberty of rehearsing their titles, or saying their Naggarum, before any pagoda in the Left Hand streets. But that the Comatees shall not say the Naggarum in the Left hand streets, nor shall the Chetties say their Naggarum in the Right

hand streets. And we do hereby further order
that neither the Comatees nor the Chetties
shall have the liberty of saying their Naggarum or rehearsing their titles before the great
Gentoo Pagoda. And for preventing disturbance of the like kind for the future, we do
hereby forbid all persons whatsoever, building
any new pagodas in any part of this city without leave first obtained of the President and Council. We do also forbid any flags to be used in
the public procession and solemnities by any of
the castes whatsoever, besides St. George's flag;
that is a flag with a white field and a red cross.
We do hereby publish and declare that if any inhabitants of this city do on any pretence, grievance,
or any differences amongst themselves whatsoever,
desert their habitations, and go out of the Honorable Company's bounds, without leave from the
Governor; before they have applied themselves to
the Governor and Council for redress, or before
the said differences shall be determined in such
manner as shall be appointed by us, and shall refuse to return being summoned; shall forfeit their
estates to the Honorable Company and be put out
of their protection."

Four days afterwards the termination of the dispute is thus recorded in the consultation books.

" Monday, 11th February, 1717. Colloway
Chetty, Collastry Chetty and Mino Chetty, the
heads of the Chetties that lately deserted to St.
Thomé, being come back again appear before the
Board, and ask pardon for themselves and the rest
of their caste, requesting they may be permitted

to live under the Honorable Company's protection and enjoy their ancient liberties as Inhabitants.

"Agreed that their request be granted, upon their depositing in the Honorable Company's cash for 12 months the sum of 4,000 pagodas for their good behaviour; and the heads of the caste signing the law lately established.

"Agreed that an interest bond of this day's date at 8 per cent. per annum be given to Colloway Chetty and Collastry Chetty for the 4,000 pagodas deposited as before mentioned; and that the warehouse keeper do deliver them up all their bonds, papers, accounts and goods as soon as conveniently he can; and the remainder of their money shall be paid them after the account of charges we have been at on their account can be made up."

CHAPTER XXVIII.

ENGLISH MISSION FROM CALCUTTA TO DELHI.
1715—17.

Before proceeding farther with our annals of the Madras Presidency, we shall devote a chapter to the consideration of an event, which is not only interesting in connection with the early fortunes of the English on the coast of Coromandel, but which marks an epoch in the history of all the English settlements in India, — in Calcutta and Bombay, as well as in Fort St. George and Fort St. David. This event is one to which Mr. Orme and Mr. Mill have each devoted a page of their respective histories, but yet which we have reason to believe is but little known to the majority of either English or Indian readers. It appears that about a century and a half ago, a mission was sent from Calcutta to Delhi, to carry a valuable present to the Great Mogul, and to endeavour to remove certain grievances which affected the several Presidencies, and procure such advantages as could be obtained by bribery or cajollery from the Durbar. This mission was entrusted to two of the English Factors at Calcutta, Mr. John Surman and Mr. Edward Stephenson; and with them were joined an Armenian named Cojee Serhaud, and a surgeon named Hamilton. These gentlemen remained at the Court of the Great Mogul for more than two years, during which they sent frequent dispatches to Calcutta, and some few to Madras and Bombay. Copies of most of them however appear to have been forwarded to Fort St. George, and were entered from time to time in the consultation books. Accordingly it has been the good fortune of the present writer to exhume these mouldering dispatches from the old manuscript records in the Government Office of this Presidency. We shall not however publish them in detail, for whilst a large portion refers to discussions which have long since lost all interest, another portion is wanting, and could only be recovered by a collation of the records at Calcutta with those of Fort St. George. We shall therefore simply review these old letters by the light of contemporary history ; combining our extracts and illustrations in such a manner as will best serve to render the narrative an interesting picture of the times.

But what were the times ? We candidly express our belief that in the present day there are very few who either know or care to know. Indian histories, whether of Hindoo or of Mussulman, are generally regarded with a distaste highly flavoured with contempt. The reason of this is obvious. Our historians generally fail altogether to excite our interest or enlist our sympathies. Many can dwell upon the picturesque pages of old Orme with the liveliest emotions. There the intrigues and treacheries of Native princes derive a powerful interest from the fact that the genius of our own countrymen, and perchance of our own great-grand-fathers, triumphed over all. Arcot and Plassey are to us still spirit stirring names; and a host of rich associations still hang round the old Fort at Vellore, and the precipitous heights of Ginjee. But who cares to read the history of Ferishta? Who cares to peruse that dreary chronicle of Mussulman dynasties who have long since withered in their tombs? We may yet exult in the triumphs of Englishmen over Mussulman, Mahratta, or Pindaree; but neither Mill, nor Elphinstone, nor any one else, has hitherto succeeded in exciting our interest in the old wars between Mussulman kings and Hindoo Rajahs,—in old religious dissensions between Sheahs and Sonneahs, Vaishnavas and Saivas,—or even in those seraglio stories of murder and sensuality which pervade oriental history in every direction. Yet the time has been when the annals of historians like Ferishta were the delight alike of people and of princes; when every Mussulman throughout the land listened to the old annals of Ghazni and Delhi, of Bijapore, Golconda, or Berar, with an enthusiasm only to be surpassed by that with which the Jew listens to the chronicles of the kings of Israel and Judah, and to the inspired traditions of Jerusalem and Samaria. Even the very names of places and of men, names which are a positive torture to English eyes and ears, would awaken his feelings and sympathies, in the same way that the hearts of the old Scottish cavaliers warmed at the names of Dundee, Montrose, or Killiecrankie.

We believe that this evil would be remedied if an historian possessed larger sympathies as well as a larger personal acquaintance with the country and the people; if he appealed to the affections as well as to the judgment; if in a word he not only familiarised himself with those differences which are the result of a peculiar history and a peculiar culture, but also with all those complex desires and passions, in which all men can sympathize because they are common to all the great family of mankind.

The story which we are about to relate is one which ought to largely excite the interest of our readers. The year 1715, the very year that the Highlanders and the Pretender rose against king George, the two English Factors, together with the Surgeon and the Armenian, set out from Calcutta to Delhi. The character of the honest Factors is reflected in every page of their dispatches. They displayed none of the enlightened curiosity of a Clavijo at the court of Timour, or of a Bernier at the court of Aurungzebe; but they were shrewd practical business men; and they went out like members of a Chamber of Commerce, eager to obtain certain privileges, which would not only redound to the advantage of their honourable employers, but to their own credit and reputation. In Calcutta they desired some protection against the oppressions of the Nabob of Bengal, and permission to purchase more villages. In Madras they desire to recover the out villages, which had been granted in former years, but which had been since resumed by the Nabob of Arcot. In Surat they wanted to pay a fixed yearly rent in view of the customs levied by the Mogul governor. A few other similar privileges they desired to obtain, which were of considerable importance in those days, but which would excite no interest now. In a word they went, not as political envoys, but as petitioners. Neither one of them had ever been to Delhi before, but still they were not without Indian experiences. They had formed an exalted idea of the wealth and power of the Great Mogul; and they knew something of the character of the Omrahs or nobles at the Court of Delhi. Jaffier Khan, the Nabob of Bengal, was himself a good type of an Omrah; a man who rose from nothing, by that happy mixture of intrigue and audacity, which is peculiar to the Asiatic. Originally he had been a mere Tartar adventurer, who had rapidly risen in the army during the wars in the Dekkan, and had subsequently been appointed Dewan, or comptroller of finance, in Bengal. At that time, Prince Azim, the grand son of Aurungzebe, was Nabob or Subah of Bengal; and when the sovereign died, Azim and his three brothers plunged into a war for the imperial throne. Azim was slain, and Jaffier seized the happy moment for appointing himself to the Nabobship; and this post he managed to retain until it was not thought worth while to remove him. . Towards the English Jaffier had acted the part of a petty tyrant. He had insisted upon searching their goods which were sent up country, and in levying exactions in that arbitrary manner which is especially offensive to Englishmen. This was one of the grievances for which Mr. Surman and Mr. Stephenson now hoped to obtain redress;

and it was therefore expected that the influence of Jaffier Khan would be exercised to the utmost to impede the success of the mission at Delhi.

But to return to the narrative of the mission. For some reason not explained, the hottest part of the year had been chosen for the journey. The envoys left Calcutta in April 1715, and reached Delhi on the 7th of July, after a three months journey. The report that they were carrying a large present to the Great Mogul, secured them an escort from the Governors of the different provinces through which they passed; and they even travelled through the district of the Jauts, who at that time were regarded as the most dangerous of robbers, without meeting with any serious mischance. The day after they reached Delhi, they dispatched a letter to Mr. Hedges, the Governor of Calcutta, from which we make the following extract.

" We passed the country of the Jauts with success, not meeting with much trouble, except that once in the night rogues came on our Camp, but being repulsed three times they left us. We arrived at Phwordabad the 3rd instant (July), where we were met by Padre Stephanus, bringing two seerpaws, which were received with the usual ceremony by John Surman and Cojee Serhaud. The 4th we arrived at Baorapoola, three coss from the city, sending the Padre before to prepare our reception, that if possible, we might visit the king the first day, even before we went to the house which was got for us. Accordingly the 7th in the morning we made our entry with very good order; there being sent a Munsubdar of two thousand Munsub, with about 200 horse and peons, to meet us; bringing likewise two elephants and flags. About the middle of the city, we were met by the Sciad Sallabut Khan Bahadur, and were by him conducted to the palace, where we waited till about 12 o'clock till the king came out. Before which time we met with Khan Dowran Bahadur, who received us very civilly, assuring us of his protection and good services. We prepared for our first present, viz. 1001 gold Mohurs, the table clock set with precious stones, the unicorn's horn, the gold escritore bought from Zoudee Khan, the large piece of ambergreese, the astoa and chelumgie Manilla work, and the map of the world. These, with the Honorable the Governor's letter, were presented, every one holding something in his hand as usual. John Surman received a vest and Culgee set with precious stones ; and Serhaud a vest and Cunger set with precious stones likewise, amid the great pomp and state of the kings of Hindoostan. We were very well received ; and on our arrival at our house, we were entertained by Seiad Sallabut Khan with dinner sufficient both for us and our people. In the evening he visited us again and stayed about 2 hours. The great favour Khan Dowran is in with the King gives us hopes of success in this undertaking. He assures us of his protection, and says the King has promised us very great favours. We have received orders first to visit Khan Dowran as our patron ; after which we shall be ordered to visit the Grand Vizier and other Omrahs. We would have avoided this, if we could, fearing to disoblige the Vizier ; but finding it not feasable, rather than disoblige one who has been so serviceable, and by whose means we expect to obtain our desires, we comply with it."

On the seventeenth of the same month, Mr. John Surman dispatched another letter to Governor Hedges, from which we make an extract showing the farther proceedings of the mission.

" We have lately sent to your Honor the good news of our safe arrival here, the visit of the King, and the civil treatment we met with, all which will without doubt be very welcome news. We have since visited several Omrahs, as the Vizier (Abdulla Khan) and

Khan Dowran, and Tuckrub Khan ; where we were received with all the respect that could be expected, and gives me some hopes that all will end well ; but what gives me the most encouragement (for I am well acquainted these nobles, as long as they are expecting to get any thing are always complaisant) is that the methods we are at present taking is consistent and with the advice and counsel of Zowdee Khan. We visited that gentleman the 11th current, and met with the same treatment he has always given to Englishmen, with the highest acknowledgments of the favours he has received from them, that as yet he had never been able to retaliate any of them, but hoped he had now an opportunity of doing something. He pressingly advised us to do nothing without the advice, counsel, and order of Khan Dowran (and the main instrument of our affairs) Seiad Sallabut Khan ; that the turn of affairs at the Durbar obliged us to it. This, which he told us by word of mouth, he wrote me when I sent your Honor's letter to him. We are convinced he advises like a friend, and we are intent on the method, but at the same time very cautious, how we any ways disoblige the Vizier ; we being very sure that Zowdee Khan was very intimate there, sent and advised him when we intended to visit, that he would use his interest for our better reception, intending to manage the Durbar by his means. He assured us that we might be satisfied as to the important Durbar. The good prospect we have of our affairs makes Cojee Serhaud very good humoured, and at present tractable, in hopes he shall obtain his promised reward and considered that every thing is come to its crisis. I take particular care that he remains so, and as much as possible persuade every one with me to do the like ; which I fear gains me but little good will. But as passion must now be curbed, except we expect to be laughed at, we must be very circumspect in our actions and counsels."

Three days afterwards Mr. Surman and Mr. Stephenson dispatched another letter to Governor

Hedges, complaining of the invalidity of their letters of credit, and the difficulty they had in obtaining money, which they felt to be the mainspring of their negociations. But before following the course of their proceedings, it may be as well to glance at the contemporary state of the court at Delhi.

The Moguls were Mussulmans, but they were altogether a different race from the first Mahommedan conquerors of Asia. They were Tartars, whilst their predecessors were Arabs or Afghans. During the Afghan period the Mussulmans had established several large and independent kingdoms both in Hindustan and the Dekkan. During the Mogul period, these independent kingdoms were brought under the supremacy of one sovereign—the great Mogul who reigned at Delhi. The Afghan supremacy dates back to the time of William the conqueror. The Mogul period only commenced in the sixteenth century, about the time of Henry VIII. It reached its zenith in the reign of Aurungzebe, who conquered the last Afghan dynasties in the Dekkan, and who died in 1707, after having flourished from the time of Oliver Cromwell to that of Queen Anne. But at the very moment when the power of Aurungzebe seemed to extend from the Himalayas to Comorin, a new enemy had arisen. The old Hindoo nationality flashed out in the Mahrattas, and the Mahrattas resisted Aurungzebe until the day of his death. From that hour the Mogul empire was on the decline. It became a prey to disorders of every kind, to wars without and wars within. It was threatened by the Sikhs on one side,

and by the Mahrattas on the other. Meantime
the country was desolated by internal struggles.
No sooner had Aurungzebe departed this life than
his sons plunged into a desperate conflict for the
throne, which terminated in the death of all save
his fortunate successor and survivor Shah Aulum.
The latter died in 1712, and then another conflict
arose between his sons, which likewise terminated
in the death of all, save a drunken and depraved
wretch named Jehandar Shah. The new sovereign
was even too bad for Delhi. A sort of religious revolution was got up by two Seiads, or descendants
of the Prophet, who were brothers; and after
another desperate struggle Feroksere, a nephew of
Jehandar Shah, was placed upon the throne.

Feroksere was thus the reigning sovereign when
the English mission arrived at Delhi. His great
aim was to escape from the thraldom of the two
Seiads, through whom he had obtained the empire.
These two Seiads had been amply rewarded. Their
names were Abdulla and Hussein. Abdulla was
made Vizier, and Hussein was made Bukshi, or
paymaster of the forces. We may add that the
Omrahs of the Court were as ready as their royal
master to procure the ruin of the two Seiads.
Amongst these must be especially mentioned a
particular favourite of the king, named Emir Jumla. But as we shall see, all their machinations and
intrigues were defeated by the energy and genius
of Hussein.

It will have been seen by the extracts already
made from the despatches, that the great friend of
the English at the court was an Omrah named

Zowdee Khan, the same who had carried on an amicable correspondence with Mr. Pitt, the former Governor of Madras. By his advice, the envoys endeavoured to obtain the favour both of Abdulla, the Vizier, and of a powerful nobleman named Khan Dowran. But Khan Dowran was a strong supporter of Emir Jumla, and a great enemy of the Vizier. This circumstance, and others which will be presently noticed, served to delay the negociation of the English envoys for a very considerable period.

The intrigues against the two Seiads were in full play at the moment of the arrival of the mission at Delhi. Emir Jumla had made an effort to separate the brothers, but without inflicting any blow upon their power. Hussein had been raised to the rank of Commander-in-Chief, and sent to reduce Ajeet Sing, Rajah of Marwar;—a Rajpoot prince, who had rebelled during the recent troubles, and had likewise distinguished himself by destroying Mussulman mosques and erecting Hindoo pagodas. The Court party however was not ashamed to intrigue with this worshipper of idols. Accordingly, private advices were sent to the Rajah, assuring him that the king Feroksere would be infinitely obliged to him, if he would use his best exertions to resist Hussein. But this little plot proved a failure. Hussein triumphed over the Rajah, and the Rajah did not deem it expedient to sacrifice himself for the good of the Court party. Terms were concluded between the two in a manner worthy of a passing notice. Notwithstanding the influence of caste prejudices, it had been the

fashion throughout all the later conflicts between
Mussulman and Hindoo, to cement every peace
by a royal marriage; that is, the defeated Rajah
was persuaded, or constrained, to give one of his
own blooming daughters as a bride to the Mussulman sovereign. This custom was followed on the
present occasion; and the Rajah Ajeet Sing gave
not only a large peiscush, but promised also to
give his youthful daughter to the king Feroksere.
Hussein hurried back to Delhi with the welcome
news, and was once again all powerful at court;
and Emir Jumla was compelled to retire to Patna
and undertake the Government of Bahar. Feroksere however still fretted under the domination of
the Seiads, and meditated upon the best means of
escaping from the constraint they imposed. At this
juncture Hussein obtained the appointment of Viceroy of the Dekkan; and about the same time the
English Factors reached Delhi and were admitted to
an audience. Three days afterwards however, they
were astonished by the news that Feroksere had
left Delhi; but the following extract from a letter
which they addressed to Governor Harrison at
Madras on 4th August, 1715, will sufficiently explain the state of affairs.

"Three days after our arrival here, the king left the
city, under pretence of visiting a sacred place, about 6
coss from thence. But the true reason (we are of
opinion) was to clear himself of a kind of confinement,
which he thought he suffered whilst in the Fort. Afterwards on the petition of his Omrahs to return to the
city, the time of the rains being improper for travel-
ling, he showed himself resolved to proceed either to
Lahore or Ajmeer. Neither could all the arguments
used avert his intended journey. This startled us,

and considering with how great trouble and risk we had brought the present thus far, and how to carry it on at this time of the year, we were something at a stand. At last we concluded to give the gross of our present in, notwithstanding the king was abroad. But in delivering some of the fine clocks, they were ordered to be returned and kept in good order till he came back to the city, he having now determined only to visit a sacred place about 40 coss from Delhi; after which he would return. This stopped our presenting the remainder of our goods, but we concluded that it was necessary to attend his Majesty in this tour. We now continue in the camp, leaving Mr. Stephenson and Mr. Philips to take care of what goods remain in the city; and in case that the king should proceed further, that they may concert measures to bring the goods after us. We are in this interval preparing petitions to be delivered to his Majesty, hoping we shall do something for our Honorable Masters that has not been yet obtained. The patronage and management of this negotiation is in the hands of the greatest favourite at Court, Khan Dowran, and under him Sciad Sallabut Khan. Withal, we being no ways unmindful of an old friend Zowdee Khan, without whose advice, we enter upon nothing. But he being at present in so low a station is not able to obtain the King's ear. However we are satified that in whatever lies in his power, he does and will assist us, but particularly in the Vizier's Durbar.

Hussein Ali Khan Bahadur Ameer-ul Omrah is lately gone into the Dekkan country, having the entire command of all that part of his kingdom. Your Honors have undoubtedly heard how great he has made himself even to vie with the command of his imperial Majesty, as lately appeared in the disputes between himself and Emir Jumla whilst at Court, when he obliged his antagonist, contrary to the King's desires, to remove from Court to Patna, whereby through the interest of Hussein, and his own mismanagement, he is quite ruined. Wherefore we humbly recommend a very good correpondence with Hussein. Otherwise, whatever we shall be able to do here will be of very little service before him."

Another pleasant intrigue awaited Hussein Ali in the Dekkan. Emir Jumla had been sent to Patna to undertake the Government of Bahar, at the time that Hussein had set out for the Dekkan. Before leaving Delhi, Hussein had assured the king, that if any mischief were aimed at his brother Abdulla, he would be at Delhi within twenty days to avenge him. But the blow was aimed not at Abdulla but at Hussein. Our old friend Dawood Khan had been appointed Governor of Guzerat; and he was instructed to pick a quarrel with Hussein and cut him off if possible. The further progress of affairs is fully illustrated in the dispatches. On the 31st August, 1715, Messrs. Surman and Stephenson wrote as follows.

"We have advices here that Hussein Ali Khan and Dawood Khan are come to a rupture in Barrampore, so that it is likely a battle will ensue, the latter having engaged many of the Dekkan country to his party. It is whispered at this Court that this is a design laid to involve Hussein Ali Khan in trouble, and retrench his grandeur which of late has not been very pleasing.

"The king proceeding no further than Paniput,* returned to the city on the 15th, but being a little disordered in his health has not made any public appearance. So that we have not had an opportunity to

---

* The shrine of a Mahommedan saint of great repute, and famous in history as the scene of two of the greatest battles ever fought in India; viz. that which overturned the Afghan dynasty and established the Mogul emperors in 1525; and that which nearly crushed the Mahrattas in 1761.

deliver the remaining part of our present, or commence our negotiation, which shall be done by the 1st proxm."

On the 6th of October, the envoys wrote to Governor Hedges as follows.

"We designed to have presented our petition on the first good opportunity; but his Majesty's indisposition continuing, and Mr. Hamilton having undertaken to cure him, it has been thought advisable by our friends, as well as by ourselves, to defer delivering it till such time as it shall please God that his Majesty in some measure returns to his former state of health. Which advice, we intend to follow, considering that, whilst he is in so much pain, it can be but a very indifferent opportunity to beg favours of him. The first distemper the Doctor took him in hand for, was swellings in his groin, which thanks be to God he is in a fair way of curing; but within these few days last past he has been taken with a violent pain, which is likely to come to a fistula; it hinders his Majesty from coming out, so naturally puts a stop to all manner of business, wherefore must have patience perforce.

"Your Honors will have heard of the death of Dawood Khan in the Dekkan, slain in a battle with Hussein Ali. (This was a desperate conflict, in which a matchlock ball struck Dawood at the moment when victory had declared on his side.) This has given a great deal of uneasiness to this court, it being quite otherwise laid by the king and his favourites; and that which was designed for Hussein Ali's ruin, has proved a great addition to his former glories. The king at first seemed to resent it to his brother Abdulla, who not taking it so patiently, as he expected, he has altered his resolution to sending Hussein Ali Khan a Seerpaw and other marks of favour. We have advised in our letters to the Governor and Council of Madras to have particular regard to the friendships of that great Omrah; otherwise whatever we shall be able to do here for that coast will be of little service, unless backed with his favour."

The dispatches are here silent upon a point of considerable interest. The king laboured under a disease, which was not only painful in itself, but which prevented him from completing his marriage with the daughter of the defeated Rajah. After some months Dr. Hamilton succeeded in curing him; and according to the popular story the gratitude of the sovereign was unbounded. Feroksere is said to have promised to grant any favour which Dr. Hamilton chose to ask; and we are told that the generous surgeon requested no rewards for himself, but simply asked that the requisitions of the Company might be complied with. The king it is added, immediately granted this favour, and also directed that all the fees of office should be remitted. No such story however appears in the dispatches; nor indeed is it likely that the envoys would have given prominence to a fact, which was calculated to deprive them of all the personal credit which would otherwise have accrued from their successful negociations. The following extract of a letter to Governor Hedges, dated 7th December, 1715, contains all they had to say upon the matter.

"We write your Honors the welcome news of the Kings recovery. As a clear demonstration to the world, he washed himself the 23rd ultimo, and accordingly received the congratulations of the whole court. As a reward for Mr. Hamilton's care and success, the King was pleased on the 30th to give him in public viz. a vest, a culgee set with precious stones, two diamond rings, an Elephant, horse, and 5000 rupees; besides ordering at the same time all his small instruments to be made in gold, with gold buttons for his coat and waist coat, and brushes set with jewels. The same day Cojee Serhaud received an Elephant and vest as a reward for his attendance on this occasion.

"We have esteemed this as a particular happiness, and hope it will prove ominous to the success of our affairs, it being the only thing that detained us hitherto from delivering our general petition. So pursuant to the orders we received from Khan Dowran, the King's recovery was succeeded by the giving in the remainder of our present (reserving a small part only till the ceremony of his marriage should be over); and then delivered our petition to Khan Dowran, by his means to be introduced to his Majesty. Sciad Sallabat Khan, who has all along managed our affairs under Khan Dowran, being at that instant, and some time before much indisposed, we were obliged to carry it ourselves; not without taking care to have his recommendation annexed. Since the delivery Cojee Serhaud has been frequently with Khan Dowran, to remind him of introducing it to his Majesty; but has always been informed, no business can go forward till the solemnization of the king's wedding is over, when he has promised a speedy dispatch. All offices have been shut up for some days, and all business in the kingdom must naturally subside to this approaching ceremony, so that we cannot repine at the delay.

"The Rajpoots are likely to receive great honor by this wedding; the king having consented to all their desires in respect to the ceremonials; and this evening goes on his throne attended by his whole nobility on foot, to receive his spouse. All the Fort and Street, through which he passes will be made resplendent with innumerable lights; and in fine all will appear as glorious as the riches of Hindoostan and two months indefatigable labour can provide."

We are surprised that we cannot find in the dispatches any further notice of this celebrated marriage. According to Mussulman historians, the festivities on the part of the bride were conducted by Hussein Ali, and "the marriage was performed with a splendour and magnificence till then unseen among the sovereigns of Hindustan. Many pompous insignia were added to the royal train upon this occasion. The illuminations rivalled the planets, and seemed to upbraid the faint lustre of the stars. High and low shared the festivity, and joy thrilled through the veins of all. The Emperor Feroksere came to the palace of Hussein Ali, where the ceremony was performed; after which, he carried the princess in the highest splendour of imperial pomp to the citadel, amid the resoundings of musical instrument and acclamations of the metropolis.*

It was now to be expected that the cure of the king by Dr. Hamilton, would have led to a speedy consideration of the petition; but no such good fortune happened to the embassy. The king's marriage, and the general dilatoriness which prevailed,—every Omrah at the Court being far too much occupied in plotting and intriguing to pay any attention to the petition of the Feringhees,—led to a delay which threatened sometimes to imperil the success of the mission. On the 8th January, 1716, the envoys wrote to Governor Hedges as follows.

"As to the course of our negotiations, we can give but a very slender account of their progress; for although our affairs are fallen into the patronage of one of the most able men in this court to dispatch them, if he pleases, yet his dilatory methods of proceeding are such as must make us pursue our designs with patience

---

* Scott's History of the successor of Aurungzebe.

for the present. Our petition is returned, after having passed the examination of the books; the next that follows will be the King's signing; after which we shall take care to give your honors a particular account of it.

"We have lately been surprized with the King's designs of departing from this place, but God be thanked he is delayed for some days at least. We shall make the best use we can of the delay, if possible to effect our business before his departure, but which we cannot rely on.

"Two nights ago Emir Jumla arrived in this place from Bahar, attended by about 8 or 10 horsemen, much to the surprize of this city; for it is but at best supposed that he has made an elopement from his own camp for fear of his soldiers who mutinied for pay. The particulars of all which we are not yet acquainted with, nor what reception he is like to meet with from his Majesty."

On the 10th March, 1716, Messrs. Surman and Stephenson again wrote to Governor Hedges as follows.

"Your Honors will doubtless have heard by flying reports the troubles that have possessed this place for the past month, occasioned by the coming of Emir Jumla and all his forces, as it is said without the king's order. All the Tartars mutinously joined to demand their pay, which they gave out they would force either from the Vizier or Khan Dowran. This was certainly the grounds of gathering forces on all sides, the Vizier himself having not less than 20,000 horse; all which continually filled the streets and attended him when he went to the king. Khan Dowran and the rest of the Omrahs, with their forces and all the kings Tope Conna, kept guard round the Fort for about 20 days. The Vizier was obstinately bent not to pay the Tartars any thing, without very particular examinations and accounts to be made up for the plundering the town of Patna; which conditions the Tartars did not think to comply with till such time as they found the Vizier was not to be bullied; when they seemed to be willing to come to a composition, which was effected by breaking their party, and the king's orders for Emir Jumla's procedure for Lahore. The king ordered Chicklis* Khan to go and see Emir Jumla out of the city; divesting him of all his posts at Court, as also of his Munsul, Jageers, &c. with his glorious additional titles, which are ordered for the future never to be used. It is the general observation of this city, that this has only been a scheme laid if possible to entrap the Vizier, and take away his life; but he has been so continually on his guard, that nothing could be effected. So once more all is calmed, much to his (the Vizier's) Honors, and the entire disgrace of all Tartars in general; they being almost all turned out of service, a few great ones excepted. Emir Jumla is now 20 coss off this place in his way to Lahore, at present without any Munsul or post. But it is reported he will enjoy the former by the king's favour. These troubles occasioned the shutting up all the Cutcherries for this month, so that no business could possibly go on; in which ours met the same fate, with the rest, being just in the same state as a month ago. Khan Dowran very frequently promises that he will make an end with all possible expedient; but he is such a strange dilatory man, and withal inaccessible, that we have occasion to summon the utmost of our patience. There is no help for it, for with all this dilatoriness, he is the only reigning man in the King's Durbar, so that we hope he will at last consider and for his own honor see us handsomely despatched with all full grant to all our petitions.

"The great rebel Gooroo (Bandu the Seikh) who has been for these 20 years so troublesome in the Subahship of Lahore, is at length taken with all his family and attendance by the Subah of that province. Some

---

* This man afterwards became famous as Subah of the Dekkan, under the name of "Nizam-ool-Mulk."

days ago they entered the city laden with fetters, his whole attendants which were left alive being about 780, all severally mounted on Camels, which were sent out of the city for that purpose, besides about 2000 heads stuck upon poles, being those who died by the sword in battle. He was carried into the presence of the king, and from thence to a close prison. He at present has his life prolonged with most of his Mutsuddies, in hopes to get an account of his treasure in the several parts of his kingdom, and of those that assisted him, when afterwards he will be executed for the rest. There are 100 each day beheaded. It is not a little remarkable with what patience they undergo their fate, and to the last it has not been found that one has apostatised from the new formed religion."*

It is scarcely possible to conceive of a more wretched state of affairs than that depicted in the foregoing extracts. The leading events are already known to the historical student; but these notices, written on the spot by Englishmen who were probably eye witnesses of many of the scenes they describe, seem to bring the events more clearly to our eyes. The revolt of a Tartar army in the streets of Delhi is bad enough; but that terrible procession of 780 Sikh prisoners, with two thousand bleeding heads elevated on poles, is something too terrible to contemplate. We may add that the whole 780 were subsequently beheaded on seven successive days. We learn from Elphinstone that Baudu the chief was reserved for greater cruelties. "He was

---

* This religion was a sort of compound of Hindooism and Mahommedanism, in which the leading doctrines of both were reconciled by a strange kind of compromise.

exhibited in an iron cage, clad in a robe of cloth of gold, and a scarlet turban; an executioner stood behind him with a drawn sword; around him were the heads of his followers on pikes, and even a dead cat was stuck on a similar weapon to indicate the extirpation of everything belonging to him. He was then given a dagger, and ordered to stab his infant son; and on his refusing, the child was butchered before his eyes, and its heart thrown in his face. He was at last torn to pieces with hot pincers, and died with unshaken constancy, glorying in having been raised up by God to be a scourge to the iniquities and oppressions of the age."

But to proceed with the story of the English mission. The following extract from a letter dated 21st March 1716, is a singular description of the procrastination which generally pervaded the court of the Mogul.

"We have frequently complained to your Honors of the strange dilatoriness of our patron Khan Dowran. He is never known to sit out in public, and return answers to any manner of business; so that what can be said to him in the way from his apartment to his palankeen, is all that can be got; which is so very little for a man of a great business, that many days pass before an opportunity can be had even for the least answer; and that his own servant, Seiad Salabut Khan, who has the management of our affairs under him, and is as intimate as any one with him, can do as little that way as other people. Wherefore the main part of all our business has been managed by notes. This has been a great occasion of the dilatoriness of our affairs; all which we were obliged to bear with abundance of patience; still having very fair promises that our business should be done to our satisfaction. Nay Khan Dowran himself, very often both by word of mouth, and in several notes, promised to do it. A few days ago when Serhaud went to pay his respects as usual to Khan Dowran, and put him in mind of our petition, he was very surprizingly asked what petition? " Have not I done all your business?" To which Cojee Serhaud answered; but the time and place not allowing of a further explanation, he got into his palankeen and went away. This strange forgetfulness made us in very pathetic terms enquire of Salabut Khan, what we might expect after so many promises of having our business effected to our satisfaction, when we had so long and patiently waited, and been at so great an expence, to be thus answered was very surprizing, and what we did not nor could not expect in the least. We were answered that daily experience might convince us of the strange carriages and forgetfulness of that great man. Still bidding us not to despond, but that every thing would go very well after so many fair promises as we before had received. This gave us but small satisfaction, and the rather made us the more inquisitive, which gave us this further light, viz. that Khan Dowran had been advised by his own Mutsuddies that it was not his business to persuade the king to sign our petition, but that it was better to get the Vizier to advise the king what things were proper to be granted us. We were in hope that in case we would have got those petitions granted us by the means of Khan Dowran, that afterwards the Vizier would not gainsay it, as at least by a little bribery it might have passed. There has been several endeavours made to get an opportunity to speak with Khan Dowran so as to convince him; but more has been procurable. We fear the petition in this interim may be gone in, and will come out signed by the Vizier as before mentioned.

" Yesterday the King contrary to the advice of the Vizier, and purely on his own will, went out a hunt-

ing; and all the Omrahs to their tents. The place at
present mentioned is about 18 coss off; but God
knows what may be the designs of it, or where he will
march to. This obliges us to follow him to-morrow
or next day, leaving Mr. Edward Stephenson and Philips
behind to take care of the Honorable Company's
effects here. Should the petition come out signed as
above mentioned, we shall be obliged to make a new
address to the Vizier; which will not only protract
this negotiation, but must lay us open to a denial, and
at the best very expensive. We shall advise your
Honors as soon as we have any hopes of success (which
God send) or what we shall be obliged to recede from."

It would be useless to inquire into the various
motives which induced Khan Dowran to hand the
English embassy over to the Vizier Abdullah.
Sometimes it was supposed that the bribes to the
subordinate officers had been insufficient; sometimes that Khan Dowran was desirous of escaping
from the responsibility of advising the king. One
rumour reached the ears of the English envoys,
and seems to have been more likely a cause than
any of the others. It was said that the mysterious disease with which the king had been attacked
the preceding year, had again made its appearance,
and threatened to become annual; and that the
king had given private orders that the business of
the embassy should be delayed, in order that he
might retain the services of Dr. Hamilton. Meantime the results were most unfortunate to the embassy. Mr. Surman and Mr. Stephenson, strongly objected to being handed over to the Vizier as
the "cast-off favourites" of Khan Dowran. At
this moment an incident occurred, which so plainly
illustrates the disorderly state of the court, that we

extract the account from one of the dispatches, dated 20th April, 1716.

"Whilst the king was encamped 14 coss from Delhi in order to hunt, there happened a quarrel between the people of Khan Dowran and Mahamud Amilkhan as they came from the Durbar; which, after their masters got into their tents, ended in a downright fight, herein they fired with small arms, boms and great guns for about 2 hours, notwithstanding the king's repeated command to forbear, yet was it at last made up after about 100 men were killed and wounded. The king was highly displeased with the liberty they took, and resented it to both of them. But the munsal of all the actors took the trumpet from his favourite; who was not admitted to his presence for three days, and threatened much more. But at present all is made up and his Majesty again reconciled to them."

The story of the delays which followed in accomplishing the business of the embassy, would be somewhat amusing were it not also interminable. Khan Dowran was at last induced to stir himself; but again the envoys were disappointed, for their petition was only in part granted, and then was only signed by the Dewan. At length the news reached the Court that the English at Bombay intended to withdraw from Surat altogether, in consequence of the oppressions of the Mogul Governor of the district; and fears were entertained that the English fleet would immediately appear in those seas, and retaliate upon the Mogul ships, as it had done on a previous occasion. This intelligence appears to have had an extraordinary effect. The Vizier Abdulla, began to take an active interest in the petition; and accordingly he is men-

tioned in the dispatches as the " good Vizier."
All the forms of a royal firmaun were gone through
as rapidly as could be expected. The petition was
signed without any further demur, by the Vizier,
and finally by the king Feroksere. But when the
royal firmaun was an accomplished fact, and the envoys prayed to be permitted to return to Calcutta,
another difficulty arose. In consequence apparently of another unaccountable exhibition of dilatoriness on the part of their patron, Khan Dowran,
they could not obtain permission to leave Delhi.
At length even this difficulty was apparently sur-
mounted, and the envoys were admitted to a fare-
well audience with the king. But the event is best
described in a letter addressed by the envoys to
Governor Hedges, dated 7th June, 1717.

"The 23rd ultimo, John Surman received from his
Majesty an horse and Cunger, as was pre-appointed;
and the 30th ult. we were sent for by Khan Dowran
to receive our dispatches, which we had accordingly; a
seerpaw and culgee being given to John Surman, and
seerpaws to Serhaud and Edward Stephenson, as likewise to the rest of our companions. We were ordered
to pass one by one to our obeisance; then to move
from the Dewan. We did so. But when it came to
Mr. Hamilton's turn, he was told the king had granted
him a vest as a mark of his favour, but not for his dispatch. So he was ordered up to his standing again.
Whilst he was performing this the king got up. We
were highly surprized at this unexpected motion, not
having the least notice of it till that minute, either
from our Patron or any of authority; it being near
a twelve month since Mr. Hamilton had been in private
with the Majesty, and in all this time not the least
notice taken. We were very much concerned at his
detainment, and the more because we were assured of

his firm aversion to accepting the service, even with
all its charms of vast pay, honour &c.; that if the king
did detain him by force, if he outlived the trouble of
his esteeming imprisonment, he might be endeavouring at an escape, which every way had its ill consequences. To free our Honorable Masters from any
damages that might accrue to them from the pas-
sionate temper of the king, our patron Khan Dowran
was applied to for leave, twice or thrice; but he positively denied to speak or even have a hand in this
business, till our friend Seiad Sallabut Khan had an
opportunity to lay the case open to him, when he
ordered us to speak to the Vizier, and if by any means
we could gain him to intercede that he would back it;
nay if the Vizier refused, he would make one effort
for the doctor himself. Nay Sallabut Khan promised
to convince the king himself in case of any delay, pursuant to our patron's directions. We made a visit to
the Vizier the 6th instant, and laid the case open to
him in a petition from Mr. Hamilton, of how little
service he could be without any physic, language or
experience in the country medicines, or their names;
besides which the heart breaking distractions of
being parted for ever from his wife and children would be insupportable, and entirely take
away his qualifications for the king's service;
that under the favour of his Majesty's clemency,
with the utmost submission, he desired that he might
have leave to depart with us. From ourselves we informed the Vizier that we should have esteemed this
a very great honour, but finding the Doctor under
these troubles not to be persuaded, we were obliged
to lay the case before his Majesty, and we humbly desired he would use his intercessions to the king,
that his Majesty might be prevailed upon to despatch
him. The good Vizier readily offered to use his utmost
endeavours; and since the case was so, the business
was to gain the Doctor's dispatch without displeasing
the King; and he ordered a petition to be drawn up
to his Majesty in the same form as that given to

himself. It was sent him and the Vizier was as
good as his word; writing a very pathetic address
to his Majesty, enforcing Mr. Hamilton's reasons,
and backing them with his own opinion, that it
was better to let him go. The King returned
an answer which came out the 6th as follows: since
he is privy to my disease, and perfectly understand his business, I would very fain have kept him,
and given him whatsoever he should have asked. But
seeing he cannot be brought on any terms to be content I agree to it; and on condition that after he has
gone to Europe and procured such Medicines as are
not to be got here and seen his wife and children, he
return to visit the court once more, let him go. We
hope in God the troublsome business is now blown
over."

Such then is the history of this curious embassy.
We leave our readers to moralize upon the contrast
of those days with the present; and merely conclude
our narrative, by dismissing the dramatis personæ.
Dr. Hamilton died of a putrid fever soon after his
return to Bengal; and a curious anecdote respecting
his memory was told to Jonathan Scott, the trans-
lator of Ferishta, by the celebrated Warren Hastings.
The emperor Feroksere was not satisfied with the
account of Hamilton's death, which he received
from the Governor and Council at Calcutta. Accordingly he sent an Officer of rank to Calcutta to
examine the truth from the Natives, whose solemn
testimony and that of the Europeans were carried
to the emperor. This circumstance was afterwards
engraved on the tombstone of the deceased surgeon. The other English envoys returned in safety
to Calcutta, and we trust " lived happy ever
afterwards." The end of the principal actors

in the Mogul court forms a part of the tragical history of the times. Three years after the visit of the English embassy, Feroksere was suddenly placed under confinement by the two Sciad brothers, Abdulla and Hussein; but the story of his death belongs to a future chapter. During the succeeding reign Hussein was assassinated by the connivance of the then sovereign; and shortly afterwards Abdulla was also thrown into hopeless captivity, and his life is said to have been only spared out of respect for his descent from the prophet. Thus ends our story of the English embassy from Calcutta to Delhi a century and a half ago.

CHAPTER XXIX.

GOVERNORSHIP OF MR. JOSEPH COLLET.

1717—18.

Mr. Collet succeeded Mr. Harrison as Governor of Madras on the 8th of January 1717. His administration only lasted three years, for on the 18th of January 1720, Mr. Collet retired in his turn, and was succeeded by Mr. Francis Hastings. The annals of those three years, 1717-20 are marked by events, which are well worthy of preservation. The English at that time possessed a great many slaves, and accordingly two Charity Schools were erected for the children of those slaves. Then again the reception and proclamation of the Firmaun, granted by the emperor Feroksere to the English envoys at Calcutta, was evidently regarded as a most important affair; and it is interesting to note the ceremonies and rejoicings which took place on the occasion. We have also a lively account of some serious and sharp fighting which took place respecting the possession of the out-villages which had been guaranteed by the Firmaun; together with notices of various incidents which serve to enlarge our picture of those primitive but stirring times.

Before however we proceed with the annals of Madras, it will be necessary to briefly explain the position of affairs in Southern India. Sadatulla Khan was still Nabob of Arcot; but Cheen Kulich Khan, better known as the Nizam-ul-Mulk, had been recalled from the Dekkan, and the Seiad Hussein Ali Khan, had been appointed in his room. Hussein Ali, as Subah of the Dekkan, thus exercised supreme authority over the whole of Southern India in the name of the Mogul emperor Ferokserc.

We shall now place our extracts before our readers in chronological order. The first refers to a curious case of forgery, one however which appears to be more common in our own times than in the generation which has just passed away.

"Thursday, 4th April, 1717. The President acquaints the Board that on Monday in the afternoon, Captain John Powney having made a complaint to him of Mr. John Richardson, writer in the Honorable Company's Service, for counterfeiting his hand, by drawing out a false invoice of goods; pretending to have sent them by the said John Powney on Ship " Britannia" to Siam; writing a receipt on the bottom of said invoice, and counterfeiting Captain Powney's name thereunto. That he, the President, had upon the said John Richardson's acknowledging of the fact, closely confined him to his room. The said invoice, with another note, whereunto Richardson forged Mr. Benjamin Walker's hand, being given to Soondrum, a Conacapily, in pawn for the sum of 200 pagodas lent to Richardson; Soondrum is called in, and produces the true notes to the said John Richardson; who being shown the same, and asked whose hand writing the notes were of, and the names signed thereunto, acknowledged both the notes and the names to be of his own hand writing; only excusing himself, by saying he was greatly put to it for money, and hoped to have recovered his notes before they were due. The said John Richardson being thereupon ordered to withdraw, the Board came to the following resolutions in relation to him.

"That he be immediately discharged from the Honorable Company's service; that he be close confined to the cock house, and sent for Great Britain (with the consent of his creditors) by the first ship; and the Secretary is ordered to endorse the said John Richardson's true counterfeited notes on the back side of them, declaring they have passed this Board's examination, and are found to be forged."

The next extract explains itself.

"Monday, 29th April. The President reports to the Board, that he has been acquainted with very great inconveniences which the soldiers suffer, by being obliged to give their whole pay to the Steward of the Hospital, for sustenance during the time of their continuing sick in it; and being also obliged to pay half a pagoda per month towards their clothes, as many months as they stay in the Hospital for recovery of their healths. By paying so many half pagodas, they of course become in debt, which is so great a hardship upon them, that when they leave the hospital, the payment of the debts they thereby contracted takes away great part of what they should buy provisions with. To avoid which, many poor fellows have ruined their healths rather than go into the Hospital to be cured, when their distempers have been but in their infancy.

"Ordered that for the future the soldiers be obliged to pay the Steward no more than two pagodas per mensem for sustenance, during the time they continue in the hospital; it being found upon a scrutiny into the matter, fully sufficient to furnish the men with good provisions."

The next extract refers to a piece of immorality we should have hesitated to publish, were it not curious as illustrating the light in which such proceedings were regarded five or six generations ago.

"Monday, 6th May. Petition from Benjamin Skinner, Serjeant at Vizagapatam, complaining of Thomas Wilford, Factor in the Honorable Company's Service for having used too much familiarity with his wife; as fully appears by the deposition he now produces, taken upon oath before Mr. Robert Symonds, Chief, and Mr. John Emmerson, Second of Council at Vizagapatam, which is entered after this consultation.

"Agreed that the said Thomas Wilford be sent for up from Vizagapatam, and that he be suspended the Honorable Company's Service till their pleasure be known concerning him."

"The deposition of Stephen Whinship taken before the Chief and Council of Vizagapatam.

"The deponent declares upon examination in the case between Benjamin Skinner and his wife Anne, that he, the above said Stephen Whinship, with his wife, Mary, inhabiting in the house with the above said Benjamin Skinner and his wife Anne; that Mary the wife of deponent did tell him her husband, that Anne the wife of the above said Benjamin Skinner held a familiarity and an unallowable communication with Mr. Thomas Wilford, one of the Right Honorable Company's Factors; and that said Mr. Thomas Wilford used to climb over the wall at unreasonable hours, and enter into the apartment of Anne, wife to the above said Benjamin Skinner; which the deponent taxing her with, and threatening to acquaint her husband of her evil practices, when she with tears confessed the fact, entreating him to conceal it from her husband's ears. Afterwards, upon some difference between the wives of the deponent and the abovesaid Benjamin Skinner, Mary the wife of the deponent revealed it to the above said Skinner."

Our next extract is far more pleasing. It refers to the erection of the two Charity Schools for the education of the children of the slaves.

"Monday, 27th May. The President lays before the Board a paper of proposals delivered him by Mr. Grundler, one of the Danish Missionaries lately arrived from Tranquebar, for erecting two Charity Schools in this city. It is agreed that liberty be given for erecting two Charity Schools, one for Portuguese in the English town, and another for Malabars in the Black-town. The proposals are as follows:—

1. Whereas the slaves belonging to the English Inhabitants of this place have a great many children, who have no manner of care taken of

them, but are kept entirely ignorant of the Christian Religion ; it is humbly proposed that a Charity School be erected, wherein such poor children shall be taught to read and write the Portuguese language (which is the only one they understand) and be fully instructed and trained upon practical knowledge of religion and the true doctrines of the Gospel.

2. There being some reason to hope that the knowledge of Christianity may also be propagated among the Natives of this country, it is likewise proposed that a Malabar Charity School be erected in some convenient place in the Black-Town, for instructing poor children in the principles of Religion, and to teach them to read, write, and cast accounts, after the way and manner used among the Malabars.

3. That these two Schools be allowed the protection and patronage of the Honorable Governor and Council, without whose consent and approbation nothing of moment relating to the said Schools shall be transacted.

4. That the immediate care and directions of the said two Schools shall be committed to two or more Trustees, to be appointed by the Honorable Governor for the time being.

5. That leave be given to such Trustees to build or buy two School houses, one for the Portuguese School within the English town, and another for the Malabar School in the Black-Town.

6. That what money, gifts or legacies shall be given by Charitable persons for the support of the said two Schools, or either of them, shall

duly be registered by the Trustees in a book to be kept for that purpose.

7. That the Trustees shall have power to make what particular orders and regulations shall be found necessary for the better management of the said two Schools, provided that said regulations shall be approved of by the Honorable Governor and Council."

We now come to the all-important event, the reception and proclamation of the imperial Firmaun. The history of the embassy from Calcutta to Delhi, by means of which the Firmaun was obtained, has already been given in the preceding chapter.

"Wednesday, 24th July. This day being appointed for proclaiming the Royal Firmaun or charter, granted by the Great Mogul King Ferokseré to the Honorable English East India Company, for enjoyment of several privileges in his dominions (received from Bengal the 21st instant) the following orders for the ceremony are to be observed.

"All the Soldiers of the Garrison are to be upon duty, and one company to be drawn up under arms before the Fort gate.

"The Mayor with all the Aldermen and city officers to attend on horseback at the Fort Gate, where the Firmaun will lie in the Governor's state palankeen, till the Governor comes down and orders the Secretary to read it in the English language, and the Chief Dubash in the Moors and Gentoo languages, in presence of all the inhabitants of the city. After which, the palankeen with the Firmaun, attended by the Mayor, Aldermen, city officers on horse back, a company of foot soldiers, all the English with music, are to move forward down Charles Street to St. Thomas' Gate, where the Registrar is to proclaim His Majesty's Firmaun. From thence to proceed to the Sea Gate, proclaiming it there; and soon to the Middle Gate repeating the proclamation over again; from which Gate the Mayor, Aldermen and city officers are to return to the Governor in the Fort, and the Firmaun to be carried forward from this Middle Gate through the Black Town to Attapollium Gate in manner following : viz. First the Pedda Naik, or watchman of the city, to be on horse back with all his Taliars and the country music, then one company of the English Guards, next two trumpets, after which the Chief Dubash on horse back, the palankeen with the Firmaun guarded by six Serjeants after him; and then all the Moors and Gentoo merchants on horse back close after the palankeen to the aforementioned Attapollium Gate ; where the Chief Dubash on horse back is to hold up the Royal Firmaun, and proclaim it by expressing himself in the following words.

"This is His Majesty King Feroksere's Royal Firmaun, wherein he confirms to the Honorable English East India Company all former grants and privileges, enjoyed by them heretofore ; and further grants many new privileges, with the possession of several lands in many parts of India, with such favour as has never before been granted to any European nation.

"Then he, the Chief Dubash, is with the re-

tinue to go out at the said Attapollium Gate, and
enter the town at Tom Clarke's Gate, proclaiming
the Royal Firmaun a second time there ; and thence
to proceed within the town at Bridge Foot Gate, in
order to proclaim it a third time ; and from the said
Gate to return to the Choultry, where the Taliars
and Black Music are to stay without, and the
guards with the Dubash and palankeen to return
to the Fort and deliver up the Firmaun to the
Governor ; the Black merchants being permitted
on foot to attend it back from the Choultry gate :
and for the more regular management of this
solemnization the following orders were delivered
the Gunner of the Garrison for discharging his
part of the ceremony.

" To Mr. Frans Hugonin, Gunner,

"As soon as the Firmaun is read before the
Governor at the Fort Gate, you shall begin to fire
from St. Thomas Bastion, and proceed from thence
to the Westward and on the Northward till you
come round to the said St. Thomas Bastion ; and
then to continue firing round the walls of the
Black Town to the numbers of 151 guns. As
soon as the fire is gone round the White Town,
Captain Matthew Martin, Commander of the "Marlborough," must take up the fire ; and when he has
done, all the Europe Ships in the road must fire one
after another ; and the country ships, upon the
Europe Ships finishing, to fire altogether as fast as
they can ; the ships being handsomely dressed out
with their colours and streamers.

"When the Governor and Company come to
the garden at Tiflin, the Governor will begin the

Mogul's health, when you must begin to fire from the Garden point, and continue the fire round the town to the number of 101 guns; after which you are to prepare against Dinner to fire 101 guns at King George's health, 51 guns at the Prince and Princess and Royal Families health, and after Dinner 31 guns for the Honorable Company's health; the ships in the road to fire at drinking the Mogul's and King George's healths, in the same manner as they did upon proclaiming the Royal Firmaun.

"After the ceremony of proclaiming the Firmaun in the English and Black Town was over, the Honorable President with the Gentlemen of Council proceeded to the Garden house through the Black town, attended upon by all the Gentlemen of the city on horse back with handsome accoutrements; where all they, English, Portuguese, Armenian and Moors Inhabitants, were splendidly entertained at Dinner; and the day concluded with feasting of the soldiers, with tubs of punch, and a bonfire at night; and the Black Merchants, to show their joy at the Honorable Company's receiving so much favour from the Mogul, made abundance of fireworks upon the Island."

The next extract refers to the projected occupation of Divy Island, off Masulipatam, by the English. Possession had been granted in the Firmaun, but some difficulties rose in the way. The extract is chiefly interesting as illustrating the feelings of the Natives towards the English of that period.

"Monday, 26th August. The President delivers to the Board a translation of their letters from Masulipatam, one by Cunsum Pera, who had been formerly Chief Dubash to the New East India Company there, the other from Khan Colonoo Buggawan, an eminent Brahmin in those parts, advising and pressing us to take speedy possession of Divy Island. They both agreed that all the inhabitants wait impatiently for us, and that we may depend upon having an accession of people from the continent; the inhabitants being very desirous of living under the English Government, and that there are already eighteen towns and villages upon the Island.

"After full debating the matter, it is agreed that Cunsum Pera be sent for hither to give us a more full account of the state of affairs there; that he be taken into the Company's service and employed in that business; and that in the meantime, the President do give orders for providing all necessaries ready for taking possession of Divy Island."

The following extracts exhibit the operation of the imperial Firmaun, as regards regaining possession of the out-villages.

"Monday, 2nd September. The President produces translates of letters from the Nabob Sadatulla Khan, Sunka Ramah, and our spy Brahmin at Arcot, relating to the demand he had made of Trivatore and other villages lately granted by the Royal Firmaun. The Nabob's letter is wrote in general terms, with a great many compliments, but refers to Sunka Ramah and the spy Brahmin for an answer to the business in hand. They both advise that in conversation the Nabob told them, he could not deliver up possession of the villages without seeing the original Firmaun, but that he was desirous to maintain good understanding with the English.

"On a full consideration of the matter it was agreed that the President should write to the Nabob, rendering him thanks for the assurances of his friendship and favour, and acquainting him that 21 days after this date, he designs to take possession of the said villages ; and together with his letter to send the present, usually made upon a new President's accession to the Government of this place ; which has been suspended so long, that we might be assured of the Nabob's keeping his post ; which has been very unlikely, and if a new Nabob had been established, we should have been obliged to have given it over again. The sum agreed on is 500 pagodas, and one piece of superfine scarlet cloth to the Nabob, and 200 pagodas with some cordial waters to Ducknaroy, the Nabob's Secretary and Son-in-law, who has the chief management of his affairs. To whom also it was agreed the President should write a short compliment. It is further agreed that the President do write to Sunka Ramah to make the several presents ; and at the same time to acquaint the Nabob that it is an express grant in the Royal Firmaun, that neither he, nor any of the King's officers, should demand to see any of the original papers ; but that copies, duly attested by the Cazi, shall be a sufficient claim on our parts for the several privileges and grants bestowed upon us ; and that himself and all other officers are obliged to yield obedience to such attested copies."

"Thursday, 19th September. The President proposes to the Board the taking possession of Trivatore, &c. (five villages granted the English Company by the Mogul) on Monday and Tuesday next, and begin with Trivatore, and in case of opposition (which is hardly expected) to repel force by force."

"Monday, 23rd September. Early this morning the Honorable President (attended by most of the Gentlemen in the place) set out for Trivatore, whereof he took possession, stayed there and dined and returned in the evening, having in the interim taken possession of two more villages.

"Tuesday, 24th September. Early this morning Mr. Richard Lordon set out with a party of men, and took possession of the two other villages without any opposition, and returned about noon."

"Sunday, 29th September. The President represents that this morning he has received advices from the Nabob's Court at Arcot, and from Peersada at Poonamallee, that the former would not accept of the 500 pagodas present, we had sent to Sunka Ramah for that purpose; and that less than 1000 would not content him. That Peersada had stopped the roads to this city from Poonamallee, and would not permit merchandize, or the common necessaries of firewood, &c. to be brought into Madras; and that he had sent to Diaram, the Head Renter of the country under Hussein Ali Khan, for assistance to distress us further.

"On mature deliberation upon these advices it was agreed to make the Nabob's present 1000 pagodas for the following reasons.

"First, that we might divide the interest of the country Government about us, and thereby prevent their joining together to distress us.

"Secondly, the present last made by our late President amounted to that value, and might give them the fairer pretence to demand the same now.

"Thirdly, the present is conditional on his giving a letter confirming to us the peaceable possession of the villages we have lately taken."

"Wednesday, 9th October. The President produces a letter which he received from Diaram yesterday, wherein the said Diaram demands by what authority we have taken possession of Trivatore and the other villages; and adds that unless we have a sunnud under Sadatulla Khan's seal or Seiad Hussein Ali Khan's Perwanna, to warrant our so doing, we must restore the villages to his order.

"The President's answer to the aforesaid letter is also read, signifying to the said Diaram, that what we have done in relation to the villages is by virtue of his Majesty's authority; and that we will not give up our just rights on any pretence whatsoever, but on the contrary will defend them to the utmost of our power. The President's conduct on this occasion is approved by the Board.

"The President likewise communicates to the Board a letter which he lately received from some of the inhabitants of Divy Island, pressing him to despatch the Deputy Governor thither with all speed, to prevent the countries being laid waste by Apporrow the Renter, who is now plundering the inhabitants, as apprehending their desertion from him upon the arrival of our people there. The President's answer to the said letter is also read and approved ; encouraging them as much as possible to wait with patience till the rains are over, when they may expect the Deputy Governor with a sufficient force to rescue them from the oppressions of Apporrow and to redress their grievances.

" Wednesday, 16th October. The President communicates to the Board a proposal which was made him by Sunka Ramah and the other late joint Stock merchants, to rent the five new villages granted by the Firmaun, viz. Trivatore, Satangodu, Catawaucha, Vezallawarrow and Lingambauca at 1200 Pagodas per annum for 12 years. Whereupon the yearly amount of that Revenue being examined into, when the said villages were granted the Honorable Company in President Pitt's time, and found to be just the same, it is agreed that they be let to the aforementioned persons for 12 years, at 1200 pagodas per annum ; and that the Secretary do prepare a lease against next consultation."

Diaram the Head Renter was not disposed to see the villages taken out of his hands, without making an effort to force Governor Collet to give him a present. The following extracts in reference to these proceedings will be found very curious.

" Friday, 18th October. The President acquaints the Board that he has just now received advice from Trivatore, that Diaram's son has entered that town with 250 horse and 1000 foot, and had cut down our flagstaff and posted himself in the town. He adds that in the morning a Brahmin belonging to Diaram had been with him; and after a very long harangue wide of his purpose, delivered his errand, which was to demand a present of 1000 pagodas to Diaram, in consideration of which he would quit all pretentions to the villages we were possessed of. He declared withal that unless we would comply with that demand, Diaram's forces would take possession of them the next day. It appeared in fact that the forces were on their march to Trivatore whilst the Brahmin was delivering his message.

"The President then proposed to the Board to consider whether we should comply with their demands of money in order to buy a peace; or whether we should tamely sit down with the affront they had given us in cutting down our flag, and wait to see how much further they would proceed; or whether we should make a vigorous charge with our forces, and endeavour to drive them out of the Town by force of arms.

"After mature deliberation it appeared to be the unanimous opinion of the whole Board, that we should endeavour to drive the enemy out of Trivatore by force, for the following reasons.

"First, that Diaram has no pretence to make any demands on us on account of the said town; that we are not directed by the Firmaun to demand possession of them from him, but from the Nabob; his business being only to collect the rents for Sciad Hussein Ali Khan; and that to give him money upon this occasion would be a precedent for him to make demands on any other, or perhaps without any pretence, whenever he should think fit.

"Secondly, that to sit down quietly without resenting the affront, would but encourage the enemy to proceed to greater injuries ; and give them reason to apprehend that we were doubtful of our own strength, and must submit to whatever terms they should think fit to impose on us.

"Thirdly, our men having of late been pretty well disciplined, and being now completely officered, we do not doubt their being able to drive the enemy out of the town and maintain the possession ; which we hope will have so good an effect as to deter them from attacking us rashly again.

"Agreed that the direction of the Military be left to the Governor singly."

"Monday, 21st October. The President reports that after closing the consultation on Friday evening, he held a consultation with the military officers ; the result of which was, that he gave orders to Lieutenant John Roach to draw out 150 men of the Garrison, to be in a readiness to march by two o'clock in the morning of the 19th to Trivatore ; that he should endeavour to enter the town about break of day, and if he found the enemy there, to attack them immediately, and endeavour to drive them out of the town, and to keep possession of it till further orders. The President adds that about 9 o'clock in the morning he received advices from Lieutenant Roach, that he had entered the town exactly at the time appointed, and found the enemy in possession ; but that after about an hour's dispute he had obliged them to quit the town and take to the plains. That after this they made some attacks, but were constantly drove back ;

and Lieutenant Roach pursuing some of them to the plain, saw a fresh body of horse coming from the northward, which he then guessed by view to be about 500 in number. On these advices the President ordered Lieutenant Fullerton to draw out 100 men more of the Garrison, and with a sufficient quantity of provisions and ammunition, and two field pieces, to march immediately in order to join Lieutenant Roach. By 12 o'clock at noon all things were in a readiness, and Lieutenant Fullerton began his march. In the meantime the President ordered the militia of the town to be raised, who took possession of the White town; while the out-guards were strengthened by the remainder of the Garrison; and Gunner Hugonin, with the Governor's Horse Guards (being six in the whole), were ordered to patrol about the Washer town and Tondore, to prevent the enemy from burning or plundering on that side. At 3 o'clock in the afternoon, the President received further advices from Lieutenant Roach, dated half an hour after 12, advising that the enemy had kept skirmishing with them till near that time, but then were all drawn off, and marched towards Satangodu, after he had recovered the Flag Staff, and Flag, which he again hoisted in the middle of the Town. Soon after arrived further advices that Lieutenant Fullerton had joined Lieutenant Roach with his body, and that the enemy were marched off to some mile distance. On which the President sent order to Lieutenants Roach and Fullerton to march back in the evening or early the next morning; it being difficult to supply them with necessaries at that distance. They returned the same evening, and arrived at Fort St. George about 8 o'clock.

"It appeared that on Lieutenant Roach's entering the town the boors were not prepared to receive him, presuming we durst not march out of the reach of our own cannon. As soon as he gained the middle of the town, he saluted them with three vollies which did some execution. As fast as they (the enemy) got into order, they possessed themselves of the Avenues which are numerous, and endeavoured to regain the middle of the town; it being a very large square containing a Tank and a Pagoda; but in about a hour's time they were obliged to quit the town and take to the plains, though they afterwards made several attempt to re-enter the town but were obliged to retire about noon.

"In the whole action, which lasted about six hours, there was not one man of our Garrison killed or wounded by the enemy; one only of our Europeans was shot in the arm by his comrade's error in firing; three of our peons were slightly wounded, but none killed. The enemy left in the place one camel, 6 horses killed; six horses were taken alive by our men. Five men only of the slain were left, the rest being carried away; so that we do not know the certain number, but suppose there might be about 10 or 12 killed in the action.

"The President adds that he received advices yesterday from Poonamallee, that when the enemy had marched about 3 miles from Trivatore towards

Poonamallee, they encamped and continued there till 9 o'clock at night; and then marched one hour (contrary to their custom) without lights; fearing, as it appeared, to be attacked in the night; for when they thought themselves out of reach of pursuit, they light their duties and proceed on their march towards Poonamallee. Advices from thence further adds that Diaram's son, who commanded the party, was shot through the shoulder blade and his life endangered; that the commander next to him had several balls in his thigh; that thirteen more of their men were wounded, and eleven horses, besides one camel and two horses which dropped on the road.

"The President concluded that this great success without any loss must, next to the blessing of God on the justice of our cause, be ascribed to the good conduct of Lieutenant Roach, who had posted his men in such a manner that the enemy was not able to make any attack without certain loss to themselves, as at the same time they were unable to do us the least injury. He, therefore, proposes to the Board to consider of some honorary reward to be given Lieutenant Roach, who to his former merit at Fort St. David, has added this new and eminent service.

"Agreed that in consideration of Lieutenant John Roach's former services at Fort St. David, for which the Honorable Company have in their letters ordered him a gratuity, which has never yet been given, and also in consideration of his eminent service at Trivatore on the 19th instant, in defeating the enemy, with so much loss on their side, and without the loss of one man in ours ;—that the President by his Commission constituted Lieutenant John Roach, Major of all the Honorable Company's forces on the Coast of Coromandel and Island of Sumatra ; and that a Gold Medal, with the Honorable Company's arms set round with diamond sparks, with an inscription on the reverse suitable to the occasion, (the value about 300 pagodas) be given him.

"Agreed that his pay as Major be 20 pagodas per mensem.

"Agreed that it be left to the discretion of the President to order smart money to the wounded, and some gratuity to the inferior officers, who all behaved themselves very well in the engagement."

Thus ended this gallant little affair, which must have created no small excitement amongst the denizens of Fort St. George.

The following story of a spy is very curious as illustrating the life of an adventurer in the olden time.

"Friday, 7th February. The President informs the Board that he had for sometime past kept one Francisco Ferera, a pretended Doctor, close prisoner in the Fort, on an information he had received that the said Doctor had performed the part of a spy, and given information of our circumstances to the Moors during our quarrels with Diaram. That as to his personal character, he had formerly been a Jew in Italy, and Constantinople, and at Grand Cairo ; and that in the latter place he turned Turk, and married and had children, who now reside there. That he has been sometime in these parts, and professing himself a Christian, married a Portuguese woman an inhabitant of this city. The President adds that he has been very much solicited to release the prisoner, who is not capable of doing any further hurt with respect to Diaram. He proposes to consider whether the prisoner may not be freed on giving security for his behaviour, and that he shall not go out of the English bounds without leave of the Governor. All the circumstances being considered, it is agreed, that on giving good security as above, that the said Francisco Ferera be discharged from his imprisonment.

"The prisoner proposing one Francisco Gregorio, an inhabitant of this place of some substance, to be bound with him in the penal sum of 1000 pagodas for his good behaviour;—it is ordered that the Secretary make out a bond accordingly."

The next story of a murder gives us an insight into the working of the police peons under the Pedda Naik.

"Monday, 9th June 1718. The President reports that some Guzerat Merchants had been with him this morning, to advise him that one Frivadee, a Surat Merchant Inhabitant of this place, was found this morning with his servant hanged in his own house, and that it was supposed they had hanged themselves. That on this information he had ordered the Secretary, in the presence of the Company's merchants and the Guzerat merchants, to take an account of the deceased's effects and secure them for his relations.

"Wednesday, 11th June. The President ac-

quaints the Board that yesterday morning he had
discovered that Frivadee and his servant, who
were supposed to have hanged themselves, were
murdered by robbers, who had carried off a very
large booty in money; that he had immediately
given out orders for a strict search after the murderers; and that just now three persons were
brought before him, charged with that murder;
that the case being extraordinary, he had summoned them together to hear the examination of
the prisoners, and such witnesses as should appear
against them.

"The prisoners and witnesses, with a considerable number of the principal inhabitants, Europeans
and Natives, were called in; and the money and
jewels which had been taken by the prisoners from
Frivadee were produced, having been taken in
possession of the several prisoners to the amount
of five or six thousand pagodas.

"On a full examination it appeared to the whole
Board that there was sufficient reason to put the
prisoners upon trial for their lives for murder and
robbery; and it was accordingly agreed that they
should be tried in the Mayor's Court according to
the charter, and that an order be given the Mayor
in the following manner.

"On a full examination of Cadojee, Perscram,
and Kisnados, who stand charged with the murder
of Frivadee and his servant on the night between
eighth and ninth instant, and several other witnesses concerning that murder,—we do find full
and sufficient cause to put the said Cadojee, Perscram and Kisnados on trial for their lives; and

in order thereto, we do hereby authorize you, the Worshipful John Legg, Esq., Mayor, to summon a court to-morrow, being the 12th instant, for the trial of the said prisoners, and to acquit them, or on their conviction of murder and robbery, to condemn them to suffer death in such manner as shall seem to you most proper to deter others from committing the like crimes."

Short work was made of these gentlemen, for two days afterwards we find the following significant entry.

"Friday, 13th June. This morning about 9 o'clock Cadojee, Perseram, and Kisnados were executed upon the Island."

This event directed the attention of Governor Collet's attention to the inefficiency of the Pedda Naik. We extract the proceedings at length.

"Monday, 7th July. The President reports to the Board that Pedda Naik, the chief Watchman of the town, has forfeited his Cowle by open and notorious transgressions of every part thereof; that he is become utterly incapable of discharging the duty of that post, having by his extravagance rendered himself unable either to maintain a sufficient number of Taliars to watch the city, or to make good any losses that shall happen as by the Cowle he is obliged to do; that through his incapacity as a watchman to discharge his duty, frequent robberies have happened of late, and one instance of what is unusual in these parts of a merchant and his servant murdered in their own house by robbers. The President added that if a speedy stop was not put to this mischief it would increase upon us till it become past remedy.

"The Cowle was then read, and the violation of every part thereof by Pedda Naik was notorious to the whole Board.

"The Pedda Naik being called in, and acquainted with the sentiments of the Board on his conduct, was asked if he had any thing to say in his own defence. He only replied that he was not able to do better, and left himself to the judgment of the Board.

"Agreed that Pedda Naik, chief watchman of the city, having forfeited his Cowle, and being incapable of performing the duty of his office, be dismissed the Honorable Company's Service.

"Agreed that Koonugoree Timapa, Naik of the same cast and family with Pedda Naik, be constituted chief watchman of this city of Madras, under the same obligation of duty, and with the same privileges and revenues as the former enjoyed.

"Agreed that the revenues from the Sea Gate, Choultry and Bazar appropriated to the Watchman, be to the end of this month carried to Pedda Naik account, they being mortgaged to the corporation; and the beginning of the next month delivered up to the new Watchman; and that all these other revenues be immediately delivered up to the new Watchman."

Towards the end of the year 1718, Governor Collet appears to have concluded a definite arrangement with Sadatulla Khan, Nabob of Arcot, as regards possession of the out-villages. The following extracts will sufficiently explain the matter.

"Monday, 10th November 1718. The President represents to the Board the present state of affairs with respect to the country Government; that he has been for sometime past, as they know, threatened with forces from the Nabob, in case he would not deliver up Trivatore and the villages granted by the firmaun. But that for about a fortnight past the Nabob had by some of his agents begun privately a treaty of peace with him. The first terms that were offered were that the villages should be delivered into the hands of Sunka Ramah till a sunnud could be procured from Sciad Hussein Ali Khan; which being rejected by the President, the Nabob proposed that the President should write to him in general terms to this purpose; viz, that he had taken possession of the village by virtue of the king's grant, and that the Company would give orders to return the king thanks for his bounty, and to procure a sunnud from Sciad Hussein Ali Khan. If not that the Nabob was at liberty to act as he should think fit. To which the Nabob was to answer, that if the Company procured a sunnud from Sciad Hussein Ali Khan, it would confirm the peace between us. The President adds that the sum insisted on for presents is 2000 pagodas for the Nabob, and 1000 pagodas for Ducknaroy his Secretary, and prime minister; of which he proposes 1000 to be paid out of the tax levied for building the choultries, and the other 2000 out of cash. The President further adds that he has not yet returned an answer to this proposal, being willing first to know the sentiments of the Board concerning it.

" After mature deliberation the whole Board unanimously agreed that the President should accept of the Nabob's proposal, and make peace with him accordingly, for the following reasons.

First. Hereby we fully assert our right to the possession of the villages by virtue of the King's grant, without entering into any engagements of receding from that right, even though a sunnud should not be obtained.

Secondly. That three years time of settled peace (as far as such a thing can be with the Moors) is hereby gained, and thereby time sufficient for the Honorable Company to give their orders for our future conduct.

Thirdly. We hereby assert the Honorable Company's right to all the grants made in the Firmaun, in which that of Divy Island is included.

Fourthly. By making peace on these terms, we effectually prevent all future demands upon us on account of our new fortifications on the Northside of the Town, and of our fortifying Egmore, which used to be always esteemed a ground of complaint and cause of quarrel. It also prevents all claim on account of the goods recovered out of the wreck of the Ship " Success," and the manner of our doing it, that is by open force. A peace being once concluded without any claim on these accounts, there can be no pretensions raised on them hereafter.

"The President then told the gentlemen of the Board that this negotiation required the utmost secrecy till it was effected. Besides that, though he does believe the Nabob to be in earnest, yet the

Moors so much affect a mysterious conduct, that it is not to be depended on till perfected. It being very usual for them to enter on a Treaty when they design a surprizing blow. He added that to prevent any danger of that kind, he had placed a sufficient Garrison in Egmore Fort, and doubled the guards at all the Choultries; and that he had employed several spies in the enemy's camp as well as in the country round about."

"Monday, 15th December. The President reports to the Board that this day the peace concluded with the Nabob was fully ratified; that Aga Mogheen, who had negotiated that affair with him, came to the Garden about 10 o'clock this morning with two elephants, fifteen horses, and about three hundred peons; that one of the elephants carried a chair of state with a canopy, in which sat two persons who brought two Seerpaws for the President, with a perwanna in answer to the letters wrote sometime since, expressing the Nabob's agreement to the terms of peace, and desiring a sunnud might be procured from Seiad Hussein Ali Khan as soon as it could be done conveniently. The Nabob sent also a horse which Aga Mogheen delivered to the President. The solemnity was greater than usual on the occasion on the Moors part. We received them with a body of nearly 500 men in arms; all the Honorable Company's servants and most of the inhabitants being present, with great numbers of the Natives. The presents being received, the Nabob's health was drank and 31 guns fired."

During this year Governor Collet was engaged in a long and troublesome inquiry into the conduct of the Governor of Sumatra, who by irregular proceedings had brought on a war with the Sultan, which had terminated in the forced retirement of the English. The particulars would afford but little interest to our Madras readers; but the following certified statement of the inhuman conduct of an English supervisor at this time, furnishes such a sad picture of the atrocities which occasionally occurred, that we cannot pass it over. The entry is to be found in the consultation book of 14th August, 1718; but the event itself had taken place at the beginning of the year. The statement is as follows.

" To whom it doth or may concern,

" This is to certify that on Sunday the 2nd of February 1718, before noon came on shore at Bantall, Mr. James Morris (supervisor from the Malborough) some thing in liquor. After dinner, he being drunk, he sent for two of the men prisoners of war out of the cock house; when having asked a few questions, he ordered them down upon the parade, himself attending, where he ordered one of them to be beheaded first, and then the other inhumanly to have his fingers and thumbs hacked off joint by joint, and at last his head cut off; after which, or next day, he obliged Sultan Cutcheel to sign their death warrants; in attestation of which we have hereunto set our hands this 9th day of August 1717 in Madras.

BENJAMIN GRAVES.
ROBERT WYNN.
AUGUSTUS WYNN.
ROBERT BARRET."

CHAPTER XXX.

GOVERNORSHIP OF MR. JOSEPH COLLET.

(Continued.)

1719—20.

The closing year of Mr. Collet's governorship seem to have passed tranquilly away; and the domestic incidents which occurred at Madras thus present a striking contrast to those tragical revolutions at Delhi which were heralding the fall of the Mogul empire. In a previous chapter, we noticed the state of the court at Delhi in 1715-17, when the English embassy was despatched from Calcutta to the emperor Feroksere. We now purpose to bring out in bold relief the contrast already indicated. First stringing together the concluding annals of Madras under Governor Collet; and then taking a glance at the contemporary events which were being enacted in the empire of the Mogul.

Our first incident is simple enough, and the extract will explain itself.

" Monday, 5th January, 1719. Augustus Burton, who came out in the Honorable Company's Service upon the "Mary" the last year, on his coming on board the ship brought with him clandestinely a young man, named Edmund Massey, his brother-in-law; without permission of the Com-

pany or Captain, who was ignorant of it till the
ship was under sail, when it was too late to send
him ashore. The Captain, since his arrival from
Bengal, applied to the President for permission to
carry the said Edmund Massey back again to England, to prevent his having to pay the penalty for
bringing out any passenger to India without the
Company's permission, which he is obliged to by
his charter party. But the said Edmund Massey, having likewise requested to be entertained in
the service here as a writer, and being a sober lad
and capable of business,—it is agreed that we do
give Captain Hobben a permission to leave him
here, and that he be admitted into the service till
the Honorable Company's pleasure can be known
concerning him."

Our next extract illustrates the peaceful state of
the relations between the Government of Fort St.
George, and Sadatulla Khan, the Nabob of the
Carnatic.

"Wednesday, 11th February. The President
represent to the Board that Ducknaroy, who is
prime minister to the Nabob Sadutulla Khan, and
Fyre Khan the Nabob's general, came to St Thomé
last Saturday, with a body of 400 horse and 1000
foot, in order to perform a religious ceremony of
washing in the sea at the time of the Sun's Eclipse
the next day; and that he (the President) had
sent the Company's black servants and merchants
to welcome him into this part of the country, and
to sound the inclinations of Ducknaroy, whether
he was inclined to accept an invitation to see the
Fort; and that he had received a very civil answer

from Ducknaroy and Fyre Khan, with assurances of their friendship, and an intimation that they were inclined to give him a visit.

"These two persons having the greatest influence both in the direction and in the execution of the Nabob's affairs, it is thought convenient to receive them in such a manner as may establish the good understanding between us and them begun on making the peace; and that presents be made them in such a manner as may be most acceptable to them to the amount of 1000 pagodas; that they may be admitted into the White Town with 20 palankeens, 100 horse, and 200 foot; that the President receive them at the foot of the stairs in the inner Fort, and lead Ducknaroy into the Consultation Room; that 51 guns be fired by the Fort; and then taken up by the ships; that on his departure out of the White Town the same number of guns be again fired, and taken up by the ships also; that the Secretary and Captain Fullerton be sent to St. Thomé to invite them to come into Town to-morrow morning."

"Thursday, 12th February. About 9 o'clock this morning Ducknaroy, the Nabob Sadatulla Khan's Prime Minister and favorite, together with Fyre Khan his General, entered the Town with 100 horse and 200 foot (in pursuance to the invitation) and came to pay a visit to the President. They were welcomed into Town with 51 guns from the Fort and afterwards from the "King George" and other ships in the road with a proportionable number. The President attended by the gentlemen of Council, covenanted servants and most of the inhabitants of the place, conducted them into the Consultation Room, where the Nabob's health was drank, and after a short confabulation, they took their leaves (being saluted with 51 guns from the Fort and afterwards by the ships as above) and went to a house in the Black Town prepared by Sunkah Ramah for their reception; where they were sumptuously entertained at the Honorable Company's Expense till 5 o'clock in the evening, when they went to take a view of the Garden house and from thence returned to St. Thomé."

The following incidents are so simple that we leave the records to tell their own story.

"Monday, 23rd February, 1719. The President acquaints the Board that being informed several Patan Merchants were come from Bengal on a ship bound to St. Thomé, he had used means to induce them to settle at Madras and to land their goods here; that he had prevailed with them, on condition they had a cowle granted exempting them from paying the Pagoda or Musqueet duty. They alledged that to pay to the Pagoda would be contributing to the promoting of idolatry; and that they cannot consent to contribute to the Musqueet in this place, which belongs to a different sect of Mahommadans.

"Agreed that in consideration the granting such a cowle will be no detriment to any part of the Honorable Company's revenues, but on the contrary will increase them by the addition of foreign Merchants becoming inhabitants, such a cowle be granted them."

"Thursday, 26th February, 1719. Chinna Chetty, one of the Chetty Caste, was brought before the Board and charged with the breach of the law made the 7th February 1717, for preventing disputes and differences between the several Castes; wherein it is provided that all the several castes shall, on their public festivals and solemnities, make use of St George's flag and no other. In violation of which law the said Chinna Chetty did hoist a Gentoo flag at Trivatore on Sunday last. He confessed the fact, but pleaded ignorance of the law, which could not be true; that law having been promulgated with the utmost solemnity, being affixed to all the gates of the town for some months, and made on so remarkable an occasion as the desertion of the Chetty caste.

"The Board, not being informed of the criminal's circumstances, fully agreed to defer pronouncing sentence till the next consultation; designing, if he be a man of some substance, to impose a proportionate fine upon him; otherwise to inflict a corporal punishment and turn him out of the bounds; it being necessary to make an example of such offenders on the first breach of that law; the preservation of which is so requisite to prevent all disturbances that may otherwise arise on caste affairs.

"Monday, 2nd March. The President reports to the Board that according to agreement in last consultation, he had enquired into the circumstances of Chinna Chetty, and found him incapable of paying a fine which would be large enough to deter others from committing the like offence.

Wherefore the Board gave sentence that he should stand in the pillory for the space of an hour the next choultry day, with a label before him to signify his offence, and that then he be expelled the Bounds."

The next incident is particularly interesting, as illustrating the growth of religious toleration in the English settlement at Fort St. George. Some of our readers will remember that in the year 1680, when Mr. Streynsham Master was Governor of Madras, the intermarriage of Protestants with Roman Catholics had excited the attention of the English Government; and the two English Chaplains being taking into Council, the following atrocious order was forthwith promulgated. " That upon the marriage of a Protestant with a Roman Catholic, both the parties to be married shall solemnly promise before one of the Chaplains of the place, before the Banns shall be published, and also in the Chapel or Church upon the day of marriage, that ALL the children by them begotten and born, shall be brought up in the Protestant religion." How this narrow-minded regulation worked for the benefit of the Protestant religion, will be gathered from the following circumstances which transpired some thirty years afterwards.

"Thursday, 2nd April, 1719. The President represents that the Portuguese priests of St. Thomé had very lately taken the liberty to marry some English people belonging to this city without leave; which practice he apprehended to be of dangerous consequence; many of the young Gen-

tlemen in the Company's Service being of good
families in England, who would be very much
scandalized at such marriages as were likely to be
contracted here, without the consent of the President; particularly that one Crane, late chief Mate
of our ship "Falconbridge", was married to a
French man's daughter of this place on Sunday
last; and in order to it renounced the Protestant
religion, which he had professed all his life till
within a few days before. The other was one
Dutton, an ordinary fellow, who was married a
week before at St. Thomé to Ann Ridley, whose
father was formerly Governor of the West coast.
Her small fortune being in the hands of the Church,
the minister, as one of her guardians, refused his
consent; on which they went to St. Thomé, and
found a priest to marry them there. The President
adds that, to show his resentment of such a practice,
he had ordered the Mettos not to suffer any of the
Portuguese Padres, belonging to St. Thomé to
come into the English bounds. He further proposed
to the Board to consider of some proper orders to
be given for preventing the like practices for the
future. After some consideration, it was agreed
that an order be published in the English and
Portuguese languages, and put up in writing
at the Sea Gate and at the Portuguese Church,
that if any Christian inhabitant of Madras
shall be married in this city, at St. Thomé,
or elsewhere, without leave from the President; that if he be in the Company's service
he shall be liable to such penalty as we shall think
fit; but if the person so offending shall not be in

the Company's service, and only a free merchant or inhabitant of the Town, he shall be expelled the English Government on the Coast of Coromandel. Also any parent consenting to, or promoting such marriage, without leave as aforesaid, shall be liable to the like penalty of expulsion."

"Monday, 6th April. The President informs the Board that on a full enquiry into the marriage of the Mate Crane, mentioned in last Consultation, he finds that the said Crane had been bred a Protestant, and continued to profess a Protestant religion till within a few days of his marriage ; and then the woman whom he married refused to have the ceremony performed in the English Church, because all Roman Catholics married there are obliged to subscribe a declaration that they will bring up their children in the Protestant religion, by an order of Council dated the 25th of March 1680 ; and that on her refusal there to comply with that obligation, he had renounced the Protestant religion and declared himself a Roman Catholic in order to marry her. The President therefore proposed to the consideration of the Board, whether that order of Council, dated 25th of March 1680, should be repeated or not ; which being freely debated, it was unanimously agreed to repeal the general order, for the following reasons.

"First, that the obligation is in its own nature unjust, and a violation of that natural right which all parents have to educate their children in that religion they think most acceptable to God. Secondly, that such a promise can be no obligation on the conscience of any person, being unlawful in itself. Thirdly, that the requiring such a promise may be attended with ill consequences, as in the instance now before us; the woman refusing to be married in the English Church for that reason only; the consequence of which was, Crane's renouncing the Protestant religion and declaring himself a Roman Catholic.

"Ordered that the Secretary acquaint the Honorable Company's Chaplain of the place in writing, with the repeal of the aforesaid order, and that he is not any more to require such subscription."

"The President also acquaints the Board, that the severe methods which he had taken to show his resentment to the Protuguese priests of St. Thomé, for marrying any subject of this Government without his consent, had produced a very good effect; for that the Padre Governor at St. Thomé had sent him a very submissive letter or address, wherein he obliges himself, and those of his fraternity subject to him, not to marry any persons subject to this Government for the future, without asking his previous consent."

The following entry refers to the general history.

"Thursday, 16th April, 1719. General letter from Masulipatam dated the 26th ultimo read, advising that it is reported that there is an insurrection amongst the Sciads, who have dethroned and imprisoned King Feroksere. The said letter further advises, as a confirmation of that news, that the Nabob of Golcondah who was advancing towards Masulipatam, immediately upon that intelligence returned to Golcondah, in order to draw in his effects with all possible expedition."

The Nabob of Golcondah here mentioned, does not appear to have been the Seiad Hussein Ali, Subah of the Dekkan; for he had gone to Delhi to assist his brother Abdullah, the Vizier, in dethroning Feroksere, and setting up other puppet kings in his room.. Nor could it have been Cheen Kulich Khan, better known as the Nizam-ool-Mulk; for he had retired from the Dekkan on the appointment of Hussein Ali, and was at this time merely Governor of Malwa. We therefore infer that by the Nabob of Golconda was meant Mobariz Khan, the local Governor of Hyderabad. But we shall have more to say upon this subject further on.

To return to the annals of Fort St. George. The following incident does not speak much for the philological attainments of the English inhabitants at this period.

"Monday, 25th May, 1719. The President represents to the Board that there is not any person in the Honorable Company's Service in this place, who is able to translate a letter out of the Portuguese and French languages into English; or *vice versâ*, to translate English into those languages; which has rendered it difficult for him to maintain the necessary correspondence in the Honorable Company's affairs; the Portuguese language being the common language of India amongst all Europeans. He therefore proposes to admit a young man, named George Foriano, son of Mr. Nathaniel Foriano (Super Cargo of the Honorable

Company's Ship " Hertford" to China), who is wellqualified for the purpose aborementioned, being skilled in both those languages, to be a Factor in the Honorable Company's Service here.

" Agreed that Mr. George Foriano be admitted a Factor, Mr. Elwick offering to be security for him, and that the Secretary make out his Indentures for three years."

The next entry is worth preserving as illustrative of the times. Singularly enough it expresses the same fears on a small scale, as those which have been felt in some quarters in reference to the reductions which are now going on in our Indian army.

" Thursday, 9th July. The Honorable Court of Directors having, in the 5th paragraph of their letters to us by the " Marlborough," thought fit to order that the Garrison of this place should be reduced to 360 men and the Garrison of Fort St. David to 340. The manner of doing it is taken into consideration.

" It appears to us,—First, that this limitation is only designed for a time of established peace, which is not the case at present; there being by our last advices from Delhi, two princes with large armies contending for the Empire, the event of which may very probably affect us.

" Secondly, it appears dangerous to disband the whole number of supernumerary forces at once, even in a time of peace, much more so in a time of famine. Such number of men must be put upon violent measures, or else be obliged to go in a body into the service of the Moors, which may be very dangerous to this settlement.

"It is therefore agreed that the President give orders to the officers to disband gradually the worst of the Topazes, from about twenty to forty in a month as he shall think fit."

In the last chapter we noticed that the Pedda Naik, or Chief Watchman, was dismissed from his post on account of neglect of duty. It will be seen from the following entry that it was soon found necessary to restore him to his former employment.

"Monday, 17th August. The petition of Coonogozee Timapa Naik read, desiring liberty to resign his employment of Chief Watchman to Coonogozee Pedda Naik, who officiated in that office before him, and was very capable of executing it, but was dismissed for his extravagance. The said Timapa Naik being unfit to do the duty of that post any longer, by reason of his old age; and the former Pedda Naik, being very much reclaimed by the hardships which his extravagance brought upon him, promises a faithful discharge of his duty for the future, and tenders the duties belonging to the office of Chief Watchman as a security for his fidelity and good behaviour.

"Agreed therefore that Coonogozee Timapa Naik be discharged at his request from the office of Chief Watchman of this city; and that Coonogozee Pedda Naik be appointed in his stead."

Another entry occurs the same day which illustrates the summary method of proceeding with pirates in Governor Collet's time.

"The President acquaints the Board that on Tuesday 11th instant, he, with the rest of the Commissioners for trying of pirates, did bring Roger Bullmore, one of those that ran away with the "George" Brigantine, to his trial, by virtue of King George's Commission; and that having found him guilty of piracy, felony and robbery, they had passed sentence of death upon him, and that he was ordered to be executed on Wednesday next."

The hot winds this season appear to have been too much for Governor Collet and accordingly he determined to retire. But we leave the records to tell the story.

"Thursday, 15th October, 1719. The President acquaints the Board that having found himself indisposed during the last season of the land winds; so that it is with difficulty that he has been able to discharge the duty of his station; and that therefore he has determined to return to Europe on the next ship to be despatched from hence; and acquaints them with his purpose so early that there may be time for settling the Government according to the Honorable Company's standing orders.

"He then proposed that Mr. Francis Hastings should be sent for up from Fort St. David, as soon as he could conveniently, in order to take the chair upon the President's going off; and that Mr. William Jennings, second of Council here, should go down thither with a Commission for Deputy Governor, and that Mr. Nathaniel Elwick, who will then be second here, take on him the office of accountant.

"The President then produced a letter wrote to himself separately by the Honorable Court of Directors, dated the 8th January 1717, and read the first para ; by which it appears that they designed Mr. Elwick for the Export Warehouse-keepers employ particularly, as being well skilled in the sorts of calicoes sent from hence to England. He therefore, proposed that Mr. Elwick should keep the Export Warehousekeeper's employ, and that Mr. Richard Horden Sea Customer should take the Import Warehousekeeper's employ upon him ; and that this regulation should continue in force till the arrival of the next letters from Europe.

"To all which proposals the Board agreed unanimously."

The last measures of Governor Collet are of such a simple character that they require no preliminary explanation, and it will be sufficient to lay the entries themselves before our readers.

"Monday, 2nd November, 1719. According to order of last consultation, Vizago, the Choultry Dubash, was brought before the Board on his trial, for extorting exorbitant fees beyond what had ever been practiced, particularly on the register of slaves. The most that had ever been allowed was 20 fanams in the whole, including the Company's duty ; whereas he had obliged great numbers of people to pay him 24 fanams, and took the 4 fanams to his own use ; also in house bills registered at the choultry, where the true fees are 2 pagodas and 2 fanams per cent., he extorted 2 pagodas and 18 fanams, and in many instances a larger proportion; and also in house bills registered at the court, he extorted in general about 16 per cent above the usual fees; and that besides the above mentioned, he has been guilty of great neglect in his office, by putting off the poor people and refusing to do their business.

" A great number of persons of all ranks appeared to prove the several branches of the charge; but there was no occasion to hear any witness except to the last article, he confessing all the rest on their being proposed to him; some witnesses were called for the proof of that, who very fully convicted him of delay, and putting off their business from time to time without any reasonable excuse.

" The prisoner and witnesses being withdrawn, it was considered that the practice was in itself scandalous and abusive, and particularly oppressive to the poor; many of them being obliged in this time of famine to sell their children for rice; and the extorting 4 fanams in the fees was a considerable hardship on them; that, therefore, it was necessary to put a stop to such abuses by making the offender a public example.

" Accordingly it was resolved that Vizago, the Choultry Dubash aforementioned, be turned out of the Honorable Company's service, and disabled from any future employment therein; that he stand in the pillory the next Choultry day; and that he be fined 500 pagodas, one-half to be paid to the Charity School, and the other half to the Choultry Stock for the maintenance of prisoners.

"The criminal being called in, sentence was pronounced accordingly.

"To prevent such abuses for the future, it is ordered that the after written statement of Choultry fees, being agreeable to ancient custom, be hung up in the Choultry by the Chief Justice.

"For registering houses and land in the Mayors Court register, situated in the Black town, pettahs, or out gardens; for every bill to pay one per cent to the Chief Justice, and half per cent to the Registrar on the value of the house or land.

"And whereas most of the buildings in the Christian Town do far exceed those without in value, to prevent the charges running too high: for every bill value under 500 pagodas, is to pay the same fees as above; but all bills exceeding that sum are to pay 5 pagodas to the Chief Justice, and $2\frac{1}{2}$ pagodas to the Registrar, and no more.

"For registering houses and land in the Choultry Register; for every bill to pay one per cent. to the Chief Justice, and one per cent. to the Registrar, on the value of the house or land.

"For Registering slaves; for every slave the Honorable Company are to receive 8 fanams, the Registrar 3 fanams, and the Chief Justice 2 fanams.

"And all bills, either for houses, land, or slaves, are to pay to the Choultry Dubash one anam, and to the Chief Justice's Taliars one fanam, for their trouble in getting the bills registered.

"And whereas some small houses in the Black Town, not exceeding 5 or 6 pagodas in value, are made over by bills of sale wrote in Gentoo on Cajan leaves, which are entered in the Register kept by the Town Conicoply for that purpose; for every Cajan bill the Town Conicoply is to receive 2 fanams; besides the one per cent as above to the Chief Justice and Registrar.

"The bricklayers for measuring of ground are to receive for their trouble 2 fanams for all valued at 100 pagodas or upwards, and one fanam for all under."

"Thursday, 26th November, 1719. The President acquaints the Board that he had some time since published an order for registering all houses and gardens in the Black Town, or the adjacent parts, in the Mayor's Court or Choultry, for prevention of frauds in sale and mortgages; but that some of the poor having complained to him that during the present dearness of grain it would be hard upon them to pay the charges though small, he therefore, proposes that all houses under 50 pagodas value should be exempted from the obligation of that order, till plenty returns, which the Board agrees to."

"Wednesday, 23rd December, 1719. The President being about to depart for England, demands for his justification hereafter, a certificate from the accountant that he stands not indebted upon the Honorable Company's General Books. He likewise demands a certificate from the Sea Customer that he has paid all their customs due from him, one from the Receiver to the same purpose, and another from the Land Customer. All which are ordered to be drawn out against next consultation and delivered him, the Board being satisfied that he is not in any way indebted to the Honorable Company.

"Monday, 28th December, 1719. The President delivers in a list of the inhabitants of a new pettah or town raised near Trivatore, consisting of 105 houses which are inhabited by 489 persons, male and female, besides children, ranged under the usual divisions of Right hand and Left hand Caste. He acquaints the Board, that the town, in which there is also a handsome pagoda, is called at the desire of the people "Collet's pettah;" and that the inhabitants consist of weavers and painters, which he encouraged by degrees to come and live near this place, that they might be serviceable to the Honorable Company. That in order to prevail with them to a compliance, he promised them, so soon as the town was completed, a Cowle should be given them to secure to them such privileges and immunities; and the said Town being now finished, and the inhabitants well settled, he proposes that his promise which is now claimed, should be performed, and a Cowle given them accordingly; the conditions of which being approved by the Board, as well as the President's management in this affair, the Secretary is ordered to prepare."

"Monday, 18th January, 1720. Early this morning the Honorable Joseph Collet, Esq., President, embarked on Board the "King William;" whereon the Goverment fell to the Honorable Francis Hastings, Esq.

Having thus closed the narrative of the tranquil state of affairs at Fort St. George during the last year of Mr. Collet's administration, it may be as well to take a brief glance at the contemporary state of the ruling power at Delhi. All those influences which indicate the decline of an empire, were in full play in the empire of the Mogul. Vice and sensuality at the court, frequent rebellions in the provinces, a puppet king struggling for power, overbearing ministers, a mercenary army without the slightest sentiment of loyalty, incessant intrigues ending in open assassinations;—these, and a thousand other significant circumstances, were transpiring in India. Indeed it must have been evident to all that ever since the death of Aurungzebe in 1707, the Mogul empire had been hastening to its dissolution; worn out by premature old age brought on by its political crimes, and vainly struggling to retain the appearance of strength and beauty when it was fast sinking into the grave.

It was during this gradual decay of the power of the Mogul, that a man arose, whose name, and that if his descendants, must ever take a prominent place in the history of this Presidency. This man was Cheen Kulich Khan, better known as Nizam-ool-Moolk, the first Nizam of the Dekkan. His father Ghazee-oo-deen was one of those Tartar adventurers, who had migrated into India at a comparatively recent period, and risen to eminence during the wars in the Dekkan. The future Nizam was born in 1644, and like his father had distinguished himself in the wars of Aurungzebe. During the reigns of the immediate successors of Aurungzebe,—Shah Aulum and Jehandar Shah,—he had fallen into obscurity, in consequence of his rivalry with Zulfikar Khan,—that great king maker to whom both the last mentioned princes owed their thrones. But in 1713, when he was fast approaching his seventieth year, his fortunes were again on the rise. Jehandar Shah had been dethroned by the two Seiads; and both he and Zulfikar Khan were put to death. The two Seiads set up Feroksere as a puppet of their own; and Cheen Kulich Khan, being well known as the enemy of Zulfikar Khan was first appointed Nizam of the Dekkan.

Most of the intrigues of Feroksere to escape from the thraldom of the Seiads, have already been noticed in the narrative of the English mission from Calcutta to Delhi. But the last of all, the one which led to the downfall of Feroksere, deserves especial notice; for it is one which strikingly illustrates the desperate state of public affairs, whilst it is closely connected with the rising fortunes of Cheen Kulich Khan. But the last and most and important plot of all, the one in which Cheen Kulich Khan was implicated, and which led to the ruin of Feroksere about the very time that Governor Collet left the Madras Presidency, deserves especial mention.

Very early in the reign of Feroksere, Cheen Kulich Khan had cause to hate the two Seiads,—Abdullah, the vizier, and Hussein, the commander in-chief. He had held the government of the

Dekkan little more than a year, when he was removed to the small government of Moradabad, and the Dekkan was handed over to Hussein. Under such circumstances the disappointed Nizam was likely to prove a powerful supporter to Feroksere. Accordingly he was summoned to court, and the emperor promised to make him vizier in the room of Abdullah, provided the Seiads were overthrown.

A plot was speedily formed, and was soon ripe for execution. Hussein was away in the Dekkan, and Abdullah was alone in Delhi. Accordingly it was determined to assassinate Abdullah at that great festival which terminates the Ramazan; for on that day the king went in state to the Mosque, attended by a train of nobles and troops far exceeding in number the guards of the vizier. But all went wrong through the criminal weakness of Feroksere. He had a favourite, a low profligate minion, who was naturally hated by the whole court. The influence of this favourite was all powerful. By his advice Feroksere was induced to postpone the plot. Worst of all, Feroksere forgot his promise to Cheen Kulich Khan, and actually engaged to make this wretched favourite vizier as soon as the Seiads were overthrown. Lastly the emperor was mad enough to give to this favourite the district of Moradabad as a private jaghire; being the very district of which Cheen Kulich Khan was Governor.

These circumstances came out in time, and then Cheen Kulich Khan was more exasperated against such an infatuated king than he had previously been against the Seiads; whilst the vizier Abdullah saw that Feroksere was incorrigible, and that his own life would be in constant danger so long as Feroksere continued on the throne. Accordingly he drew over Cheen Kulich Khan by the promise of the government of Malwa, and immediately summoned his brother Hussein Ali from the Dekkan.

The doom of the emperor Feroksere was now sealed. In his alarm he sought a reconciliation with Abdullah, and the vizier engaged with the emperor in mutual oaths of fidelity and attachment. Of course such oaths were utterly worthless. Abdullah merely desired to gain time for the arrival of his brother; whilst the cowardly Feroksere continued to lay plots for the assassination of the Seiads. Meantime Hussein Ali had made a peace with the Mahrattas, and at last reached Delhi with thirty thousand horse, ten thousand of whom were Mahrattas.

The whole city was now filled with dread. Every one felt, from the highest Omrah to the lowest dealer in the bazaars, that a terrible convulsion was at hand. The very appearance of the Mahrattas, Hindoo robbers as they were, suggested ideas of massacre and plunder to the Mussulmen of Delhi; whilst no one could foretell who would gain the ascendant, the Seiads or the emperor. Meantime the wretched Feroksere began to see his own folly. He was however far too weak and cowardly to attempt the slightest resistance to the two Seiads, and therefore helplessly submitted to their mercy. They demanded that the royal guards should be withdrawn from the palace, and that their own soldiers should be posted in their room. Feroksere obeyed. Hussein Ali then paid him a formal visit, and the poor miserable emperor made a desperate effort to conciliate his enemy. He received the Seiad with the greatest distinction. He burst into tears and placed his own turban on the head of Hussein; and even took the jewels from his dress and pressed Hussein to accept them. But the Seiad refused, and upbraided the fallen monarch with his ingratitude. He then left the palace without paying any of the ordinary ceremonies of respect due to the person of his sovereign.

In a few days more all was over. On the 15th of February 1719, Feroksere expressed a wish to hunt, but the Seiads suspected him of designing an escape, and obliged him to postpone the intention. The next day the Sciads surrounded the palace with their troops, and the vizier entered the presence of the Emperor, and demanded that all the offices of the palace should be given into his hands. Feroksere promised compliance, but prayed for delay; and the evasion threw the vizier into such a passion, that the terrified emperor retreated to the haram, which he hoped would be respected by the rebels.

The story of the night which followed is one of the most thrilling narratives in all the Mussulman histories. The vizier Abdullah remained in the palace, and so also did Ajeet Sing, Rajah of Mewar, whose daughter had been given in marriage to Feroksere as a token of submission to the Mogul supremacy. The army of Hussein

Ali, including the ten thousand Mahrattas, remained under arms the whole night. Early in the morning a rumour flew through the city that the vizier had been killed by Ajeet Sing, who had resolved to protect the emperor his son-in-law; and accordingly several omrahs prepared to rise against Hussein Ali. Meantime a party of Mahrattas had engaged with some soldiers whom they had mistaken for an enemy; and the still more frightful rumour spread through Delhi that the Mahrattas were plundering the city. At once the whole population of fiery Mussulmen arose as one man against the idolatrous Mahrattas. Fifteen hundred Hindoos were massacred in the streets, and the whole city was thrown into frightful disorder. Those omrahs who supported the cause of the Seiads, in their alarm at the supposed death of the vizier, were preparing to make their escape from the scene of anarchy. Plunder, fire, and massacre had already begun, when the news spread that Abdullah was still alive. Hussein Ali and his friends now recovered their spirits and restored order. The royal servants were dispersed after a brief resistance; and it was proclaimed from the walls of the citadel that another prince had ascended the throne.

Whilst these events were being transacted in the city, still darker horrors were being perpetrated in the palace. Feroksere utterly refused to leave the haram. Meantime Abdullah was informed that the people were already in revolt, and that no time was to be lost. In this extremity he commanded some Afghans to force open the doors of the haram. There was a short conflict with the eunuchs and other attendants, and then the vizier and his rude soldiery rushed into the sacred apartments. The unhappy emperor, surrounded by his mother, wife, daughter, and other princesses, was soon discovered. The royal ladies filled the air with their shrieks and prayers for mercy, whilst Feroksere himself was in an agony of terror. But Abdullah turned a deaf ear to all entreaties, and pounced upon his prey. The emperor was dragged from the arms of the half frantic women, and thrown into a dark chamber. A child was taken from the confined princes, and immediately seated upon the throne; and the booming of cannon and customary strains of music announced to the people of Delhi that Feroksere was deposed and that another puppet king reigned in his stead.

The end of Feroksere may be related almost in the very words of the Mussulman historian. For two months he was confined in a dark chamber, enduring various calamities. The hot iron, by which so many princes had been incapacitated from reigning, was drawn over the eyes of Feroksere; but strange to say it did not utterly destroy his sight. He sent the most piteous messages to the Sciads, praying to be restored to the throne on any terms they chose; but not the slightest attention was paid to his prayers. Then he promised immense rewards to his keepers, provided they would connive at his escape. The Sciads were now alarmed, for Feroksere was still lamented by the lower orders amongst whom he had squandered his treasures, and an escape might be followed by a revolt and a revolution. Accordingly they resolved on his death. On two different occasions poison was mingled with his victuals, but without effect. The third time he was thrown into violent agonies, and began to invoke God against his murderers. The bow string was then sent for, but the emperor struggled against his executioners with all the violence of desperation. He seized the bow string with his hands, and it was only after he had been beaten down with clubs, that the string was passed round his neck, and he at last expired. On the following evening the body was interred in the tomb of Humayun, followed by a large crowd, cursing the Sciads and lamenting their beloved Ferokscre.

The new child emperor only reigned four months, and then died of a consumption. Another child was taken from amongst the confined princes, but he shared the same fate. At last a healthier young prince was selected, who ascended the throne under the name of Mohammed Shah. He began to reign before the end of 1719, and before the end of 1720 the power of the Seiads was entirely over. This event is so intimately connected with the final establishment of Cheen Kulich Khan as Nizam of the Dekkan, that we can scarcely avoid narrating it here.

On the deposition of Ferokscre, Cheen Kulich Khan had obtained his promised reward, namely, the government of Malwa. There he found everything lapsing into anarchy;—the Zemindars asserting their independence, and the people either suffering from robbers or becoming robbers themselves. These disorders justified him in raising and maintaining troops; but the Seiads soon suspected that he was aiming at something far beyond the mere defence of his province. Accordingly they tried every friendly means to remove him. Hussein Ali was still viceroy of the Dekkan, and they hinted to Cheen Kulich Khan, that as Malwa lay half way between the Dekkan and Delhi, so it would form a very convenient residence for Hussein Ali; inasmuch as from that spot Hussein could both superintend his vice royalty in the Dekkan, and watch the progress of affairs at the capital. Accordingly they offered Cheen Kulich Khan four other Subahs, any one of which he might have in exchange for Malwa. He sent back an insulting refusal, and then marched an army over the Nerbudda into the Dekkan, where he had many old connections both amongst the Mussulmans and the Mahrattas. There he achieved a brilliant success, and the Seiads became alarmed. An army was sent against him, but he defeated it. At the same time, the new king Mohammed Shah, saw in Cheen Kulich Khan, one who might deliver him from the thraldom of the Seiads. Accordingly he sent secret messages assuring him that he should receive royal support in his resistance to the Seiads.

In this extremity the Seiads resolved that Hussein should march against the self-constituted Nizam of the Dekkan, whilst Abdullah remained at Delhi. To make matters doubly sure, it was also resolved that Mohammed Shah should accompany Hussein. This circumstance proved the ruin of the Seiads. A conspiracy was formed for assassinating Hussein during the march. A savage Calmuck named Hyder Khan was pitched upon to strike the blow. Whilst Hussein was passing along in his palankeen, Hyder attracted his attention with a petition; and when Hussein commanded him to present it, he drew out his dagger and inflicted a mortal blow upon the Seiad. Hussein suspected the author of the conspiracy, and cried out " Put the emperor to death." But it was too late. The necessary preparations had been made for the defence of Mohammed Shah, though the assassin himself was cut in pieces on the spot by a hundred swords.

Here closes the story of the famous usurpation of the Seiads. Mohammed Shah returned to Delhi, and Abdullah was utterly defeated, and imprisoned for life. How the Mogul empire rapidly faded away, until it seemed to expire in the funeral pyre heaped up by Nadir Shah, belongs to a future episode in our annals of the Madras Presidency.

CHAPTER XXXI.

GOVERNORSHIP OF MR. FRANCIS HASTINGS.

1720—21.

The Governorship of Mr. Francis Hastings, the successor of Mr. Collett, was short and turbulent. It lasted little more than a year and a half, namely, from the 18th of January, 1720, to the 15th of October, 1721. The foreign relations were quiet enough at this time, and for some years afterwards, as both Sadatulla Khan, Nabob of the Carnatic, and Cheen Kulick Khan, Subah of the Dekkan, were far too busy in establishing themselves in their several governments to pay much attention to the little Factory at Fort St. George, so long as it paid the annual rental on the day it was due. But the internal affairs of the settlement were marked by many irregularities and disorders during the administration of Mr. Hastings, and of his successor Mr. Elwick; and thus necessitated those rigid inquiries and thorough reforms which were subsequently carried out by one of the most remarkable of all the early Governors of Fort St. George, namely, Mr. James Macrae.

The first incident under the rule of Mr. Hastings is connected with an extraordinary dispute with an Havildar in the neighbourhood of Egmore, which was brought to a tragical conclusion; the Havildar being shot dead in the midst of the quarrel by the Company's Chief Peon. The following is the official narrative of the affair.

"Saturday, 20th February, 1720. The President acquaints the Board, that last night the Havildar of the Metto near Egmore had stopped some oxen, loaden with bricks and straw, which belonged to the Honorable Company, which were coming into Town. This morning, being complained to about it by the Paymaster, as also of the people being beat and imprisoned that were driving the oxen and refused to pay some money, which the Metto people would have extorted from them;—he (the President) sent the Chief Dubash, with some others, to know the reason of such an insult, and to demand the delivery of our people whom he had imprisoned. The President adds that instead of receiving answer to that message, the Havildar returned him a very saucy one, and refused to let the Honorable Company's goods and people pass; though the Chief Dubash used many mild persuasive arguments with him for that purpose. At length, not being able to prevail, the Chief Dubash returned and gave the President an account of what had passed; whereupon he ordered the Chief Peon, with some others, to go and expostulate with the Havildar further, and in case of any resistance to force the Havildar to a compliance. But when the Chief Peon went to him, he found him at the head of about 50 of his peons and people in a fighting posture; and upon going up to him to deliver the President's message, the Havildar drew his scimetar and struck at him, which he warded off with his target, and thereby evaded being cut down. The Chief Peon immediately drew a pistol from his side, and shot the Havildar; which when he had done, he with his people fell upon the rest and killed two more, which terrified them all so much that they ran away.

"The President adds that he thinks the Chief Peon has by this action showed himself a trusty servant to the Honorable Company, and deserves encouragement; that if he had sat tamely down under this first insult, we should not have failed of receiving many more of a higher degree; and that our showing our resentment upon this occasion will have a good influence upon all the Metto people, and Junkameers for the future; that lest the matter should be represented to our prejudice to the Nabob, he has taken care to transmit an exact account of it to our Vakeel at Arcot; and for the security of the garrison has given orders to the Officers to be upon a very strict guard for fear of surprise."[1]

"Monday, 14th March, 1720. The President acquaints the Board that he has received very friendly letters from the Nabob and Ducknaroy upon the subject of the Metto Havildar being unfortunately killed by our peons; and that apprehending no disturbance will ensue, he has ordered in the guards which he had joined to those at Egmore and the Choultries, in order to put a stop to the expence occasioned thereby."

The next event is narrated at a length far exceeding its importance, and can be best told in a few words. It seems that a discovery was made that some sort of correspondence had been going on between the principal Chetties in Madras and the Portuguese Viceroy of Goa. From a perusal of the papers it would seem that this correspondence only referred to some presents that the Viceroy of Goa wished to send to Hussein Ali, the previous Subah of the Dekkan; but Governor Hastings appears to have suspected that the correspondence had for its object the " revolt of the Chetties," or in other words their removal from the English Government of Fort St. George to the Portuguese Government of St. Thomé. The matter assumes an undue importance in the records, inasmuch as it was the cause of a tremendous quarrel between Governor Hastings, and Mr. Nathaniel Elwick, who was at that time third in Council; Governor Hastings being inclined to deal harshly with the Chetties, whilst Mr. Elwick declared that no proof whatever had been furnished that they were really guilty. Under such circumstances Governor Hastings placed the Heads of the Chetties under confinement, and then ordered the following proclamation to be posted on the Sea Gate, with the view of obtaining further evidence against them.

" Monday, 25th April, 1720. Whereas a discovery hath lately been made of a design sometime since formed by the inhabitants of the Chetty caste of this place, to revolt from this Government and to take protection under the Portuguese at St. Thomé; and whereas there is just reason to suspect, by the Viceroy of Goa's letters to the Heads of the Chetty caste, that they signified under their hands their resolution to desert this place and shelter themselves under the Portuguese at St. Thomé, in case he could have obtained a grant of that place from the Nabob; and whereas, furthermore, the said Chetties upon examination have confidently denied their engagement in any such conspiracy;—the Honorable Governor and Council have therefore thought fit to issue out this proclamation, that if any person or persons concerned in the said conspiracy will make discovery to the President, or to any one of the Council, so as that the rest of the persons concerned may be fully convicted, such person or persons shall receive a handsome reward and full pardon for themselves."

"By order of the Honorable Governor and Council."

The Proclamation had no effect whatever. No one came forward to volunteer evidence, and the Chetties themselves obstinately denied all knowledge of such a conspiracy. Accordingly Governor Hastings desired them to sign a paper, in which confiscation of all property and the forfeiture of all protection were declared to be the penalty of desertion. This however the Chetties refused to do, and then the Governor proposed that the two head Chetty merchants, who conducted the Company's investments, should be suspended from their office. The following extract from the consultation of the 30th May, 1720, will show the nature of Mr. Elwick's opposition.

"Mr. Elwick offered security for the two Chetty Merchants, as far as 10,000 pagodas, for their appearance six months hence; but being asked if he would sign the security paper in their behalf aforementioned (involving the pain of confiscation and forfeiture) ; and being also asked if he would suffer the penalty which the Chetties must suffer in case their accusation should hereafter be turned into a conviction ; — he refused them both ; and being told by some of the Board, that the security which he offered was no more than bail for their appearance six months hence, and that according to the laws of our nation all persons taken up upon suspicion of treason are forthwith imprisoned without bail or mainprize, Mr. Elwick's notion was thereupon rejected."

Mr. Elwick continued to be very earnest in his opposition to the suspension of the two Chetty Merchants, and declared that the sorting of the cloth, and the business of the Company generally, could not go on whilst they were in confinement. The records of the dispute are far too voluminous for publication, but the following extract from the consultation book of the 19th of July will sufficiently illustrate the party spirit which prevailed.

"The President acquaints the Board that Mr. Elwick, the Warehouse keeper, has been very remiss in his business in not having given in any account of the contract ever since it was made, and in not having sorted any quantity of cloth since the "Dawson's" dispatch ; though out of perverse, obstinate humour Mr. Elwick pressed him once or twice, while the merchants were confined, for their releasement in order to go to sorting. Mr. Elwick, finding his plea for not sorting proved to be nothing else but an excuse for idleness, began to be much enraged; and told the President that it would draw very strange stories on the stage, and that the consequence must take its course, desiring those words might be minuted verbatim; to which the President made no reply, but ordered the Secretary to minute them accordingly."

About this time the attention of the Government was excited by the murder of a Chetty whose name is not mentioned. It was a cold blooded affair. The murderers were two soldiers, named Robert Grott and Richard Righting, who appear to have killed their victim for the sake of drink. The depositions are lengthy, but the following extract will suffice to show how such cases were adjudicated on in the Council Room.

"Monday, August 1st, 1720. The affair of the murder is now resumed. The President acquaints the Board, that a Dubash boy (belonging to one of the prisoners suspected to be guilty of the murder) was apprehended at St. Thomé; who being sent for in, deposes that he went with Robert Grott, his master, from his house in company with two white men, and a woman, whose names he could not tell, to drink toddy at a toddy house; where they stayed till past 12 o'clock at night, at which time the two men and the woman left them. Then the prisoners Grott and Righting went to a choultry and carried a bottle of arrack; where they saw a man covered over with a clout, fast asleep; whom soon after they awaked by giving him a blow with a cane, and at the same time asked for fanams to buy arrack. The man answered he had

none. But receiving a blow or two more from
them, he gave them one fanam, then another, and
afterwards a third. Upon continuing their usage
to him, and repeating their demands, he drew
down his purse and bid them look if there was
any more. Then the prisoner Righting told him if
he had no more than three fanams, he would give
him more if he would go with him to the Governor's Garden; but instead of carrying him thither,
they led him to another garden near the Choultry,
where he afterwards heard him cry out. The
Dubash further deposes that when he would have
followed them, they struck him and bid him be
gone; and as he was going away he saw Righting
take the club from Grott. After this they went
to Town, and a soldier, by name Clark (whose
house they were in) asked them, how came they so
bloody; who said they had been fighting. The
Dubash afterwards went to look for a mat to sleep
on, and saw Righting look over some silver things;
and upon demanding leave to go home, he denied
him. Clark again asked them how came they so
bloody; who replied as before that they had been
fighting.

"Righting being sent for in and interrogated
concerning what the boy had deposed against him,
says that he never had the club in his hand, but
carried the Chetty into the Garden; upon which
he was ordered to withdraw; and Grott being
called in says that Righting took the club away
from him and killed the man.

"Righting being brought in again, and acquainted with what his comrade had alleged against him, declared that they had been drinking, and that the Dubash boy told Grott that this Chetty fellow had money; upon which Grott went to him and asked him for some, when he gave him two fanams; then he demanded two more, but he would not give it them. The deponent Righting, seeing that, took him into a garden, and told him if he would not comply he would carry him to the Governor's Garden; and as they were talking together Grott struck him with the club and killed him. Grott being called in, again denies what is laid to his charge; and being asked where the Chetty's silver girdle, his earrings, and other things were, avers that Righting took them and he has heard nothing of them since. Upon which Righting was again sent for and asked the same question; who answered that the Dubash boy took them off, which is all that he knows of the matter."

"The prisoners being all dismissed the Room, the Board debated upon the affair for some time, and then unanimously pronounced them guilty of the murder. But the Honorable Company, having not yet procured a power to bring to an Execution, it was agreed they should be continued in prison and whipped very severely every week as a punishment for the disorders they committed as soldiers."

The murder case being thus deposed of, Governor Hastings poured out the vials of his wrath upon Mr. Elwick. He brought forward a declaration that he would no longer sit at the Council Board whilst Mr. Elwick was present.

But the story is best told in the language of the records.

"Monday, 8th August, 1720. The President acquaints the Board, that he has called this consultation on a very extraordinary occasion, in order to lay before us a declaration concerning the repeated affronts that he had received from Mr. Nathaniel Elwick, a member of this Board, and also his incapacity for the service of the Honorable Company. The said declaration being read before the Board, and duly considered; Mr. Elwick was ordered to withdraw; in pursuance of the Honorable Company's orders, that no member of the Board should continue sitting while such cases relating to himself were examining.

"Mr. Elwick being withdrawn the President's declaration was more maturely considered; and most of the members of the Board agreed that one or other of them was assured of the truths of all the facts charged on Mr. Elwick by the President, in relation to his behaviour at this Board as well as in this place.

"The facts alleged to prove his incapacity were then considered, and thereupon Mr. Draper the Secretary delivered in a report, which was read and observed to prove one article of Mr. Elwick's remissness. All the other instances of his negligence were well enough known to most of the members of the Board, and therefore did require no other proof.

"The latter clause of the President's declarations was then considered, wherein he pleased to publish his full resolution to sit no longer as President at this Board, if Mr. Elwick should continue as a member of it.

"Upon recourse to the Honorable Company's letter in order to find out some directions in such out of the way cases, no such appeared; and therefore, we judged it a case of an extraordinary nature. We observed, however, that suspension is made the penalty of a refractory disorderly behaviour, as well of negligence and remissness in business; and therefore the President desired the opinion of the Board, if Mr. Elwick had not incurred the penalty of suspension.

"The matter being debated for sometime, the Board thought fit to come to the following agreement.

"That as Mr. Elwick, on account of his refractory disorderly and insolent behaviour to the President, has most justly incurred the penalty ordered by our Honorable Masters to be inflicted in such cases, as well as on account of his negligence and remissness in his business, which penalty is no less than suspension. And as the Honorable President has been pleased to put the matters upon so important an issue, as to declare to us all that he will not sit any longer as President, if Mr. Elwick is continued at this Board; we think ourselves under a necessity of suspending Mr. Elwick, who has been guilty of remissness in his business as well as of indecent behaviour to the President and to the rest of the Board; rather than to part with the President, who has so long suffered Mr. Elwick's insolence and passed by his remissness, as well as behaved himself to us all with the greatest candour, mildness and decency imaginable. It is therefore, agreed and resolved that Mr. Nathaniel Elwick be suspended forthwith from the Honorable Company's Service (officio et beneficio) till the Honorable Company's pleasure be known concerning him.

"As every Member of the Board was allowed to give his opinion on this, as well as on all other occasions very freely, Messrs. Turner and Benyon declared that they could not agree to suspend Mr. Elwick; because they thought the Honorable Company's orders did not allow of a sufficient latitude for so doing, although they could not but confess that he had not behaved himself to the President so respectfully as he ought to have done."

Mr. Nathaniel Elwick subsequently protested against the proceedings, and then the matter ended for a while.

The next incident to which we have to draw attention is a very curious one. Charles Davers, a young gentleman who came out as a writer in 1717, died this year; and left an extraordinary will so illustrative of the times that we give it at length. Mr. Davers had come out in his eighteenth year, and was not twenty-one at the time he died. He was the fourth son of Sir Robert Davers, Baronet. His salary appears to have been only £5 a year, and yet he seems to have been already engaged in several commercial adventures. The desire of the young man to have his name and memory perpetuated is very striking; but we leave the will to tell its own story.

"Thursday, 22nd September, 1720. In the name of God, Amen, I, Charles Davers, now of Fort St. George in East India, Merchant, being of sound and perfect mind and memory, do make and ordain this my last will and testament in manner and form following.

"Imprimis, I recommend my soul to God who gave it, hoping through the merits of a crucified Saviour to obtain a joyful resurrection; and my body I commit to the earth to be decently interred; and for all such worldly estates, as these which it has pleased God to bless me with, I give and bequeath as follows; viz.

"Imprimis, I leave unto the Charity School of this place 200 pagodas; and desire the boys belonging to this School may attend me to the place of burial. Item, I leave unto the Master and Mistress of said School 20 pagodas each for mourning. I wish all piety and learning may attend them, and that they may infuse the same into the children, by the help of our Blessed Lord and Saviour Jesus Christ, Amen.

"Item, I leave unto my friend Mr. Thomas Wright 20 pagodas for mourning. I wish all health may attend him in this world and happiness in the next.

"Item, I leave 200 pagodas for a tomb to be erected in the burial place in form as follows. Four large pillars, each to be six covids high, and six covids distance one from the other; the top to be arched, and upon each pillar a cherubim; and on the top of the arch the effigy of Justice. My body to be laid in the middle of the four pillars, with a handsome stone a top of me, raised about four feet; and this inscription in the stone:—" Here lyeth the body of Charles Davers, fourth son of Sir Robert Davers, Bart, who departed this life the———of——Anno Domini———aged———." The four pillars to be encompassed in with iron rails, which are to go from pillar to pillar; and at every square, steps to be raised with stones, so as people may read the inscription.

" Item, I leave the Hono.able Governor, Council, and Secretary of this place, each a Gold ring of one pagoda and a half each value, with these words to be engraved in them, " Charles Davers, obiit," etc. To whom I wish all tranquility, health, and prosperity.

" Item, I leave unto Dr. Pitchers, the sum of 30 pagodas in case I die of my present illness, and that I did not pay him before I died.

" Item, I leave unto my friend, Mr. Paul Foxley 20 pagodas for mourning; to whom I wish all health in this world, and happiness in the next.

" Item, I leave unto the Minister that attend me 20 pagodas for a ring.

" Item, I leave unto my friend Mr. John Maubers 20 pagodas for mourning.

" Lastly, I leave my two trusty and beloved friends Mr. George Sittwel and Mr. Catesby Oadham, my two executors of this my last will and testament, and desire them to see me carried to the place of burial in the manner following viz.

" My Corpse to be carried from the Town Hall

at seven o'clock at night. I desire that all the free merchants of my acquaintance to attend me in their palankeens to the place of burial; and as many of the Company's servants as I have had any intimacy within my life time; that all that attend me may have scarves and hat bands decent. I desire that Mr. Main, and the Charity Boys, may go before my corpse, and sing a hymn; my corpse to be carried by six Englishmen or more; if occasion, the minister and the rest of the gentlemen following. I desire of the Honorable Governor that I may have as many great guns fired as I am years old, which is now almost twenty-one. In case it is customary to pay the great guns firing I desire you to do it. I desire the favour of the Captain of the guard to attend me; and that you present him with a gold ring the same as the Governor and Council. And now as to my Estate, I have 1086 ounces of silver, which my father sent me out this year. I am concerned with Mr. Thomas Theobalds in a respondentia bond in the "George" Brigantine. I have also an adventure with Captain James Hurdis, the prime cost being 72 pagodas and a half. I have at this time in my escritore about 100 pagodas, besides clothes and linen; an account of which I always keep in my escritore. I desire of my two executors to accept of 30 pagodas each for mourning; and each a ring of 15 pagodas value, with my name and time of death engraved upon it.

"After my corpse is buried, which I desire may be done very handsomely, the remainder of my estate I desire may be laid out in rice, and be given to the poor at the burial place, as long as it lasts. This I declare to be my last will and testament."

CHARLES DAVERS."

In the early part of 1721, an event transpired in Black Town which appears to have given no little trouble to the Governor. The Warehouse Conicopily had seduced a Rajpoot woman residing at Madras; and the strictness of the ideas of honour prevailing among the Rajpoots, led her relations to demand the severest punishment against the offender. The story is sufficiently told in the following extract from the consultations.

"Thursday, 23rd February, 1721. Petition from Venkatarauze, an inhabitant of this place of the Rajpoot caste, was presented to the Board; the import of the said petition, being a complaint against Davaroy, the Warehouse Conicopilly for seducing his sister from her lawful husband, and forcibly detaining her when she was demanded by himself and her said husband. The President thereupon acquainted the Board that this complaint had been made to him singly a few days since; whereupon he confined him to the Choultry, with a resolution to re-examine the case at the Board; the complainant being very pressing and importunate for justice; and being so much exasperated at the shame and disgrace which their family was like to suffer on the occasion, that they could scarcely be restrained from murdering themselves as well as the woman; the caste or tribe to which they belong being so nicely strict in their rules with regard to matters that concern their honour, that they choose much rather to suffer death than ignominy or reproach. Davaroy being brought before the Board, and examined upon the occasion; he replied that Venkatarauze came about ten days ago to him and told him that his sister had returned from the place, to which he sent her up in the country, but that he could not find her. Devaroy added that thereupon he sent to one Eyamoi-Villevochum a Washerman's wife and bid her look for the girl; and when she had found her she told her that her brother desired she might be carried to Davaroy's house. Davaroy added that when the girl was brought thither it was very late, and that therefore he asked the Washerwoman why she brought her at that unseasonable time of night, and bid her go away; but that they desired to lodge in the house that night, for fear of being taken up by the rounds. That in the morning, just before he went to the Fort, he enquired which was the Rajpoot woman; who when she saw him desired his protection from her friends, who, she said, would use her ill whenever she returned to them. He affirmed that he then bid her go a second time, but she replied, she was afraid and could not go; and then the Washerwoman told him that if he did not keep her from her relations she should suffer very much. Whereupon he came to the Fort. Davaroy further declared that he could not deny but that Venkatarauze came to his house the next day, and demanded his sister, as having heard that she was there; and that he replied that it was not in his power to deliver her up, but that he might go to his master. That the third day the said Venkatarauze met him in the street, and demanded his sister again; and that he replied, that he had been hard at work in the Fort, and was very much fatigued, but that he would talk with him in the morning; when the said Venkatarauze went and made his complaint to the Governor.

"Venkatarauze, the Complainant, being called in, and asked concerning the matter in dispute; he declared that about four months since, having heard that his sister frequently went to the aforementioned Washerwoman's house who bore no very reputable character, he began to be apprehensive, lest his sister should be seduced by her, if he did not timely prevent it; and that therefore he sent her up in the country to some relations there, but that lately returning again very privately (which however came to his knowledge) he sent to the aforesaid Washerman's to enquire where she was. The Washerwoman at first replied, that she knew not; but afterwards assured him she was in the house of Davaroy; whither he accordingly went, and meeting him at home, intreated him to deliver up his sister in order to prevent shame and infamy from falling upon their whole family, which the detention of his sister would unavoidably occasion. The said Venkatarauze further declares, that the defendant Davaroy then returned him for answer, that she was not in his house, but some where in the street; that thereupon being exasperated, he persisted in his demands of the girl; telling him without that if he was resolved, himself and family should kill themselves or leave the bounds; they would do either of the two. To which Davaroy replied, they might do what they would, but that he could not make up the matter in less than eight or ten day's time, when the Ships were gone for Europe.

"The Washerwoman being called in, and asked concerning this matter, she declared that the Plaintiff Venkatarauze did go to Davaroy and demand his sister; and that thereupon she herself was sent for by him, who bid her look amongst the cooly washerwomen for the girl; which she did accordingly, found her, and brought her to Davaroy's house, who bid her go away; that they replied it was late, and that they were afraid of being taken up by the rounds; for which reason they desired to lie there that night. This deponent further alleged, that then Davaroy permitted them to stay, but ordered her to take care of the girl, and stay with her. In the morning they asked Davaroy what they should do with her; who replied she might go. The deponent added that she told Davaroy, that if the girl returned to her relations they would murder her. Whereupon Davaroy gave them leave to continue in his house for three days; two of which, this deponent adds, she remained with the girl; but confesses that the third day she was absent.

"The sister to the Plaintiff Venkatarauze, being brought before the Board, was asked if Davaroy was guilty of the several particulars wherewith he now stood charged. In answer whereto, the woman declared in the affirmative and offered her oath to the same.

"The foregoing depositions being heard and fully considered; Davaroy was remanded to the Choultry, and the several persons concerned in this affair, dismissed the room."

This affair was debated at very great length, and occupies an important place in the records. The case was subsequently handed over to the arbitration of the heads of the castes, and Davaroy was sentenced to pay the sum of four hundred pagodas.

Our next extract refers to the general state of affairs in the Dekkan. It has already been mentioned that Hussein Ali Khan had been assassinated, and that Cheen Kulick Khan, alias Nizam-ool-Moolk, was Subah of the Dekkan. The entry though short may be useful to the historian.

"Tuesday, 21st March, 1721. The President acquaints the Board that he has received repeated advices from our spy peons at the Nabob's Camp, relating to Cheen Kulick Khan's coming this way with a very powerful army; that he (Cheen Kulick Khan) had summoned all the Nabobs of this country to come to him to give an account of their management; and that it is thought he will come to Ginjee. The President therefore proposes to every one to consider, whether his coming this way may not prejudice the Honorable Company's affairs, if we do not send a present, attended with proper persons to treat with him. The President further acquaints the Board that it is reported Diaram is with him; but as there is no certainty of it at present, he intends to make further enquiry."

About this time Governor Hastings was engaged in an enquiry into the murder of two Englishmen at Syriam in Pegu. The event excited considerable attention at the time, but has long since been devoid of interest. The main features however may be related as illustrative of the mode in which the British traded with Pegu about a century and a half ago.

In 1720 a Captain Heron resided at Syriam, a few miles to the south-east of Rangoon, in the character of British Resident; and it had been customary on the arrival of any of the Company's ships at the Syriam river, for Captain Heron to transact all the necessary business with the Prince of Syriam, or even the King of Pegu, and to give the supercargo such aid and advice as lay in his power. About this time the Company's ship " Lusitania," with Mr. Stephen Orme as Supercargo, arrived at the Syriam river. For the first day or two Mr. Orme lodged at Captain Heron's house, and all things went on smoothly. Mr. Orme however refused the proffered assistance of Captain Heron, and acted for himself. He made his own presents to the Prince of Syriam, and rejected the aid of Captain Heron's overseer whilst conducting the repairs of his vessel. A coolness naturally sprung up between the two, which was greatly increased when Mr. Orme not only took a separate house, but hoisted the English flag in his compound. The quarrel soon extended to the subordinates; and whenever the Lascars of the " Lusitania" went ashore they were obstructed and affronted by the Lascars of Captain Heron. The former requested Mr. Orme that they might be permitted to resent these affronts; but he replied that he should severely punish any one of his crew who should make any attack upon Captain Heron's men unless he had received the first blow.

Under these promising circumstances the time came round for the Mussulman feast called "Hossein Jossen," and the "Feast of Jamsee;" better known as the Mohurrum. This festival is celebrated by dancing round large fires in the vicinity of the Mosque, together with mock fighting which generally ended in real blows. Accordingly Captain Heron had never permitted any Englishman to go near these festivities, and had very often prevented the Lascars from doing so. Above all it was strictly forbidden that any one should carry English colours on the occasion. It seems however that a number of Lascars from the "Lusitania," together with others from some Moors ships, went to the feast, followed at a distance by five Europeans. Whether colours were carried or not appears to be uncertain. But an affray broke out, in which Cojee Zackary, an Armenian merchant at Syriam, interfered at the head of his Lascars; being also accompanied by the Lascars of Captain Heron. It was in this affray that the Chief Mate and Gunner were murdered at the direct instigation of Cojee Zachary. We quote the deposition of one of the witnesses as a sample of the whole.

"I, the under written Manoel DeMonte, inhabitant and married in this city of Madras, do hereby declare that I being in Syriam in the time that the Moors made their feast; we, the Lascars belonging to the Frigate called the "Lusitania," and some Moor's Ships, joined at night and were going to the place where the feast was kept; and when we came to the Street wherein lives the Moors Calafa, we met the Lascars of Cojee Zachary and Captain Heron. The streets being very narrow, we could not pass by them in a body, and the Pilot of the Frigate (who was in our Company) went and desired them friendly to go forward, or grant us liberty to pass them. Instead of hearing his petition, one of the Moors insulted him and gave him many blows. We seeing that, we all arose against them and made them presently run away; and so continued our march to the place where the feast was kept. A little while after came Cojee Zachary on horse back, with a lance in his hand (made after the country fashion); and after him his Lascars, and some of the natives, all armed with sticks and stones. The Pilot of the Frigate perceiving Zachary, he went to him and took the reins of his bridle in his hand, and begged of Zachary not to take notice of what had happened. Zachary gave him no answer, and shaking his head he went round the fire crying, "Beat the dogs;" and immediately the quarrel began, which grew so great that our people all run away, except the Pilot and Gunner of the Frigate. Zachary, spying them out ordered his people to beat them; and he went himself to assist them, and with the lance that he carried in his hand, he wounded the Pilot, of which wound the Pilot fell on the ground. Zachary perceiving that, and that the Gunner was yet safe and running away, he ordered his people to run after him and bring him back ; which they did and beat him in the presence of Zachary till the Gunner fell dead ; which Zachary perceiving, and it being near the fire round which the Moors celebrated the ceremony of their feast, he ordered to bring a light; and looking on and examining the two corpses, and finding they were dead, he retired to his house. To the truth of which, being acted in my presence, I standing all the while in a house near the place, where all this was acted, I do hereby declare and certify, and take my oath on the holy Evangelist in Madras, this 8th day of May, 1721."

The next day Mr. Orme, appealed to the Prince of Syriam for justice against Cojee Zachary, but appears to have been greatly obstructed by Captain Heron. The information was transmitted to the king of Ava, and the latter ordered " that Zachary should be in the sun three days, be bored through his cheeks and cut in his back seven times, and pay a hundred viss of silver ; and that each one of all the others concerned should receive one hundred blows ; provided that Captain Heron would declare in the public Ronda that the whole story was true." It would seem that Zachary escaped punishment ; and on reaching Madras Mr. Orme charged Captain Heron before Governor Hastings with having been bribed to screen the murderer. It will be sufficient to say that the charge of bribery fell to the ground, but that Captain Heron received a severe reprimand from the Court of Directors.

It was soon after this inquiry that the Governorship of Mr. Francis Hastings was brought abruptly to a close. The quarrel with Mr. Elwick was brought to an unfavorable termination; for instead of his suspension being confirmed, he was appointed Governor of Fort St. George and Mr. Hastings was removed. The proceedings are somewhat obscure, the General letters from the Court of Directors being missing. We can therefore only extract the following entry, after which Mr. Nathaniel Elwick took his seat in the President's chair.

"Sunday, 15th October, 1721. Ships "Heathcote" and "Marlborough" (belonging to the Honorable Company), arrived this afternoon from Great Britain; by whom received two packets from the Honorable Court of Directors, directed to the Honorable Nathaniel Elwick, Esq., President and Governor, William Jennings, Nathaniel Turner, Richard Benyon, Catesby Oadham, John Emmerson, Randal Fowke, James Hubbard, and George Drake. All except Mr. Jennings immediately met in the Consultation Room in the Fort; where all the Company's servants, both Civil and Military, and other inhabitants, were summoned; and on their appearance the packet was opened and the Commission read to them, after which they withdrew."

CHAPTER XXXII.

GOVERNORSHIP OF MR. NATHANIEL ELWICK.

1721—24.

Our readers will already have remarked that during the period now under review, Fort St. George was singularly free from any interference on the part of the Nabob of the Carnatic or Subah of the Dekkan. This tranquil state of affairs continued for some years. The rent was paid regularly, and at intervals compliments and presents were interchanged, but no differences appear to have arisen like those which mark the early annals of Madras. A change also is perceptible in what may be called the domestic history of the Presidency. Much of the roughness of the early period had passed away. Manners became less quaint and simple, but more refined; and altogether there is a better tone in the consultations. Decorum was more strictly preserved, whatever doubts may be entertained as to any real improvement in the morality of the times.

The first event in the new administration was however an extraordinary one. On the very Sunday, the 15th of October, 1721, that Mr. Elwick took the place of Mr. Hastings in the President's chair, the new Governor asked the Secretary for the Cash book, in order that he might see the balance; but found that it was closed up only to the end of the previous month, and that no entry of receipts or disbursements had been made for the month of October. Accordingly, as it was too late to examine the actual state of the cash that evening, the cash chest was sealed up, and the key of the Godown in which the silver was kept, called the Silver Godown, was delivered up; and Mr. Hastings, the late President, and Mr. Cooke, the Secretary, were requested to be present in the morning to see them both opened.

On the following morning the council assembled in the Consultation Room. Mr. Hastings was not present, but Mr. Cooke was sent for to see the Silver Godown opened. The proceedings may here be described in the language of the official entry.

"Monday, 16th October, 1721. Mr. Thomas Cooke being sent for, pursuant to an order of yesterday's Consultation, to see the Silver Godown opened and the treasure delivered, acquaints the Board that there is none at all in the Godown; he having sold the last 29 chests by an order of Mr. Hastings, since the Consultation of the 2nd instant, at 14 dollars per 10 pagodas; which he intended to have reported the first Consultation that should have been held. He was asked to pay in the produce of the silver, but he answered he had not received it. The Board then told him that, as he had sold it without any authority, they looked upon him to be accountable for it; and demanded what security he could give for the payment of it. In answer to which he desired time till the afternoon, when he doubted not he should be able to give security to our satisfaction. He was then ordered to withdraw, and acquainted we should want him by and by."

" The President then acquaints the Board that he sent to Mr. Hastings, to desire to speak with him upon the matters of his cash account. Accordingly Mr. Hastings attended the President at the Fort, where they had a private conference in the President's room; the result thereof from Mr. Hastings was, that he was deficient in the cash account, but that he would in seven days time make it good and deliver in the cash account with the balance. In the mean time he desired to reside at the garden for his health and convenience; and likewise desired leave to retire to the Mount till the next ship sails for England, on which he hopes to embark.

"Mr. Thomas Cooke was again sent for to the Board, and the money for the 29 chests of silver demanded of him. He answered he could not at present comply therewith, but that in twenty day's time he would make good the amount of what the 29 chests sold for. Upon which the Board insisted on security till he has paid the money. He answered at present he had not any to offer, but that he would go and get security. Accordingly he was acquainted we should meet again at four o'clock, and that then we shall expect he brings it with him."

Four o'clock came, when the following discussion took place in the Consultation Room.

"Mr. Cooke attends the Board (according to order in this morning's consultation), and acquaints the Board that the late President will be answerable for the amount of the sale of the 29 chests of treasure; and if the Board does not think the late President's bond for the same sufficient security, that he is willing to enter into the bond with him for the amount of the same; and being pressed for a sum of money forthwith in part, he answered, he hoped in five or six days to be able to pay in on account of the said silver about ten or twelve thousand pagodas. Upon which he was ordered to withdraw till the Board had considered further on the affair.

"Agreed that the late President and Mr. Cooke's joint bond is no security to the Honorable Company for the 29 chests of treasure; for a bond, without assets being joined with it and made over to the amount of the said treasure, is no more than an acknowledgment of the debt.

"Agreed that as the President designs this evening to return Mr. Hasting's visit to him this morning, that he does discourse Mr. Hastings on the subject of his debt on his cash account, and Mr. Cooke's debt account, viz. the 29 chests of treasure; and that the President desires to know of Mr. Hastings if he will give security for his debt on account of the cash; as also for Mr. Cooke's debt on account the 29 chests of silver; and that the Board do wait the President's return, in order to debate further on this matter which has already taken us up a great deal of time."

Late in the evening there was another consultation, the proceedings of which are thus recorded.

"The President reports to the Board, that he having been with the late President Mr. Hastings to return his visit of the morning, did according to agreement discourse Mr. Hastings on the affair of his cash account, and the 29 chests of treasure disposed of by Mr. Thomas Cooke; and that having demanded the money, or sufficient security for each, the late President did thereupon reply to him, that he would certainly on the day after to-morrow (which he said was as soon as an affair of that nature could be transacted) pay him the balance of the cash account in money, diamonds, or other sufficient security; and that as to the affair of the 29 chests of silver, he desires till the time is elapsed which the said silver was sold at; and concluded with desiring that no unkind expressions or entries be made upon our Consultation Book to slur his reputation. To which the President replied, he found no member of the Board any way inclined thereto.

"Agreed that the Board will wait till the day after to-morrow, and expect the late President Mr. Hastings' performance of his promise, unless in the meantime there should appear cause for the contrary."

During the interval Mr. Hastings was taken dangerously ill. Accordingly on the Wednesday, being the day fixed for paying the balance of the cash, the following entries are recorded.

"Wednesday, 18th October, 1721. The President reports that upon hearing of the late President's dangerous illness, he sent for Mr. Cooke, and demanded of him security for the 29 chests of treasure which he has disposed of out of the Warehouse. He replied he could not give in security for the same. Whereupon the President thought himself obliged to deliver him to the Captain of the Guard's charge; but that upon his request, he had permitted him to remain in the lodgings of the Warehouse under sentinels."

Mr. Cooke being thus confined as security for the 29 chests of silver, the next thing to be considered was what was to be done about the cash balance. On perusing a rough draft of the cash book, it was discovered that Mr. Hastings was indebted to the company more than seventy-two thousand pagodas; whilst the amount of cash actually remaining in the treasury may be gathered from the following extract of the same date as the foregoing.

"Wednesday, *continued*. Mr. Walsh brought the key of the cash chest and opened it; upon which there was found, in money one Fanam, and some Firmauns and Husbulhookums; being 29 from the Mogul, and the Commission for trying the pirates; also a paper with blue seals, said to be a purse belonging to Dalton deceased in Pegu. These were all the things found in the chest, except some empty pagoda bags. Mr. Walsh being asked if he brought any message from Mr. Hastings, answered he had none.

"Agreed that to-morrow morning the late President's cash account be drawn out, sent to him, and the balance demanded to be forthwith paid ; and after having had a long debate upon the matter, it was also agreed that the President do give orders to the Captain of the Guard for securing the person of the late President from making his escape from the place till such time as that he has paid the Honorable Company, what he owes them on his cash account and the 29 chests of silver reported to be sold by Mr. Cooke."

Notwithstanding this singularly empty state of the Silver Godown and Treasury Chest, Mr. Hastings scarcely appears to have been a dishonest man ; and it was only the sudden manner in which he was required to vacate the chair that caused the deficiency. On the next day he paid in ten thousand pagodas ; on the Saturday following he deposited diamonds to the value of twenty thousand pagodas more, and a few days afterwards gave ample security for the remainder. Unfortunately for him the illness with which he had been attacked proved fatal. The following simple entries tell their own story.

"Tuesday, 12th December, 1721. Mr. Francis Hastings, late President, desires leave to go home on the "Marlborough," which is granted, believing the security we have on the Honorable Company's account more than sufficient to answer their demands ; the very ill state of health he is in, and the little likelihood of his life if he continues here, being sufficient motives thereto. We have also permitted his servant, Thomas Newton, to go with him; he being as Mr. Hastings says a very useful servant to him, and has long since served his time to the Honorable Company.

"Friday, 15th December, 1721. This evening died the late President, Francis Hastings, Esq."

The year 1721 was rendered memorable by a great storm, which took place during the North East monsoon, and occasioned very great damage. The records describe exactly the same kind of weather which still visits the coast of Coromandel at intervals; but in addition to the terrors of the storm, it would seem that in cases of shipwreck some fears were entertained of the Moors, though not to the same extent as in former years. The following extracts will describe the commotion which attended such an event a hundred and forty years ago.

"Monday, 13th November, 1721. The Captain of the "King George" having yesterday in the afternoon received his dispatches, was this morning to take his leave of the President, who went with him to the Sea Gate to see him off; but the surf running very high, he could not get over, but hoped for meeting with an opportunity in the afternoon; but the wind and weather increased rather than abated, growing very thick to the north east. As the evening approached rain came on and wind in greater abundance, which prevented him from going off that night.

"14th November. All last night and this day the wind and rain continued with more violence than yesterday, and increased towards noon to a great storm. The rapidity of the waters out of the country was so great that it broke two of our bridges, that next to the Fort and the other on the road towards Triplicane. At the former of these there was at least two feet fall, which must be a prodigious stream to so small a bridge; and as to the other it was hardly dry, so consequently the more liable to this disaster. The whole Island was overflowed, and nothing all round us to be seen but water, tops of hedges and trees. The rains and floods have carried away most of the Macquaw and poor peoples' houses in the suburbs of Madras. The weather at one o'clock in the afternoon was so thick and hazy that we could not see a stone cast round us; and notwithstanding we are extremely alarmed at frequent firings from the ships in the road all this afternoon, yet we cannot do anything for the security either of our Honorable Masters' goods, ships or treasure; the surf flying quite up to the gates, and impossible for almost anything to live upon the sea.

"15th November. This morning the wind began to abate and the weather to clear up; but on our looking out into the road we could perceive only one ship remaining, which in the afternoon we heard was the "Heathcote." The Chief Mate writes ashore that the brigantine he had not seen all yesterday, nor the "King George," nor the "Dartmouth" since that day at noon. As for the "Marlborough" she drove about 5 in the afternoon; and he judged that ship which was then at an anchor within half a mile of the surf off St.

Thomé, to be her. Captains Elliston, Warden, and
Crossing, and Mr. Bates, Chief Mate of the
" Marlborough," desired horses to go down and
see her, and look if any more were to be seen to
the southward, but after all that they could do it
was impossible for them to get over the river, so
they were obliged to return. We endeavoured
immediately after that to send off anchors and
cables to the " Marlborough," who made frequent
signals of distress; but the boat we put the cable
into (and in which the Chief Mate was going) filled and split to pieces. However we with much
ado got off a cable that afternoon, and the Chief
Mate went aboard. As soon as he was there he
hoisted his Ensign in the fore shrouds, the signal
agreed upon in case of another ship in distress
below there; but notwithstanding all that we could
do, we were obliged to defer sending an anchor till
the next morning.

" We also ordered three boats to be got ready
and seven soldiers to go in each boat; Captains
Warden, Elliston, and Crossing, whose ships and
brigantine were missing, went one in each of
them. But an accident prevented that wherein
Captain Warden was from proceeding, which was
her oversetting; by which misfortune a Serjeant
and three men were drowned.

" The Honorable President in the morning, perceiving the ships were missing, dispatched 100
peons to the southward along the sea side to see
if any wrecks came ashore; but the rivers being so
very deep and rapid, and the country under
water, that the peons could not pass; so that had

not any intelligence till the 17th in the afternoon from the Chief of Covelong. However it was judged necessary to have an account of the above-mentioned signal, in order to send the men as before related. Captain Crossing was in the first boat that went off that evening; when he got aboard the "Marlborough" fired one gun, which was agreed to be done if the signal on the fore shrouds in the evening was not a mistake.

"A Letter from Captain Tolson's Chief Mate to him, of this day's date, giving an account of the storm is hereunder entered.

"Heathcote," November 17th, 1721.
" Captain Tolson,
" Sir,

These are to inform you that the ship has met with no further misfortune than the loss of the Long boat and the parting of our small Bower Cable; though I must confess it is less than expected. It is impossible to relate the extremity of weather we had as to the Ships. I cannot tell further of them than that ship to the Southward of St. Thomé I take to be the "Marlborough." The "Dartmouth" I see drive yesterday in the afternoon; the weather coming on so thick saw no more of her. The "King George" I saw yesterday noon. The brigantine we saw nothing of, which impute to the thickness of the weather at that time; but heartily wish they may be well, which I much doubt. The "King George", she being a very pestered ship, or indeed the rest, I cannot see what they could do by going to sea with the wind at north east, and north east by east, and such a grown sea.

I am Sir,
Your most humble Servant,
Roger Hale."

"16th November. The Honorable President received a letter from Captain Elliston on board the "Marlborough," acquainting us she rode in six fathom water, and that since eight o'clock Tuesday morning she had seen neither of the other Ships, but she has lost four anchors, and had only their sheet anchor left; but that they had one of the Company's stocked, and desired timber to stock another, and a large Cattamaran to carry their anchors out to work further off shore. The President forthwith sent them an anchor of 25 tons weight ready stocked, on a large Cattamaran, according to their desire, and they have immediately gone out in deeper water, and now she is very safe.

"Captain Tolson also communicated to us a letter that he received from his Mate, importing the ship laboured prodigiously during all that Hurricane, which has forced all the oakum out of her upper works; that they rode almost under water which had damaged very much their provisions; that their sheet cable and best bower were both rubbed very much, and the outward cable to the best bower anchor very bad; that she had worked down all the cabins in the steerage, and the bulk head, and broke all their hen coops to pieces. Late at night the President received a letter from Captains Elliston and Crossing, two miles off Covelong, importing they had met nothing like a wreck in their way, but a Long boat and David which they believed belonged either to the "Marlborough" or "Heathcote."

"Friday, 17th November, 1721. The President acquaints the Board that, by peons sent from hence, he received advice about noon from the Chief of Covelong, that a ship is drove ashore about eight miles to the Southward of said place; and that 5 chests and 20 Europeans are come ashore and seized by the Moors; but what ship is stranded, the peons could not tell the name of.

"Agreed that the "Heathcote" be forthwith ordered under sail to the wreck; that twenty Europeans and Captain Sutherland be sent upon her to protect the wreck, with ten Lascars and ammunition, as also sixty spare arms for the Ship's Company; with all other necessaries and as many Mussoolas as can be spared, together with such as we can borrow from St. Thomé. Fourteen Europeans are already at Covelong, under command of Captains Elliston and Crossing, as also twenty Lascars."

"Friday, 17th November, 1721. Received a letter from the Chief of the Flemings at Covelong, advising that an English Ship was stranded at Mauvelipuram, and that the people that we sent down were arrived there; that the Moors at his intercession treated them very well; let them have two palankeens and a horse to go to the wreck, and enquire news of the others that were missing; that they had secured all the sailors, but upon the Captain's request had released them again; and he assures us that the Moors will not in the least hinder but rather be assisting to us in this affair."

We now turn to an incident, which is by no means without a parallel in the early history of Madras, and which at the same time is very significant. The Governors of Fort St. George appear about this period to have each had some very clever Native acting for them under the name of the Dubash; and this Governor's Dubash not only transacted all the private business of his master, such as sales and purchases, but was frequently guilty of extortion and oppression towards his fellow countrymen, of which no one can have the slightest conception who is not intimately acquainted with the native character. Of course after the death or departure of a Governor many of these acts of tyranny came out, and the Dubash was made to disgorge a portion of his ill gotten gains. Thus some time after the death of Mr. Hastings, his Dubash Mar Kistna, got into trouble; though we may remark in passing, that his evil deeds were subsequently left in the shade by another Native who afterwards acted as Dubash to Governor Macrae.

The story of Governor Hasting's Dubash is however somewhat singular from the fact of this clever extortioner being of a jocular and musical turn; and indeed seems to have been a type of a character but little known to the European, namely that of a convivial Hindoo. Dickens tells a story of a London cabman who was sentenced to solitary confinement for six weeks for having "thrashed a fare;" and who thereupon lay upon his back and sang comic songs all day. It does however seem somewhat strange that a similar character should have turned up in the records of this Presidency. We give the original entry.

"Saturday, 8th September, 1722. We have acquainted the Honorable Court of Directors that we had secured Mar Kistna, Mr. Hasting's Dubash, whom we had severe complaints against for large debts owing to sundry persons, and other indirect management. He hath now either made full satisfaction, or given security for all the demands that have appeared against him, except a debt to Amerash Tacca, a company's merchant, and to the estate of his master Hastings. His crimes are so enormous that they call for public punishment, that he may be an example to future Dubashes how they make use of their Master's power in an unwarrantable manner. He at present complains of a lameness in his limbs, how real we cannot determine; but shall leave the determination of his case till the Europe ships are gone. He always had a lodging in the Fort, and a sentry upon him, and had the liberty of his acquaintance, till the Company's Merchants reported that he lived so jocular with his singing master attending him, that he would never think of paying him his money; which was above two months since, when the President ordered him into the Ensign's room upon the Main Guard, and the door to be shut; though however he still observes a constant levee at his window every morning."

The following extract will furnish a sufficient illustration of Mar Kistna's proceedings.

"Saturday, 8th September 1722.

"A Declaration of Tombee Chetty and Moota Venkitta Chetty.

"We, Tombee Chetty and Moota Venkitta Chetty, do hereby declare that Mar Kistna sent for and told us, that as we had entered into a contract with the Honorable Company, we ought to give the Governor 5000 pagodas, which he then demanded. Upon our refusing to give the said money, he went and told the Governor some false stories, which occasioned us to be confined one day at the Gardens. About 12 o'clock that night the peons carried us to Mar Kistna's house, when we asked why we put him to so much trouble without any reason. He answered, that if we would lay down 5000 pagodas we may go free, or else we should be confined in the Choultry. Notwithstanding those threats we still refused to give any money. Then he sent us to the Choultry, and put us in a close prison, where two men can scarce stand; and ordered the peons not to let us go out without the door upon any account whatsoever, but made us eat and drink and live entirely in that little place. About four or five days after he gave orders that we should not have any provisions whatsoever, but once in four days, and then only a little rice and water, and of that not half enough to satisfy our appetites. One day we lighted a lamp in the said godown; which Mar Kistna saw, and ordered it immediately to be put out. Sometime after, we sent a man to the said

Mar Kistna to ask him how he could be so barbarous to us. He answered, that we should not be released unless we would give the said 5000 pagodas; telling the said servant that if we would give the said money, to come and tell him; if not, not to come to him again; and then he ordered the peon to push the said man out of his house. Sometime after he sent a man to us to tell us that if we would give 3000 pagodas we should be free; which we refused. Sometime after 2000 pagodas; then that we should be released for 1500 pagodas. Lastly he sent word, if we would directly lay down 1000 pagodas we should be set at liberty. But finding he could not get any thing from us he increased his barbarity to the utmost of his power, and then released us, all which was by the persuasion of Mar Kistna. Therefore we hope this Honorable Board will examine this affair."

The subsequent treatment of Mar Kistna may be gathered from the following extracts.

"Wednesday, 10th October, 1722. Agreed that Mar Kistna be, as he has petitioned, permitted to go about Town under a guard of peons and Talliars in the day time, to gather in his effects, in order to satisfy what he owes to the estates of Messrs. Hastings, Wright, and other creditors; that the Petitioners be permitted to sue Kistna in the Mayor's Court if they please, and that the peons and Talliars every night do return Mar Kistna to his confinement, till he has satisfied all his creditors."

"Tuesday, 11th December, 1722. Petition of Mar Kistna read, setting forth that being under confinement at the Fort, and not having conveniences proper to take the necessary physic for recovery of his health, it is agreed he be delivered to the charge of the Chief Peon, and Taliar, and that he remains at his own house."

After this Mar Kistna managed to satisfy all his creditors and obtained his liberty.

The following extracts regarding the Armenians will be found interesting, as throwing light upon the mode in which trade was carried on in the olden time. Our readers will bear in mind the distinction between the Company's trade, and the trade carried on by the Company's servants and merchants of the place.

"Monday, 27th April, 1724. The President told the Board that the Armenians had for a long time behaved themselves in a very insolent haughty manner; and had rendered themselves not only undeserving the great privileges granted them, but likewise obnoxious to the Government by several actions, contrary to the rules and regulations thereof; and that he had ordered them to attend the Board to answer to several facts he had to charge them with. The first was that Codejee George, and the rest of the owners of the Ship "London," had imported great part of the Ship's Cargo at Pondicherry, to the amount of 12,000 pagodas, contrary to the orders of the Company; as would fully appear from their letter of the 7th April 1708, where they order the native inhabitants to be expelled the bounds, if they carry the trade to St. Thomé to the prejudice of the customs of Madras; which by parity of reason holds the same with respect to Pondicherry, since wherever the goods are imported, still the customs are lost to them. He, the President, likewise produced the Company's letter of the 19th December 1719, where are these remarkable words, speaking of the French,—that none of our Servants, whether Europeans or Indians, nor any of our Merchants or Brokers, be permitted to buy or sell for them, or otherwise assist them, in their trade or merchandize. He added that Codejee Petrus, an Armenian lately arrived from Manilla, and an inhabitant of this place, had contracted with the French this very year for 30,000 dollars worth of goods upon freight; and that besides they had encouraged one Bassilio, a subject of Manilla, to come hither and carry away the freight from this place; all which actions tend greatly to the damage of the Company with respect to their customs, and to the place itself, by encouraging foreigners and destroying the navigation of the English. He added that this evil had been long growing to the height it now is, and that as it is daily increasing, if the Board do not take some measures to prevent it, the commerce of Madras must inevitably fall away to nothing.

" The matter being sometime debated, and the privileges granted the Armenians duly considered, they were called in and told that it was the express orders of the Company, that no inhabitant of Madras should be allowed to import goods in any foreign settlement to the prejudice of the customs of this place. Likewise that none under the English protection were to aid and assist other nations in their trade and navigation, to the detriment of the English. They affirmed that they never had done any thing of this kind; but being presssed with the importation of goods at Pondicherry, Codejee George assured the Board that he knew nothing of the doing of it till the goods were ashore and sold; and as to the contract with the French, Codejee Petrus told them that money came from Manilla for account of Spaniards there, and consigned to him and another Armenian upon the French Ship, and that his orders were to return it on the same Ship.

"They were then ordered to withdraw, and after some small debate it was agreed to overlook what was past, but to let them know that if they were guilty of such practices for the future, they should be proceeded against with the utmost rigour, in compliance with the orders of our Honorable Masters. They were called in accordingly, and told the resolution of the Board; to which they promised due obedience."

"Wednesday, 20th May, 1724. The Armenians not taking warning by the late orders given them at the Board, but growing more insolent; and having since engaged with one Agostinho Bassilio, who is a Spaniard and come to this place, where he has offered freight at a lower rate than has for many years been customary, to the vast prejudice of the trade and navigation of this place; it was proposed to put a stop to such proceedings; but this being a matter of great moment, after some debate about the methods to be used in such a case, the Board thought fit to defer coming to a resolution thereupon till they had more fully considered it."

" Tuesday, 26th May, 1724. The Board then resumed the debate concerning the Armenians, and the Manilla freight, which was deferred the last consultation day; and it was agreed by the whole Board that, if some measures were not taken to prevent it, the trade of this place would be entirely lost to the English and given to Foreigners. But as the Company have given great immunities to that set of men, it was urged that we could not, without infringing those privileges, prevent their trading on the best terms they could. To which it was replied that the contract mentioned was an obsolete one; and that even at that time it was made the Company complained that the circumstances of the times obliged them to grant greater immunities than they would otherwise have done, and that probably when those circumstances should be altered they might make some alterations therein; by which it appeared, the Company themselves did not thoroughly approve of the granting such privileges. It was added upon this side that the Armenians had long ago forfeited the privileges granted them, by carrying on their trade to and from Europe on the Danes' ships, and now more recently by contracting with the French and Spaniards, directly contrary to the conditions on which these concessions were made them. It was further added on the same side, that the Company do covenant and agree with their servants, and Free Merchants whom they permit to reside in India, that they shall have all manner of freedom in their trade, but that if ever they think fit to order any of their own ships to freight voyages, they do expect to be first served, and our ships after them. From whence it is reasonable to suppose, if they will insist upon the first plan themselves, we ought to be and are allowed the second; or otherwise we should be on a much worse foundation than any set of men in India, and obliged to leave off all trading; being under traded by the natives on the one hand and obliged to prefer the Company's ships on the other. Upon the whole of the debates, which was continued for a considerable time, it was unanimously agreed and ordered, that the inhabitants of Madras shall not be allowed to freight to Manilla any goods or money belonging to this place on any foreign ship before the English ship is laden."

The following complaint addressed to the Government of Fort St. George on the 8th June, 1724, by Mr. Drake, a member of Council, is worth preserving as illustrative of the times.

"Honorable Sirs,

"I am to acquaint you that on Tuesday night last about 10 o'clock, a Musteez belonging to ship "Moylip," did in the open street assault and most barbarously beat one of my servants. As soon as I was informed of the same, I sent a civil message to him by my Dubash, and only desired to be acquainted with his reasons; but instead of having the least reply from him he returned to me my Dubash very much beaten, and had the insolence to follow him with blows to my very door. I then could do no other than send for the Guard, who accordingly came and secured him for the remainder of the night. This no sooner was done, but Captain Hill, the Commander of the Ship this young offender belongs to, came to my house and in a most indecent manner addressed himself to me; telling me I had forfeited all good manners, and had sent a better gentleman than myself on the Guard, and that my Councellorship was my only protection for so doing, and only on that presumption I had dared to do it, and that it was well for me I had such a protection to skreen me from his immediate resentment. In short Captain Hills language and manners throughout were very foul and rude, and such as I believe your Honours upon examination will find ought neither to be given or taken, especially as I had only done my duty, and taken no more privilege than the meanest of your inhabitants may, to quell a riot in the properest manner I could. I should have been very glad if Captain Hill would have recollected himself the next morning, that I might not have given your Honors this trouble; but as he persists, and will make me no acknowledgment, I am strictly obliged to make this application, and do believe you will find I merited better usage than Captain Hill was pleased to bestow on me. But this I refer to your determination."

It may be gratifying to hear that Captain Hill, after much expostulation, was induced to make an apology.

The following entries are worth preserving on account of their historical value. They seem to refer to a confederation of different Nabobs in Southern India, including Sadatulla Khan, Nabob of Arcot, against the power of Cheen Kulich Khan, Nizam of the Dekkan. Also to a struggle between two Mussulman chiefs for the possession of Ginjee.

"Wednesday, 1st July, 1724. The President informed the Board, that yesterday he received private advices from the country that in a late engagement near Aurungabad, wherein the Nabobs of this side of the country were most of them joined against Cheen Kulich Khan, this latter had gained a complete victory. Galib Khan, commander of the forces sent against him by our Nabob, being killed; as was likewise Falum Khan son to Abdul Nabbee Khan, and almost all the Chief Officers in the Army. Sheik Mahmud Khan, Nabob of Hyderabad, was likewise wounded and his life despaired of. These letters add that a detachment of Cheen Kulich Khan's army, amounting to about 15,000 men, were on their march to seize Sattingurra, one of the passes into the Carnatta country, which had occasioned our Nabob to march to secure it; in order to which he was levying forces with the utmost expedition and at very extravagant rates. Further advices say that Abdul Nabbee Khan was marched against Fyre Khan, to take possession of the Ginjee country; and that we might shortly expect an account of the engagement from those parts."

"Friday, 16th July, 1724. The President produced another letter, giving us an account that there had happened a very bloody engagement between Abdul Nabby Khan and Fyre Khan, in which the former was killed and the latter mortally wounded, and that there were upwards of 12,000 men cut off in the engagement. That upon this, our Nabob was marched to take possession of the Ginjee country, imagining that after such a vast loss neither side will be able to oppose him; that Cheen Kulich Khan* on his march to this side of the country, and a detachment of his army consisting of 15,000 men, is now encamped at 15 leagues distance from Hyderabad, in their way hither, followed by himself with the main body.

"The President added that there are remaining of Abdul Nabby Khan's family, 23 persons, which are all resolved to maintain their right to the Ginjee country or die, so that there is little likelihood of these parts being settled again in peace for a long time."

"Wednesday, 22nd July 1724. There being a large quantity of Madeira wine in the Godowns, it was proposed to dispose of some part thereof. But the Persian Empire being so much disturbed, and the Afghans† beseiging Shiraz, it was resolved, not to sell any Madeira yet, it being very unlikely that we should have any wine from Persia this year, and consequently the price of Madeira will rise which is now very low."

About this time a crime was committed at Fort

---

* In the records he is styled Nissa Mulmuloch, who is said to be the same as "Chicklys Khan." There cannot however be the slightest doubt of his identity.

† The Afghans are here entitled "Ophgoons" in the Records. Of course in this, as in other similar cases, we have modernized the spelling.

St. David, which is worthy of some notice. A Gunner was living with a Portuguese woman; and one evening an Ensign of the Garrison made the Gunner drunk apparently for the purpose of seducing the woman. The Gunner however awoke from his drunken stupor, and after much altercation shot the Ensign dead. Many of the details are unfit for our columns, but the following extracts from the depositions are curious illustrations of the Garrison life of the period. We must premise that the Gunner's name was Jens Pitterson; the Ensign who was murdered was named Edward Key.

"Jens Pitterson declares, that the 2nd of October 1724, about 5 o'clock in the afternoon, he came from shooting; at which time Ensign Edward Key asked him what game he had got; to which he replied he saw nothing worth shooting, and so came home immediately. Afterwards Jens Pitterson declares he went home to eat, and when he had done Ensign Edward Key asked him, the said Jens Pitterson, to go to his room to drink a dram with him. To which the said Pitterson replied, that he was not used to drink and could not bear liquor, and therefore desired to be excused; but after many persuasions the said Jens Pitterson declares he went to Ensign Edward Key's room, and there drank with the Ensign two drams. After which the said Jens Pitterson says he retired into his own room, and that Ensign Edward Key about half an hour after followed him to his own room; when the Ensign told him, the said Jens Pitterson, that he wanted a companion to go with him to Bengal; for that his pay was going to be reduced, and he should be obliged to ask for his discharge. To which Jens Pitterson says he replied, that he had no occasion to leave the place while he was maintained; but that if he was discharged he must seek his livelihood where he could. Upon which Ensign Edward Key shook the said Jens Pitterson by the hand, and said to him " Comrade you must go along with me ;" and then they fell to drinking in Pitterson's room to such an excess, that the said Jens Pitterson declares he knows not what he did afterwards, only that some of the guard told him this morning that the Ensign had beat him.

"Gulielmo D. Rozario, Sentry from 12 to 2 o'clock over the gate, deposes that about half an hour after one o'clock in the morning, Jens Pitterson, Gunner of Trepopolore Guard, waked in liquor, and asked Ensign Key what he was doing. Sometime after Jens Pitterson took his cutlace, which the Ensign seeing, retired into his own room and shut the door. Upon which Jens Pitterson enraged called out, and fell a cutting and slashing the bars of the Ensign's windows. But Jens Pitterson finding he could not come to the Ensign with his cutlace, went to his room and brought a gun. Whereupon the Deponent declares Ensign Key threatened Jens Pitterson, that if he did not retire from the window, he would fire upon him without waiting for orders ; and that he the deponent called out to the Serjeants and Corporals who awaked, but were afraid to seize the said Jens Pitterson because he had a loaded gun in his hand. Whereupon Ensign Edward Key came to the window of his room, and bidding Jens Pitterson be gone to sleep, the said Jens Pitterson fired his gun in at the window, and shot him ; which alarmed the guard, but they dared not seize him because he had got another loaded piece by him ; therefore they waited till he fell asleep when they seized and bound him."

It came out in the evidence that the pay of the Ensign was only nine pagodas a month, and that of the gunner only six pagodas. It will be sufficient to say that the prisoner was sent to Fort St. George for trial, but the judgment subsequently passed does not appear in the records.

The administration of Governor Elwick was now drawing to a close. The last event in his administration worth recording, is an enquiry into the barbarous conduct of some peons who were sent to St. Thomé to arrest a man named Anconah for debt. As all the facts were fully proved, it will be sufficient if we simply publish the complaint of Anconah, and the punishment awarded to the accused. The petition is dated 16th November 1724.

" The petition of Godee Anconah.

" Humbly showeth,

" That on Saturday night, three of the Company's peons came to my lodgings at St. Thomé, and told me your Honor sent for me. To which I replied, I would wait on your Honor directly. But one of the peons called Annapah, took hold of my hand, and drew his sword, and wounded me in the side. After that he and the other two carried me into the yard, and one of them put my head under his arm and cut the tip of my ears and took my jewels. My mother-in-law, seeing what they did, asked them why they used me so ill. At which one of them drew his sword and cut my mother-in-law on the neck. Then one of my manservants, seeing me so cruelly used, begged them to let me alone. One of them presently cut off his hand and gave him a wound on the head; and after that they gave me several wounds on my belly and breast; then they beat all my woman servants and brought me into the streets, kicking and beating me on the belly. Then bringing me half way to Madras they overset me, beating and kicking me very basely; and thinking that they had killed me, they put their hands to my nose to feel if I was breathing, or whether I was dead or alive. Then they brought me before your Honor, who was pleased to order Doctor Pitcher to dress my wounds, who told me that if I had stayed but four hours longer without a Doctor I had been a dead man.

"I can assure your Honor and Council that I never wronged the Company, or am indebted to any body; but am a free merchant, and pay the Company's customs for my Merchandize. I am still very weak in my body and limbs, therefore leave it wholly to your Honor and Council to see your poor petitioner righted, and the offenders punished, according to your Honor and Council's pleasure."

Governor Elwick and Council entered upon a long and careful examination of all the circumstances connected with this outrage. In the first instance they resolved that the effects of Annapah and the two other peons should be confiscated and sold, in order to recompense the man who had lost his hand; and that the three criminals should stand in the pillory and have their ears cut off, and should then be whipped out of the bounds. Meantime however Aga Mogheen, the Governor of St. Thomé, interceded in behalf of the prisoners, and begged that they might be pardoned; and accordingly, in order to prevent the affair from being represented to the Nabob of Arcot in such a way as might prove troublesome to the Madras Government, it was resolved that the sentence should only be put in force against Annapah; and that the two other peons, who had only acted under his orders, should be discharged. Annapah however appears to have been an influential member of the Left Hand Caste, and the Heads of the whole of that Caste appeared before the Board and begged that a fine might be substituted for corporal punishment. Accordingly it was determined that Annapah should pay the following. To Auconah, whose jewels had been taken from his ears but whose circumstances were good, and who desired a public acknowledgment of the crime, Annapah was required to pay 200 pagodas. The manservant who lost his hand, being a much inferior person, would have received less; but considering that he had been disabled from getting a livelihood, " it was thought necessary to give him such a sum as might maintain him, or at least put him in a way of living easy for the rest of his life," and therefore he was to receive 200 pagodas.

Two other persons who were hurt were to be paid 50 pagodas each. Finally, in order that Annapah might make public reparation for his crime, "it was agreed to fine him further 200 pagodas, to be lodged in the Corporation Cash towards keeping the bridges in repair."

On the 18th of January 1725, Mr. Elwick resigned the President's chair, and shortly afterwards returned to England; and Mr. James Macrae of Glasgow notoriety assumed the Government of Fort St. George.

CHAPTER XXXIII.

GOVERNORSHIP OF MR. JAMES MACRAE.
1725—26.

Mr. James Macrae, Governor of Fort St. George and all the English Settlements on the Coast of Coromandel from 1725 to 1730, was one of those remarkable men who rose from poverty to affluence at the time when large fortunes were still a novelty in the commercial world. The annals of his Government will thus derive additional interest from his extraordinary career, especially in the eyes of those of our readers who come from those parts of Scotland where his name and memory are still preserved in local traditions. Accordingly, before entering upon the records of his government, it may be interesting to glance at such particulars respecting his origin as may be gathered from stories which are still current in Glasgow and Ayr.*

---

* Some interesting particulars concerning Governor Macrae and his family, and the mode in which he disposed of his fortune after his return from India, were published some years ago in the "Ayrshire Observer," and have been placed at the disposal of the compiler of these annals. It is curious to notice that all who have attempted to collect the traditions respecting this extraordinary man, dwell especially upon the fact that his Governorship of Madras, and indeed his whole Indian career, is a perfect blank. This blank will therefore now be filled up for the first time.

Mr. James Macrae was born in Ayrshire about the latter part of the reign of merry king Charles. His parents were of the very lowest class, and he himself whilst a boy is said to have been employed in looking after cattle. His father however died whilst James Macrae was still very young; and his mother then removed with her son to the town of Ayr; where they lived in a little thatched cottage in the suburbs, and where the poor widow gained her living as a washerwoman. Here young Macrae added something to his mother's earnings by running messages; but at the same time seems to have picked up some little education by means only known to Scotchmen. He appears however to have grown tired of this monotonous life whilst still a boy. Ayr was a seaport, and it is easy to understand how a young man, endowed with the energy which Macrae subsequently proved himself to possess, should have imbibed a keen desire to embark in the adventurous trading of the time, and finally have turned his back upon the poverty of home and run off to sea.

Forty years passed away before Macrae returned to his native land; and it is generally believed that throughout the whole of that period he held no communication whatever with his relations or his home. Meantime his sister married a carpenter named MacGuire, who was also in great request as a violin player at kirns and weddings, and was consequently known as "Fiddler MacGuire." The poverty of these people may be gathered from the fact that the children of MacGuire were on one occasion seen crying for bread, whilst their mother had left the house to try and borrow a loaf. But we shall have more particulars of this family to relate hereafter. For the present we must confine ourselves to the career of Mr. Macrae.

The early events in the seafaring life of the young runaway must we fear for ever remain unknown. We can learn nothing of him till about 1720, when he must already have been thirty years in India, and is simply alluded to as Captain Macrae. Most probably he had risen to the command of a vessel in the country trade, and had undertaken voyages to Sumatra, Pegu, and China. It appears however that he had been successful in gaining the confidence of his Honorable Masters, for he was subsequently sent on a special mission to the English settlement on the West Coast of Sumatra, to reform the many abuses which prevailed at that settlement. Here he acquitted himself in such a manner as to ensure his appointment to a high post. He effected savings to the extent of nearly 60,000 pagodas, or about £25,000 per annum; and at the same time carried out such reforms as promised a very large increase in the supply of pepper. Accordingly the Directors ordered that on leaving the West Coast he should be appointed Deputy Governor of Fort St. David, and thus stand next in succession to the Government of Fort St. George. The retirement of Mr. Elwick led to Mr. Macrae's advancement to the latter post sooner than could have been expected. He returned from the West Coast towards the end of 1724, and without proceeding to Fort St. David, at once took his seat as second Member of

Council at Fort St. George. At last on the 18th of January, 1725, the son of the poor washerwoman of Ayr took his place as Governor of the Madras Presidency. The proceedings on that occasion are thus recorded in the consultations.

"Monday, 18th January, 1725. The President (James Macrae, Esq.,) opened this consultation by telling the Board that, as this was the first time of their meeting since his taking the chair, he thought it would not be improper to acquaint them of his resolutions; of which the principal was, that he would prosecute the Company's interest to the utmost, and endeavour to retrieve the abuses that had crept into the management of their affairs. He added that he was determined not to interrupt in any manner the commerce of the place, but that all the inhabitants both Whites and Blacks, the Free Merchants as well as the Company's Servants, should have free liberty of trade, and that he should expect the same freedom from interruptions in what he should undertake; that he would endeavour to be as agreeable to the Gentlemen as any of his predecessors, but that he was determined to maintain the privileges and immunities belonging to the President; and he concluded by saying, that he expected a ready assistance from them in the pursuit of the above resolutions, which was accordingly promised."

Before proceeding with the annals of Mr. Macrae's administration, it may be as well to remark that he was emphatically a commercial Governor and a most laborious administrative reformer. The relations with the Nabob of Arcot remained unaltered, and what may be called the domestic incidents of the Presidency are few in number. But in all matters connected with the trade of the place, the reduction of the expenditure, the improvement of the revenues, the supervision of the mint, and the administration of justice, his proceedings are distinguished by an indefatigable industry, a display of strong sense, and above all by a fullness of record far beyond those of any of his predecessors. Nothing appeared too large or too small for Governor Macrae. Everything received his attention in turn, from such matters of detail as the sorting of cloths and the better preparation of the consultation books, up to the most difficult and complicated questions connected with the coinage, the customs, the quit rent, or the very doubtful cases of appeal from the Mayor's Court. Like most men who have risen from nothing, he was arbitrary and occasionally harsh towards his subordinates; but he proved himself a valuable servant to the Company, whose orders he rigidly respected; and no records which have as yet fallen into our hands throw more light upon the internal administration of Fort Saint George.

Our first extract seems to illustrate the determination of the new Governor to support his own dignity.

"Monday, 22nd February, 1725. The President acquainted the Board that Pondy Chetty Kistna, a person who was formerly whipped out of Fort St. David for practices against the Government, and afterwards banished from hence for the same crime; but who had lately ventured again without leave, and had wrote a letter into the country, wherein he tells his correspondent several things of the President very much to his dishonour; which coming to his knowledge had occasioned him to confine the said Pondy Chetty Kistna. The letter was produced, and the Board unanimously agreed that he ought to suffer very severely and his imprisonment was confirmed." This letter is unfortunately not entered in the records; otherwise it might have thrown some light upon the assumed faults of the Governor.

The first important matter which received the attention of Governor Macrae was that of the coinage of rupees at the Madras mint. It seems that the Native chiefs had awakened to the profit derived by the Madras Government from the coinage of rupees; and accordingly they had not only set up mints of their own, but about this time they contrived to make more rupees out of the same quantity of silver, than were made by the Company. For instance out of every hundred ounces of silver, the mints at St. Thomé and Arcot turned out to the merchant Rupees 266, annas 14; whilst the mint in Fort St. George only turned out Rupees 257, annas 7. Thus the merchant obtained nine rupees seven annas more for his hundred ounces of silver at St. Thomé and Arcot than he could obtain at Fort St. George. In other words the Madras rupee was two per cent dearer than the rupee of Arcot or of St. Thomé. The consequence was that the merchants preferred coining their silver at the latter mints; and the Company found its customs decreasing. Accordingly Governor Macrae directed Messrs. Pitt, Benyon, and Emmerson, to enquire into the whole matter. Their report is accordingly entered in the consultations, but it is not only intricate but devoid of interest to the general reader. The substance of it, rendered as clear as we can make it, appears to be as follows.

At St. Thomé, Arcot, and Covelong the charge of custom and coinage had formerly been 35 rupees per thousand; viz. 15 rupees custom to the Nabob and 20 rupees for mint charges. Both however had been recently reduced, the Nabob's custom to 10 rupees and the mint charges to 11 rupees: thus the custom and coinage were only 21 rupees per thousand, instead of 35 rupees as heretofore. It seems however that the mint charges were only nominally 11 rupees per thousand; and that actually they were 14 rupees, as may be seen from the following table.

	Rs.
Charcoal for making the powder......	1¼
Waste in melting........................	8¾
Pots..	½
Flatting the bullets.....................	½
Chopping.................................	¼
	11¼

To which was added

	Rs.
Brahmins for their care............	¾
Goldsmiths...........................	¾
Gold washers........................	1¼
	2¾

Rs. 14 per thousand.

This amount was made up thus. Every 300 ounces of silver ought to have made 974 rupees, whereas these mints only paid out 971 rupees; the difference of three rupees being about the same as the difference between 11 rupees and 14 rupees per thousand. Again there was a depreciation of weight of one rupee eleven annas per thousand, and another depreciation of standard of nine rupees per thousand; making an additional profit of ten rupees eleven annas per thousand. This fraud had been introduced ever since the reduction of custom and charges from 35 rupees to 21 per thousand; and it had proved successful, inasmuch as these native mints paid out their rupees by tale and not by weight, and the difference was so slight as to render their rupee as good in the market as the rupee of Fort St. George.

The custom and charges on the Madras rupee were as follows, two per cent. or 20 per thousand to the Company, and two per cent or 20 per thousand to the mint. Thus making 40 rupees per thousand.

The 20 per thousand mint charges were distributed as follows. First $11\frac{1}{4}$ per thousand for charcoal, waste, pots, flatting, and chopping, as in the St. Thomé and Arcot mints; and the remaining $8\frac{3}{4}$ as follows :—

	Rupees.
Brahmins for their care	$3\frac{1}{4}$
Goldsmiths	$3\frac{1}{4}$
Gold washers	$2\frac{1}{4}$
	$8\frac{3}{4}$
Other mint charges as above	$11\frac{1}{4}$

Rupees...20 per thousand.

It will be seen by the following resolution that Governor Macrae endeavoured to put matters to rights,—1st, By prohibiting the export of silver from the Company's bounds, and thus compelling the merchants to coin their silver at Fort St. George; 2ndly, By lowering the Company's custom ½ per cent and the mint charges ½ per cent, or altogether 10 rupees per thousand. Henceforth then the custom and charges at Madras would be 30 rupees per thousand; whilst the custom and charges at St. Thomé, Arcot, and Covelong would be nominally 21 rupees per thousand, but actually 31 rupees 11 annas per thousand. The original entry will serve to render the subject more intelligible.

"Monday, 8th March, 1725. Messrs. Pitt, Benyon, and Emmerson deliver in a report of the coinage, together with an account of the charges and customs collected at our Mint, and those in the country; as likewise an account of the produce of a hundred ounces of silver of the fineness of the Rupee in our and St. Thomé Mints.

"This matter being fully debated it was upon the whole agreed, that no silver except rupees shall be permitted to be exported to any part of the coast of Coromandel under penalty of confiscation, half to the informer and half to the Company; and the Secretary do give notice hereof at all the public places in the town.

"As by the calculates and reports abovementioned, it appears that our rupee is two per cent. dearer to the merchants than the St. Thomé and Arcot rupee; it was further argued that we ought to find out some method to lessen the charge of coinage, that so we may bring it nearer to a par with the country coin; and it appearing that the Brahmins actually indisburse 11¼ rupees per thousand, and that they must have something besides for their trouble, it was plain their custom could not be reduced above a ½ per cent; which not being sufficient it was agreed to strike off a half per cent likewise from the custom paid the Company; which it is hoped will be approved by the Honorable Court of Directors for the following reasons.

"First, that the present charge of coinage being 4 per cent in our Mint, and but 21 per thousand in the St. Thomé Mint, nobody will bring any silver to us, but on the contrary carry it away thither; but that when our custom is reduced to three per cent, the difference will be so much less that probably we may have the greatest part of the coinage return to us, especially since our rupee is in greater esteem in the country than theirs.

"Secondly, that we shall receive orders from Europe in two years; and if our Honorable Masters shall disapprove hereof, which we cannot believe they will, it may be laid on again.

"Thirdly, that at present the revenue is sunk to almost nothing, so that should no more silver be coined here than has been for sometime past, the difference will be very inconsiderable; whereas should we hereby regain the coinage it will be very apparently advantageous to the Company.

"Lastly, that the Company will save ½ per cent in the coinage of their own silver; which as we coin one-third generally of what goes down to the

Bay, will very near if not over compensate for the reduction of the custom on other silver.

"These being the causes why it is thought necessary to lessen the charge of the coinage, it was recommended to the President to talk with the Mint Brahmins, and bring them to an agreement for lowering the charge agreeable to the above resolve, which he accordingly promised."

How far the Government order respecting the exportation of silver was regarded by the Madras merchants may be gathered from the following entry.

"Tuesday, 30th March, 1725. Two parcels of silver having been seized last night upon some shroffs, who were carrying it out of the bounds, contrary to the late order affixed at all the gates and in all the languages, so that the proprietors could not pretend ignorance :—agreed that it be confiscated ; and Mr. Hubban offering to take it at $15\frac{1}{2}$ dollars for ten pagodas, the Secretary was ordered to weigh it off to him and receive the money, which is to be divided agreeably to the said order at the gates, half to the Company and half to the informer."

The following petition is interesting from illustrating the mode in which private property was originally acquired in the Madras Presidency. It was received by the Government on the 30th of March, 1725.

"To the Honorable James Macrae, Esq.

President and Governor of Fort St. George.

"The humble petition of Maria Pois, Widow, showeth, That a few years after the Honorable

Company's settlement here, a great many inhabitants, and your petitioner's grand father, planted gardens without any title thereto from the then President and Council. Some of their posterity have sold this ground and gardens as their own, some part to the inhabitants to build on, and some still enjoy it themselves; several have also since his Honor Harrison's time planted gardens without any title, and enjoy them as their own. But your petitioner's grand father, believing it proper to have a title to his garden, and having then an interest with the Honorable the President, Council, and Gentlemen in the place was promised the title; but in the interim he died, and his son his successor, being soft and illiterate, lost his father's interest, but got a cowle from the Honorable the President and Council for thirty-one years, contrary to his father's request and desire; and if he had not troubled the Honorable President and Council for a cowle, might have enjoyed it as the rest have done, him and his heirs for ever. All this your petitioner was unacquainted with till the time was expired. Your poor petitioner having built a house, planted trees, and brought the garden to a vast perfection, this your petitioner laid before the then President, how simply the son of the deceased managed it; to insist on a cowle but for 31 years, when the rest have ever since enjoyed the same as their own and heirs for ever.

" Now the Honorable President and Council compassionately took this, your petitioner's case, into consideration; and rented said house and

Garden to your petitioner; it being extremely hard, after having built the house and brought the garden into perfection, to lose all, your petitioner having no other subsistance. This Garden your petitioner has rented of the Honorable Company ever since the expiration of the cowle.

"Your petitioner is now informed that said house and garden is to be put up at outcry to rent; if so it is an immediate ruin to your poor petitioner, it being your petitioner's only subsistance; she, having no habitation or place of abode, most humbly begs your Honor will, out of your abundant clemency and goodness, look upon this your petitioners case with compassion, and suffer her to rent said house and garden as usual, as she answers yearly the income of the garden to the Honorable Company. If not your petitioner will be reduced to extreme want and misery. Therefore humbly begs your Honor will continue your poor petitioner to rent said house and garden, and as in duty bound shall ever pray."

Governor Macrae however showed himself to be a stern man, not easily moved by petitions whether from widows or from any one else. Accordingly the prayer of Maria Pois was rejected, and it was agreed that her farm should be put up to public outcry.

Our next extract shows that the arbitrary order for prohibiting the exportation of silver was now extended to gold.

"Tuesday, 6th April. The President acquainted the Board that several shoes of gold* had been

---

* A "shoe of gold" was ten thousand pagodas.

lately carried out of the bounds, which he believed was to be coined at St. Thomé ; and therefore he proposed that an order should be made prohibiting any gold, except what is wrought or ready coined, shall be carried out of the bounds under penalty of confiscation, the one half to the Company and the other to the informer ; which is agreed to and the Secretary ordered to affix a note at the gates accordingly."

It will be seen from the following entry how the occupations of the Governors in the olden time differed from those of the more aristocratic Presidents of modern times.

"Monday, 21st June. The President and Council met in the Sorting Godown, and examined the Fort St. David Cloth, which proved pretty good. They also examined several parcels of what was brought to be sorted here, which they found for the generality amended in the number of threads, but so thin that it was not fit for the Company's use."

The following extract shows that Governor Macrae was learning a lesson in free trade.

"Saturday, 3rd July, 1725. The prohibition some time since laid on the exportation of silver and gold into the country, which was then thought for the benefit of our Honorable Masters, having been now found to occasion a general stagnation of trade, and likewise to have fallen the price of silver very considerably, which will in the main vastly overbalance the gain by the coinage.

"Agreed that the said prohibition be taken off,

and that the Secretary do give public notice thereof at the gates."

Our next extracts, referring to the renting of the three out villages, will explain themselves.

"Saturday, 3rd July, 1725. The Lease of the Farms of Egmore, Persewauk, and Tandore being expired, the President informed the Board that he had received proposals from the present Renters, who had agreed to take them at the rent of 14,000 pagodas, provided they might have them for ten years. But that if they could not have them for longer time than the former lease, they would give but one thousand pagodas per annum, because that they actually lost in the last three years, though very plentiful ones, six hundred pagodas; but that having a long lease, they might have some encouragement to improve the lands, which they shall not have in taking them only for three years, which being considered, it was agreed that they be let on the above terms."

"Monday, 12th July. The President informed the Board that he had got the old Renters of Egmore, Persewauk, and Tandore, to give 1,450 pagodas per annum for the rent of those villages for ten years next ensuing; and that Poncala Kishna, the tobacco farmer, was security for the performance of agreements; which being the utmost he could raise the rent to, the Cowle was produced and signed to Kishna Reddee Chandra Seaca, and Chittombee."

The following extract refers to almost the only difference which ever arose between Governor Macrae and the native powers.

"Monday, 23rd August, 1725. Sometime since eight bales of goods being brought hither on one of our ships belonging to a Moorman, were attached for a debt due to Mr. Sitwell from the said Moorman, who is since run away to Covelong; and the goods have been claimed by the Nabob as his, and bought for his account; which demand being now again repeated, it is agreed that since the Nabob declares the goods are his, it is better to let them go, than make any dispute thereupon. Wherefore the President is desired to write him that upon giving up the Moorman, and paying the Company's customs, the goods shall be delivered to his order."

The Nabob however seems to have refused to deliver up the Moorman, or to pay the Company's customs. A correspondence accordingly ensued which spread over the greater part of a year; and was at length brought to a conclusion on the 21st July, 1726. We give the extract from the consultations of that day.

"The President represents to the Board that he had been long importuned by Nabob Sadutalla Khan, by pressing letters and frequent messages, to deliver up the eight bales of goods mentioned in Consultation held the 23rd August 1725, to have been attached here by the creditors of Shaak Bonlaki for the payment of his debts, as belonging to the said Shaak Bonlaki; but that the Nabob continues to claim them as belonging to himself, and insists peremptorily upon their being delivered to him; and that without his demand is complied with, he, the President apprehends a breach with him unavoidable; which in our present circumstances would be of very great prejudice to the Company's affairs.

"This matter having been considered by the Board, and the consequences a breach at this time with the Nabob might produce having been duly weighed; and it having likewise been admitted that the creditors of Shaak Bonlaki might have had reasons to believe that the eight bales in question did belong to him, yet the Nabob's right to them could not be disproved; and he continuing to insist so very peremptorily upon having them delivered to him, notwithstanding the President endeavours by repeated messages and many letters to prevail with him to suffer them to be sold for account of Shaak Bonlaki's creditors. There being no prospect of prevailing with the Nabob, it is ordered that Mr. Turner do deliver to Nabob's order the said eight bales of goods in dispute."

The following perjury cases are worthy of being preserved, as showing how false witnesses were punished in the olden time.

"Friday, 10th September, 1725. In the examination of Anconah's affair one Magdulla Kistna confessed himself perjured, by a declaration under his own hand, whereupon he was ordered into confinement; and it is now ordered that he be Pilloried to-morrow at the usual hours, and afterwards whipped at the Choultry, and then released from his imprisonment."

A year afterwards we find Governor Macrae still determined to put down perjury with a strong hand. He had been engaged upon deciding upon

a long list of appeals from the Mayor's Court,
chiefly equity cases connected of course with wills,
bonds, and disputes about property of all kinds.
These interminable and complicated cases may
have been interesting to the parties concerned, but
present not a particle of interest now, beyond the
fact that they are marked by contradictions, palpable perjuries, forgeries, and oppressions of all kinds.
Many of the cases were reversed by Governor Macrae,
whilst others were sent home to be adjudicated
on by the Directors, and even to be tried in Westminster Hall; from which we may infer that the
old stories of corruption in the Mayor's Court, so
frequent in the narratives of old travellers, were
not without some foundation in truth. How far
Governor Macrae was exasperated at this state of
things may be gathered from the following punishment ordered upon another perjurer.

"Monday, 29th August, 1726. Ordered that
Arnagery for punishment of his crime of perjury,
and for terror to all such abandoned villains, be
remanded to the Choultry prison, and be thence
conveyed to the Pillory every first day of the
month for the next six months, and set upon it
from ten to twelve o'clock; and immediately after
he is taken down from the Pillory to receive thirty-nine lashes each time at the whipping post, and
be afterwards turned out of the bounds with order
never to return again under severe punishment."

The following extract respecting the circulation
of false pagodas will explain itself.

"Monday, 27th September, 1725. The President informed the Board of a complaint the

Shroffs had made to him, that vast quantities of pagodas had been brought into the place lately, which were worse than Pagodamatt, and bore the Negapatam stamp so nicely counterfeited, that it was almost impossible to distinguish them ; and therefore he proposed that some method should be taken to stop this evil, which being for some time debated, it was agreed that the Secretary do affix a note at the gates to give notice, that whosoever should be found bringing in such bad pagodas, or offering them in payment, should be punished at the discretion of the Governor and Council, and the money be forfeited, one half to the informer and one half to the Company ; and that whatever shroff should find such pagodas should be obliged to carry them to some one of the Justices of the Choultry to be defaced, or if he did not, he should be pilloried and whipped out of the bounds."

Governor Macrae was far too fond of Committees of inquiry to let such a matter pass without the most searching investigation. Accordingly about three weeks afterwards we find the following report entered in the consultations, which will be found interesting as illustrating the condition of the country generally.

" Monday, 18th October, 1725. The following report was presented to the Honorable James Macrae, Esq., the President and Governor of Fort St George and Council.

" Honorable Sir and Sirs,

" The committee you were pleased to appoint,

to enquire into the business of the present current pagodas, and put a stop to an abuse which will at last be attended with such dangerous consequences, do now humbly lay before you their proceedings and opinion of the most proper remedy effectually to prevent this mischief without giving a shock to commerce.

"We find upon examining the shroffs that this has been a growing evil, introduced by the corruption of the country Government in conniving at the circulation of any sort of pagodas, provided their profits from those who have the liberty of coining them are answerable; and as this is so considerable an advantage to them it is not from the Nabob we are to expect any relief. Therefore we thought it most proper to have the opinion of the merchants in general which method we should pursue; who on a meeting came to this resolution, which we offer to your honors as what we likewise think sufficient to answer the design, without risking a stagnation in the circulation.

"That five shops shall be appointed in the most convenient parts of the town, for the exchanging of all money which is necessary for the currency of the Bazar; in each of which must be placed, two shroffs, a gold smith, and a Company's peon, whose stations are to be changed every day with power to cut or deface all such pagodas as are found to be bad. As to payments of large sums the merchants themselves will undoubtedly be cautious for their own security, and take such care as not to be imposed upon in what they receive, by employing such shroffs in whose fidelity they may confide.

"George Mortan Pitt.
"Nathaniel Turner.
"Richard Benyon.
"John Emmerson."

"The most convenient places for the shops are Jappa Chetty's Street, Choultry Street, Mutala Pettah, Pedda Naick's Pettah, Jaga Mulla Street."

Another point which attracted the attention of Governor Macrae at this time is also worthy of some notice. For some years past different sums of money had been lodged in the Company's cash chest at Fort St. George on account of the Jesuit Missionaries in China; for which the Government of Fort St. George, under orders from the Court of Directors, had allowed interest at the rate of six per cent. per annum. In September 1725, Father Moriset at Fort St. David wrote to Governor Macrae respecting a further deposit of cash, on the same terms; but the economical President, having plenty of money in hand, considered that this would be a favorable moment for reducing the yearly interest from six per cent. to five. The matter led to a Committee of inquiry into all the monies lodged in the Company's chest at various times by the Jesuit Missionaries in China. The following extracts from their report will be sufficient to explain the state of affairs. It will be seen that the sums deposited were not to be returned; the yearly interest paid being supposed to be a sufficient return, without any repayment of the principal. We must therefore suppose that the sums lodged at Fort St. George were of the nature of an endowment to provide for the perpetual support of the Jesuit Missionaries in China. Our report from whence the following extracts are taken is dated 21st July 1726.

"To the Honorable James Macrae, Esq.,
President and Governor and Council of
Fort St. George.

"Honorable Sir and Sirs,

"In pursuance of an order of Council, we lay before your Honors what orders have been received from the Honorable Court of Directors, relating to the receiving into the Company's cash money from the Jesuit Missionaries in China at interest; together with an account of the several sums that have been hitherto received into cash for their account, and what has been writ by this Board to the Honorable Court of Directors on that subject.

"We find that the sum of 10,000 pagodas was received into cash for their account the 31st August 1721, but no interest to be paid them thereupon till the Company's order should be had for that effect.

"The Honorable Court of Directors in their general letter dated 26th April 1722 say as follows.

"We have had application made us by Monsr. Labbe, agent for the French Jesuit Missionaries in China, to receive 10,000 pagodas of theirs into our cash at Fort St. George; that President Hastings had received the money conditionally to await our orders, though he had no occasion for any having a flowing cash; that said agent desires the money may remain in our cash and the proprietors to be for ever dispossest of the property thereof, on the Company's yearly allowing them a reasonable interest. We have considered of the whole, and in regard we sometimes have and at other times have not occasion to borrow money at Fort St. George; therefore we are willing to allow them a certain interest of six per cent. though it is one more than we pay here per annum, and hope it will be to their satisfaction."

"In consequence of which general letter a bond was executed by the Governor and Council, and delivered to the Agent to the said Missionaries, to pay them interest 600 pagodas per annum upon the sum of 10,000 pagodas received.

"The 25th February 1724 their agent paid into cash the further sum of 2,000 pagodas; and the same day the Governor and Council delivered him a bond for six per cent. interest per annum upon it.

The receipt of this sum was advised to England to which the Honorable Court answered as follows:

"Your letter advises that the Jesuits in China have by their attorney offered to deposit in our cash with you a sum of money, which you intend to receive and give bond to pay six per cent. per annum for it. Padre de Goville, lately returned to Europe, has by writing requested of us to receive 10,000 pagodas into our cash, and to pay the Missionaries for it 600 pagodas a year, which we have agreed to."

It would thus appear that at this time the Company had agreed to receive in all the sum of 20,000 pagodas on behalf of the Jesuit Missionaries in China, for which they were to pay a perpetual interest at the rate of 6 per cent. per annum, the principal not to be returned. Accordingly it would seem that the China Missionaries paid in that amount, and derived from the Company alone a yearly income of twelve hundred pagodas, or about five hundred pounds sterling.

CHAPTER XXXIV.

GOVERNORSHIP OF MR. JAMES MACRAE.
1726—27.

The commercial character of the administration of Mr. James Macrae has been already noticed, and the very lucid manner in which commercial transactions are recorded in the consultation books of the period, induces us to pay more attention to such extracts as serve to illustrate the mode in which the Company carried on their business with Native merchants, either for providing a sufficient number of bales of Native cloth for exportation to Europe, or for disposing of broadcloth, iron, and other articles of home produce which had been imported from England. These extracts however we shall not group by themselves, but simply arrange them, together with other selections, in strict chronological order; by which means the reader will be enabled to form a better idea of the miscellaneous character and general scope of the records themselves, than by any other method.

Our first extract refers to the supervision of native goods maintained in old time by the Government of Fort St. George.

"Thursday, 6th January, 1826. The Warehouse-keeper reported to the Board, that the chintzes being brought from painting (dyeing) had been examined at the Sorting Godown, and that it was the general opinion of the Sorters that both the cloth and paintings were worse than the musters; wherefore they had resolved, if the Board approved thereof, to allow the merchants only 35 pagodas per corge, instead of 40 for the cloth; and the painter 47½ pagodas per corge, instead of 60, which they used to have. This being approved, the merchants were called in and told the resolution of the Board."

"At the same time the Warehouse-keeper reported that the Pulicat Betillas, brought in by the merchants upon the muster, for which in the contract we were to give 120 pagodas per corge, were vastly inferior to the muster; and that it had been agreed in the Sorting Godown that 100 pagodas per corge was the value of them; so that he (the President) desired the order of the Board for bringing them to account at that price, which was agreed to, and the merchants accordingly told these resolutions."

The Native merchants appeared to have submitted to the reductions very quietly, for no demur on their part is entered in the proceedings. When however the Board desired to make a contract with the same merchants, as to the quantity of Europe cloth they should purchase, or the quantity of native cloth they should supply, it was not always found so easy to deal with them, as will be seen by the following extract.

"Thursday, 3d March 1726. Our Merchants were called in, and a proposal made, to them as follows.

"That they shall engage in a contract at Fort

St. George for 2000 bales of cloth, to be delivered to us one half in August, and the remainder by the last of January next."

"That they shall take all the broad cloth (from Europe) at the usual advance, to be kept under two keys, one of which to be left with themselves and the other with the Warehouse-keeper; that before they take any out of the warehouses, it shall be paid for in ready money; and that the whole amount shall be paid off by the 1st of April 1727. In consideration of which the Board (they were told) would abate the penalty of 30,000 pagodas, to be inflicted for breach of the last contract, to 10,000 pagodas; but if they would not do this they must expect to pay the whole amount of the penalty.

"Upon the hearing these proposals, the Merchants immediately declared they could not engage by any means, either to take the broad cloth, or contract for above 800 bales; and to this they adhered for a considerable time, but at last after near two hours debate, finding the Board determined to exact the whole penalty if they did not agree to the terms proposed, and being excused from any contract at Fort St. David, they consented; having first obtained a promise of the Board that if they complied within 300 bales, no penalty should be exacted."

Our next extract refers to a forged bond, found amongst the papers of a deceased Company's servant named Woolley.

"Thursday, 30th June, 1726. Captain Richard Upton, representing that a forged note, mentioning that he had received of Robert Woolley deceased 1000 ounces of Silver, for which he was to be accountable, having been found amongst said Woolley's papers, whereof payment had been demanded, signed as by him and witnessed as by Messrs. Samuel Harrison, and Richard Stephens; and that he and the said pretended witnesses were ready to make solemn oath, that neither he nor they ever had any knowledge of any such note, nor ever signed the same. Therefore craving that he and they might be sworn to the truth of what he affirmed, in order to prevent any demand being made upon him for the said 1000 ounces of Silver.

"Captain Upton and Messrs. Harrison and Stephens being called in, were interrogated as to the signing and witnessing the said note; and affirmed each of them that it was forged and without their knowledge; that there was no similitude of hand writing, and severally made oath to what they affirmed. Whereupon it was ordered that the said note appearing to be forged be cancelled; which was done."

The next entries which we consider worthy of preservation are still more curious. It has been seen that the revenues of Trivatore, and of the other out villages belonging to the Company, were farmed out to some of the Company's Merchants, on their engaging to pay a certain sum (1450 pagodas) per annum. The Merchants in their turn rented the villages to a man named Mahadin, and this Renter appears to have treated the inhabitants in a barbarous and oppressive manner. Accordingly two of the villagers sent in the following petition to Governor Macrae in which all their grievances are specified. The petition will be found to form an admirable illustration of Native administration in the olden time.

"To the Honourable James Macrae, Esq. President and Governor of Fort St. George, The humble petition of the inhabitants of Vessa Caward,

"Showeth,—That the Company has let out Trivatore and the other out villages to the Company's merchants, who during five years that they kept them in their own hands, allowed your petitioners all their privileges and allowances as usual, and they lived very happily. Then one Mahadin took these villages of these merchants, and promised to allow your petitioners the same privileges and allowances as the said merchants had done; but he has acted contrary, and not given them any privilege or allowance. Upon which they asked him the reason; and he replied that the Company had sold those villages to him, and he could do what he pleased. The said privileges and allowances due to your petitioners for these six years amounts to about 100 pagodas. Besides this he has distressed your petitioners and laid many hardships on them. He set one of their Pariahs half way in the ground, where he kept him three hours and fined him. Another Pariah he chaubucked 25 blows, put him into the stocks, and kept him there an hour. He tied one of their shepherd's neck and heals, for four or five days, an hour each day, and beat him very much and fined him. He broke a Talliar's back, and turned him out of the village. He tied a shopkeeper of the village, neck and heels,

putting a heavy stone on his back, and kept him so
an hour and then fined him. He served another
shopkeeper in the same manner. He has done too
many other barbarous actions to your petitioners
to give your Honor in writing an account of. Therefore they humbly implore to take their case into
consideration, and order them satisfaction. They
cannot go on with their business if he be continued the Renter. Your petitioners hope your
Honor will do them justice, and they as in duty
bound shall ever pray."

To this petition, a Native named Chandarasaha,
who seems to have been the steward of Mahardin,
sent in a counter-petition, denying or explaining
away the charges. This also is a gem in its way.

" The petition of Chandarasaha.

" Humbly showeth,—Whereas your petitioner
has been falsely accused that he has punished the
inhabitants beyond reason, and as to his burying
the man half under ground is utterly false; for
the man having, contrary to order, let the water
run the wrong course, was punished according to
custom; that is by laying his hand in the water
course, which filled with sand and the Company's
chop put thereon. And as for your petitioner's
forcing of unreasonable forfeits from the inhabitants, it is also false; for the inhabitants having
complained to your petitioner that a milkman's
measure was less than it should be, which your
petitioner by examining found true; therefore fined
him 6 fanams; and to a seller of tobacco and
betel, for selling contrary to the renter's order, was
fined 6 fanams. As to the Talliar, he stole away

above three pagodas worth of Mangoes, for which he paid 48 fanams ; and when the Talliar had found the thief, your petitioner told him that he might do what he would. Also the said Talliar (i. e. the Talliar who was the thief not the Talliar who had arrested him) took more than his right of the paddy, and took it away without leave ; for which fault he was tied neck and heels two hours. And as for your petitioner's putting any body in irons, it is false ; but a Pariah being taken stealing paddy, was by your petitioner's order put in the stocks. That the three persons before mentioned have sold the Company's ground, which when the Buyer came to take possession, your petitioner refused to let him take it without your Honors leave. That your petitioner for the good of the inhabitants did lend them money, and let them have paddy to the value of pagodas 260 ; and when your petitioner demands his money then they begin to make a disturbance. Now three of the inhabitants being come to this place, they have taken opportunity to say that all the inhabitants will leave the place. The Pedda Naik's allowance of ground in the said village is 4440 yards, but now he has taken 14,400 yards, which is more than his due by near 10,000 yards ; which for these four years he has not sown, nor would he let any body else, to the loss of about pagodas 229 ; and now about a thousand yards which he sowed, the paddy now lies there and he refuses to divide it. Therefore your poor petitioner most humbly requests your Honor to give him justice, and as in duty bound shall ever pray."

Governor Macrae's action upon these two petitions will be gathered from the following extract.

"Friday, 26th August, 1726. The President delivers into the Board two petitions which had been presented to him; one from some inhabitant of Vessa Cawarda, against Mahadin the present Renter; the other from Chandarasaha, who acted as steward to the said Mahadin, and put his orders in execution. Which being read, the President acquaints the Board that both parties had been before him; that he had heard them separately and also given then a joint hearing; that he had examined witnesses to the truth of the facts charged against Mahadin, and heard the Company's Merchants upon the affair. That from the whole, it appeared to him, that the said Mahadin had been guilty, and was fully convicted by evidence, of the charge delivered against him in the first petition; which is even acknowledged by the said Chandarasah in his petition, who acted by order and authority from Mahadin in all these matters, as is by Mahadin owned.

" This affair being taken into consideration, particularly the presumption of Mahadin in taking upon him to levy fines and inflict corporal punishments upon the Honorable Company's subjects without authority; which had actually frightened several inhabitants out of the bounds, as the President further informs us had been proved before him, and would deter others from coming out of the country to secure themselves and properties under the protection of English Law as usual. To prevent any such violences and extortions in time to come, it is resolved that no Renters or Farmers of Villages have authority to levy fines, or inflict corporal punishment upon the inhabitants; and that for an example Mahadin be ordered to resign his Cowle of Trivatore and the other villages into the hands of the Company's Merchants; having forfeited the same by his unwarrantable actions; and for a further punishment to him and example for others, he be fined in the sum of 50 pagodas, to be paid into the Company's Cash, and that the Secretary do demand the same."

This decision was rigidly carried out, for three days afterwards we find an entry to the effect that Mahadin had given up the Cowle and paid the fine of fifty pagodas.

Perhaps few entries are more illustrative of the character of Governor Macrae, than the following attempt at reduction in the matter of Hospital charges. The decision of the canny Scot is wonderfully suggestive. How far it contributed to the comfort of the sick we leave to the judgment of our readers.

"Saturday, 17th September, 1726. The President represents to the Board that, upon reading the particulars of the article of Hospital charges, he apprehends there are several of them too large, and others unnecessary, and ought to be reduced and discontinued; which being taken into consideration, and the several particulars again read and enquired into, it was represented that the Surgeon, who has the immediate direction of the Hospital, always insists that the present charge is necessary for entertaining and recovering the sick, and that no reduction can be made of it.

"Ordered, that whereas it hath been for some time the custom for one of the Surgeons to have the immediate care of the Hospital solely, they do in future act each six months by turns; that by their acting thus interchangeably, we may make the experiment whether the one cannot reduce the charge of the Hospital lower than the other, which it is believed out of emulation to recommend themselves, they may do."

Next follows a curious entry respecting the horses sanctioned by the Company for the use of the President.

"Monday, 7th November, 1726. The President represents to the Board, that their being now remaining alive only two Chaise horses belonging to the Company, and these so weak that to save them he had been obliged for above a twelve month to make use of a pair of Manilla horses of his own for his Chaise; that the Honorable Company had allowed his predecessor three horses for his Chaise, one of which had been dead some time, and the other two so much wore that they are not now fit to do the service of one; that the Company's piebald horse was lately dead, and that the horses for his guards were very old, and some of them quite worn out, that he was now obliged to allow two Pegu horses of his own for that service. Wherefore he proposed to the Board to purchase the said two Pegu horses for the use of his guards, and the two Manilla Chaise horses for his Chaise, on the Company's account ; being all of them young, well broke, and seasoned to the country.

"Resolved that the foresaid four horses be purchased for the Company for the service above mentioned, at 150 pagodas each ; and that the Paymaster do pay for the same ; and that one of the worst of the guard horses be sold at public outcry as soon as the season permits the usual concourse of people at the sea gate."

Whilst Governor Macrae was thus attentive to his own interests, he was by no means unmindful of the interests of the younger servants of the Company, as will be seen by the following extract, which is well worthy not only of preservation but of more general imitation.

"Tuesday, 15th November, 1726. The President represents further to the Board, that he thinks it a great discouragement to the subordinate servants, and inconsistent with that emulation we ought to excite amongst them to distinguish themselves by merit in order to their advancement, that some should be continued so long in laborious stations without any profit, while others enjoyed places of profit and that required little application. Particularly that Paul Foxley had served under the Export Ware housekeeper above five years, and discharged that trust faithfully to the approbation of his superiors ; and that Edward Croke, had continued several years Writer at the Sea gate, in which station he had had but very little opportunity of exerting himself in the Service. Therefore moved that Mr. Foxley be appointed in Mr. Croke's room Writer at the Sea gate."

"Resolved that Paul Foxley do enter upon the employ of Writer at the Sea gate the first of January next, and that Ralph Mansell do succeed him in the Export Warehouse at the same time. Edward Croke being Senior in standing to all the Servants under the Council, it was judged reasonable that he should be advanced to a station of a higher trust in the Service. Wherefore resolved that he be employed in the station of Receiver of the Honorable Company's customs, and that he do enter upon the same the first of January next."

The following petition is simply an illustration of the times.

"The humble petition of Hirdaram.

"Sheweth,—That your petitioner's brother, Nundaram, brought 2773 rupees from Arcot, and procured therewith a Bill of Exchange on Bengal from Governor Collet. Your petitioner's brother being murdered by robbers on his way to Bengal, the Bill has not yet been paid; which your Petitioner hearing came to Madras with the Nabob's perwanna to demand the repayment of the said money from Governor Elwick and Mr. Benyon, attorneys to Governor Collet; who told your petitioner that if he could bring a sufficient security to indemnify them they would pay him. Your petitioner has now brought an attestation, signed by many great Gentlemen at Arcot, witnessing that your petitioner is the next heir to the said deceased Nundaram; which your petitioner hopes is a sufficient authority for receiving the said money; and that your Honor would please to give such orders therein as your Honor shall think meet."

It will be sufficient to say that the security offered by the gentlemen of Arcot, some of whom stood high in the favour of the Nabob, was deemed sufficient, and the money was accordingly paid.

Our next extract is another curious illustration of the times; like the previous one it will explain itself.

"Tuesday, 6th December, 1726. Mr. Emmerson, Chief Justice of the Choultry, reports to the Board a late instance of a woman slave having attempted to poison a whole family; that the poison had actually been given, but operating very violently quickly discovered itself, and the effect was prevented by immediately administering proper emetics, and that the criminal had confessed the fact. That in order to strike terror into such abandoned mind's and for securing the lives of the inhabitants in future from atrocious attempts, the Justices of the Choultry were come to a resolution to punish the said criminal in the most public and exemplary manner, the approbation of this Board being first had; and that he was further empowered from the Justices of the Choultry to represent to the Board that, considering how easily poisons are procurable here, as in the late instance by low miscreants, even Sublimate Mercury, it will be highly necessary to publish a prohibition of selling or delivering poisons of any sort, but under a proper regulation; that therefore they were of opinion that no person should be permitted to sell or deliver poison, without first acquainting one of the Justices of it, under the penalty of confiscation of half of their estate, and being further liable to corporal punishment at the discretion of the said Justice.

"Approved the proceedings of the Justices in their affair, and agreed with them to prohibit the selling or delivering poison without the consent of one of the Justices, and under the penalty above mentioned, and that a prohibition be forthwith published accordingly."

Strange to say we can see no entry of the punishment which was inflicted on the woman. She was probably treated in such a fashion that the Government did not care to place it upon record.

Our next extracts will be found interesting, as exhibiting the amount of expenditure and revenue at Fort St. George and the other settlements on the Coast of Coromandel. We give an extract from the consultation first, and the Accountants' report afterwards.

"Tuesday, 6th December, 1726. Nathaniel Turner, Accountant, delivers into the Board a Report of the state of the Honorable Company's expenses and customs at their settlements upon this coast, at the balancing and closing the general books ending April last; which is read and ordered to be entered after this consultation.

"The said Report being maturely examined and considered, the Board are agreed that the reduction of the charges of their settlement, and of Fort St. David, has been carried as far as it has been hitherto practicable.

"That the increase of the expense of Vizagapatam last year, was owing to the additional number of soldiers we were obliged to send and continued there, for the security of that factory, while the country round it was ravaged and they threatened by contending armies ; that after the reduction made as advised by Mr. Symonds and Council in their letter to us dated 7th May last, the charge of that settlement will appear to have been considerably diminished upon the next years books.

"That we must likewise refer to next years books for the reduction of expense at Masulipatam and Madapallum.

"That the decrease of the Sea Customs, and the increase of the Land Customs here at Madras last year, are owing to one and the same cause ; — they having ordered the whole 5 per cent custom to be paid at the Choultry upon goods imported from the country ; whereas formerly only $2\frac{1}{2}$ per cent was accounted for there and the other $2\frac{1}{2}$ at the Sea gate upon exportation of said goods."

"That the decrease of the Customs is general last year, here and at Fort St. David, and from there account of the proceedings, seems indeed totally owing at Fort St. David to the five per cent charged in said preceding year upon so large a quantity of turned out cloths, that had been brought in there upon former investments ; and here in part to the like five per cent custom having been charged our Merchants upon a considerable quantity of turned out cloths. Besides which the customs have been considerably lessened in this fort last year, and will more considerably this, by the great decay in the trade to Manilla, and the almost total loss of the trade of the Patans from Bengal; both which trades being principally in fine goods, and formerly to a great value, were very considerable branches of the Sea Customs."

Here follows the report of the Accountant to the Governor and Council.

" Honorable Sir and Sirs,

"The General Books of this settlement ending April, 1726 being balanced and closed, and the subordinate Factory's Books, ending April 1726 beng sent up, I am to lay before your Honors the last years expense of this settlement and its subordinates on the coast, that you may please to consider whether any part of the charges can be saved to the Honorable Company.

"The Expense of this settlement of Fort St. George on the balance of our Books ending April 1725 amounted to Pagodas....................		39034 34 28
"The expense as per our Books ending April 1726 is as follows:		
"Charges Garrison.. .. Pagodas..	15779 26 77	
"Presents..	174 18 20	
"Charges cattle..	800 0 0	
"Charges Extraordinary	173 21 10	
"Fortifications and repairs	1495 29 70	
"Charges Diet	7000 0 0	
"Account Salary..	3265 34 67	
"Charges Hospital..	769 35 20	
"Charges General	6086 22 44	
		35546 8 68
"Lessened the expense of this place this year..	.. ..	3488 25 40
"The expense of Fort St. David on the balance of their Books ending April 1725 amounted to Pagodas..	.. ..	29268 28 15
"The expense as per their Books ending April 1726 is as follows:		
"Charges Garrison	13082 7 52	
"Charges Extraordinary.. ..	342 26 35	
"Peons and Servants wages	3285 6 0	
"Charges cattle	600 0 0	
"Fortifications and repairs.. ..	96 34 10	
"Charges Diet	2966 4 0	
"Account Salary..	941 30 40	
"Presents	12 33 0	
"Charges Hospital	219 28 26	
"Charges General..	5668 3 58	
		24215 29 61
Lessened the expense of that place this year.. Pagodas..		5052 34 34

"The Expense of Viragapatam on the Balance of their Books ending April 1725 amounted to.. . . Pagodas. 5836 1 61
"The expense as per their Books ending April 1726 is as follows.

"Charges Garrison..	2103	6	0
"Presents	480	6	69
"Charges Diet	578	30	0
"Charges Extraordinary	151	33	35
"Fortifications and repairs	336	33	3
"Account Salary	472	34	19
"Account Gardens	35	19	41
"Account Wax	46	34	64
"Servants' wages	1492	25	77
"Factory' provisions	25	1	16
"Account repairs	18	6	68
"Charges General	373	13	39

———— 6065 29 31

"Increased the Expence of that place this year .. .. Pagodas. 227 27 56
"Which is occasioned by 20 European Soldiers being sent down to that settlement on account of the troubles in the country in the beginning of the year; ten (10) of which soldiers are still continued there, and adds to the expense of that place; but since Mr. Symonds going down he writes us that he has in pursuance to your Honors' orders made a considerable reduction in the Peons' and servants' wages, which reduction will appear in their next general Books ending April 1727. .. .. 8313 32 24

"The Expense of Ingeram for one year ending April 1725, was .. .. Pagodas. 1315 19 18
"The Expense of Ingeram from April 1725 to May 1726 is 1182 13 63

"Lessened the Expence of that place this year,.. .. .. 233 5 35
"The Expense of Masulipatam and Madapollum was last year .. Pagodas. 628 34 40
Do. this year ending April 1726 .. .. 623 28 43

"Decreased this year in their expenses 6 5 77
"The Expenses of these two factories will next year be considerably decreased by the regulation your Honors have lately made therein.
"Lessened this year in the expenses of this settlement and its subordinates .. .. Pagodas. 8553 7 56

"Thus having given your Honors account of the Honorable Company's annual expenses on this coast, I shall proceed to lay before you an account of the produce of their customs in this place and at Fort St. David ending April 1726.

"The Sea Customs of Fort St. George.		
"On the balance of our Books ending April 1725 amounted to..	36051	8 29
"The amount Ditto for one year ending April 1726..	28560	7 46
Decrease in this revenue..	..	7491 0 63
"The amount of the Land Customs of Fort St. George.		
"On the Balance of their Books ending April 1725 was..	4455	8 29
Do. April 1726 was	10185	33 76
Increase in this revenue..		5730 25 48
"Less this year in the Customs of Fort St. George than last..	..	1760 11 15
"The Revenue of Fort St. David ending April 1726 amounted to	11941	24 75
Do. 1725..	9877	0 38
"Less this year in the Customs of Fort St. David than last	..	2064 24 37
"The Customs of Forts St. George and St. David have on the balance of our general books ending April 1726 Decreased	Pagodas.	3324 35 52

I am with respect,
Honorable Sir and Sirs,
Your most obedient humble servant,
NATHANIEL TURNER,
Accountant.

FORT ST. GEORGE,
6th December 1726.

The following record of an enterprising project in the olden time is very curious.

" Monday, 26th December, 1726. Petition read of Stephen Newcome, requesting leave to build a Sawmill, and a lease for a space of ground to the northward of the White Tower along the sea side, for building the said mill and proper sheds upon. And he being called before the Board, and heard to the benefit he proposes his mill will prove to be to the Company and the Corporation, gave sufficient reasons to believe that it will be of public advantage, and affirmed that he would saw timbers and planks 50 per cent. cheaper upon the cooly hire now usually paid. Besides that he could saw blocks of timber to much greater advantage, and prevent the waste occasioned by the unskillfulness of the present sawers."

"Granted his petition for the space of ground therein mentioned, and ordered a lease to be prepared for the same for 21 years; he paying before signing it 20 pagodas fine into the Company's cash, and annually one pagoda Quit rent during the term of his lease; and in consideration of the expence of preparing the ground, and building the mill and necessary conveniences, and the benefit it will prove to be to the Company and the place,— it is resolved that the sole privilege of sawing timber and plank by a mill be vested in him for 21 years next ensuing, and no other person have that liberty but upon an agreement with him during that time."

We hope that we shall find in future records that this Sawmill proved a successful speculation.

That Mr. Macrae was a most vigilant Governor is further proved by the following entry.

"Monday, 9th January, 1727. The President represents to the Board, that he had observed in the Sorting Godown that a great deal of cloth had been turned out this year, which he was persuaded would upon a re-examination be found as good as muster; that as he would never countenance the taking in bad cloth, so he thought it was not serving the Honorable Company well

to turn out any that was as good as their musters;
that all he proposed or desired was, that justice
might be done our Masters and the Merchants
likewise, that they may not be discouraged from
contracting with us again. He therefore moves
that in order to do justice both to our Masters
and to their Merchants the cloth turned out
this year may be restored." This was of course
agreed to.

The following consultation respecting the best
mode of improving the declining trade of Madras,
is very interesting.

"Tuesday, 31st January, 1727. The Board having taken into consideration the declining state of
the trade of this place, which appears by the
customs to be greatly diminished; and if expedients are not found for its support must in consequence affect every other branch of the Honorable Company's Revenue, and utterly ruin the
inhabitants;—It principally appears to be owing
to the following causes.

"That whereas heretofore the trade was entirely carried on by the shipping of this port, it is
now in part in the possession of the French,
Armenians, and Moors, who traffic on other bottoms and import their Cargoes into other Settlements; which they are enabled to do by the
money taken up here by Respondentia bonds,
and without which they could not carry on so
extensive a trade. It seems most probable that
the preventing this evil will most conduce to
the recovery of the customs, and make all
other ports on this coast dependent on us, though

the duties are less elsewhere ; and whereas several of our English Supra-Cargoes take up large sums of our inhabitants at Respondentia, and afterwards proceed to Bengal, where they take up as much more of persons who are ignorant of their engagements here ; so by thrusting into their private adventures greater quantities of goods than the markets where they are bound can possibly consume, they are forced to be in those ports two seasons to dispose of their own private effects ; to the great prejudice of those concerned in the stock, and puts a stop to the quick circulation ; which will effectually be prevented by letting the Gentlemen in the Bay know what engagements those Supra-Cargoes lie under here, and by degrees reduce trade to its proper bounds, which by this licentious practice has been quite overdone.

" In order therefore, to support the Honorable Company's Revenue, and to prevent the injuries this place receives from these clandestine practices ;—it is resolved that in future all Respondentia bonds, notes, or writings at Respondentia for money lent by the inhabitants of this place,—Company's servants as well as others,—upon all ships trading from this or any other port in India, shall be duly and regularly registered in a book to be kept for that purpose.

" That in case of any Supra-Cargo, Merchant, Commander, Mariner, or other, shall have borrowed money at Respondentia of any of the said inhabitants proving Insolvent, all such bonds so registered shall be accounted and deemed a preferable claim to such as are not.

"That the Sub-Secretary do keep the said Book of Register, and that he shall receive 9 fanams for registering each Respondentia bond or note under 100 pagodas principal, or 18 fanams for each such bond or note for 100 pagodas or upward; that after having registered the said Bonds or notes he shall sign them registered, the day of the month and year; and that the Secretary do put up at the Sea Gate a publication of this resolution in writing in the usual languages for the notice and observation of all the inhabitants."

Our next extracts are curious, as clearly showing how the business between the Government and the Native Merchants was transacted in the Olden Time.

"Saturday, 11th February, 1727. The President acquaints the Board that, after a great deal of management with the Company's Merchants, he had engaged them to agree to a contract for taking off the woollen goods expected upon the next ship from Great Britain, and for providing goods for Europe this season; and delivers in the Contract and the counterpart to the Board. Which being read are approved, and the said Merchants being called in, were interchangeably signed and delivered; and they promise their utmost endeavours to comply with their engagements.

"The President represents to the Board, that the Merchants having received no tasharief according to custom at signing the contract with the Company the two preceding years, and that they now insisted upon their being now tashariefed for the three contracts:—it is ordered that the Warehousekeeper deliver seven pieces fine scarlet cloth for that use. Ordered also that 10,000 pagodas be advanced them out of the 20,000 promised them in the terms of the present contract."

The following is a copy of the contract as entered in the Consultation Book.

"Saturday, 11th February, 1727. A contract made, concluded, and agreed upon this 11th day of February 1727, between James Macrae, Esq. President and Council of Fort St. George in behalf of the English East India Company on the one part, and Sunca Ramah and Tomby Chetty etc. Joint Stock Merchants on the other part.

"The said Merchants do hereby covenant, promise and agree, that they will buy of the said President and Council all the Woollen goods that they shall receive upon the next expected shipping from Great Britain, for the said Company's account, at thirty per cent. advance upon the European price; that it shall be deposited in a Warehouse under two keys, one of which to be kept by the Warehousekeeper and another by the said Merchants; that before they receive any Woollen goods out of the Warehouse they will pay the amount thereof to the Warehousekeeper, and further that they will so receive and pay for the whole quantity on or before the 1st day of October 1728.

"The above said Merchants do further promise, covenant and agree, to and with the said President and Council, that they will provide 3000 bales of cloth of the sortments; to be delivered at least 1,500 bales thereof on or before the 20th day of September next, and the remainder on or before the last day of January following. All the cloths now remaining in the Company's godown unmeasured to be counted in part of the said 3000 bales now contracted for; and the said President and Council do promise to receive the same, provided it be agreeable to our musters.

"The said Merchants do further covenant and agree that they will not demand any money upon account of this contract until the goods are delivered to the Company and embaled; excepting only the sum of 20,000 pagodas which the said President and Council do hereby promise and are obliged to advance to the said Merchants upon this contract; which said sum shall not be by them accounted for until the conclusion hereof, and the closing their accounts with the Company.

"The said Merchants do likewise covenant, and are hereby obliged in case they shall fail in complying with the terms of this contract, to pay a penalty of 20 per cent. for all the bales that they shall deliver short of the number agreed upon; unless it shall be manifestly made appear that troubles in the country have hindered them; provided always, and it is hereby agreed that in case the merchants shall comply with this contract within 500 bales of the whole 3000, that then the President and Council will remit the penalty for the said 500 bales.

"In witness whereof the said President and Council have to one part hereof set their hands, and caused the Company's seal to be affixed; and to the other part the said Merchants have set their hands and seals the day and year first above written."

"SUNCA RAMAH.
"NAIRO BALL CHETTY.
"TOMBY CHETTY.
"COLLASTRI CHETTY.
"MOODU VENKATA CHETTY."

The following story of attempted fraud will explain itself.

"Monday, 3rd April, 1727. Goodapilla Rangappah, having brought a large diamond from the mines to be sold here, and being a stranger, and recommended to Gruapah a goldsmith, to assist him in disposing of the said diamond, he had trusted him with the sale of it. But the said Gruapah, with intentions to defraud Goodapilla of the real value of the diamond, persuaded him upon several delusory pretexts to retire to Conjeveram. In the mean time, that he might carry on the fraud with the greatest security, he possessed the ignorant stranger with several groundless calumnies, to the prejudice of the President's character and to the trade of the place. Goodapilla being thus removed, Gruapah applied himself to Gopaul, a Diamond Merchant; and they entered into an agreement to have the Diamond cut without the owner's knowledge or consent, and afterwards sold it likewise without acquainting him to Mr. Parkes for 4150 pagodas, of which Gopaul and Gruapah re-received each one half; though Gruapah had been to Conjeveram, and affirmed to Goodapilla that the President had taken the stone from him, and had given him only 1500 pagodas for it ; and told him that he must not come to Madras, that if he did he would be in danger. But Goodapilla suspecting the fraud, came at last to Madras ; and having information that his diamond had been sold as above, made his complaint thereupon to the President, and craved that justice might be done him. Whereupon the President had ordered the said Gopaul and Gruapah to be committed to prison ; of all which he now acquaints the Board ; and they and Goodapilla being called before the Board, and the whole affair being particularly enquired into, it appears evident that Gruapah had imposed upon, and defrauded Goodapilla Rungapah, and aspersed the President very grossly as above narrated. Mr. Parkes being called, declared he paid so much for the diamond. Gopal and Gruapah acknowledge that it was the same diamond that Goodapilla had trusted Gruapah with to sell for him, and that they had received each one half of the money. Gruapah affirms he had paid Goodapilla 17,000 pagodas ; but the other persists to affirm that he had received only 15,000 pagodas for his diamond. It being likewise evident that Gopaul was concurring with Gruapah in this cheat, and that he knew the diamond was Goodapilla's, and had treated with Mr. Parkes about the sale of it, the Board came to the following resolution.

"That, after deducting the charge of cutting the said Diamond, and the sum already paid by Gruapah to Goodapillah, Gopaul and Gruapah do make up to him the sum it was sold for, each one half; that Gruapah being in low circumstances, the Secretary do make an inventory of his effects and sell them at the Sea Gate by public outcry, for payment of his half of the said money; and that if the amount of all his effects shall not prove sufficient, that Gopaul shall make up the sum that shall be wanting; and that he shall recover of Gruapah the sum so made good if ever he shall be found to have effects; that both be remanded to prison until the judgment is complied with, and that Gruapah be exemplarily punished for groundlessly aspersing the President's character in so gross a manner."

Here the matter ended, and we can only presume that the money was subsequently paid. It is however a significant fact that Goodapilla should be so easily induced to believe in the oppression charged against the Governor. Mr. Macrae's proceedings as regards interlopers may be gathered from the following extract.

"Tuesday, 25th April, 1727. The President represents to the Board that several persons, without indentures or license to trade as free Merchants, thrusting themselves into the several branches of the trade of India, are a great prejudice to the trade in general, and to the Company's Covenanted Servants and others that have license particularly in Pegu. That we are directed by the Honorable Court of Directors in their letter dated 7th January 1726, to send home all such Traders. Wherefore the President moves that Miles Barne and Thomas Pritchard, both now here and intended to return to Pegu, and Lewis Tornery and James

Lander, who are now there trading (though none of the four has the Company's Indentures) may be served with an order to return to Great Britain, conformably to our Honorable Masters' directions in that respect.

"Resolved that the orders for Lewis Tornery and James Lander be sent in a general letter to Captain Bercyman, Resident at Syrian, by a conveyance that now offers; with directions to him to serve the said orders and see them complied with; and that the Secretary do serve Miles Barne and Thomas Pritchard who are on the place, with the like orders."

These orders were evaded. Miles Barne and Thomas Pritchard obtained to go to Pegu for one year to recover their effects, promising faithfully to return and embark for England at the expiration of that time. However they broke their word and stayed at Pegu; and the resident at Pegu appears to have avoided taking any action in the matter.

We close the present chapter and the present volume with the following entry, which serves to illustrate the nature of the trade with China carried on by the Company's servants at Madras, and at the same time indicates the state of existing relations between Fort St. George and Poudicherry.

"Wednesday, 1st June, 1727. The President represents to the Board, that he proposes to send a ship to China this year, and is on that account in want of some silver to send on her; that as the French at Pondicherry have lately sold their silver at fourteen and three eights dollars weight per ten pagodas, he is willing to take the Company's at that price, with the allowance of a quarter more as usual for ships that go for China. Agreed to deliver the President thirty Chests of silver at those rates."

The concluding years of Governor Macrae's administration will be treated in the next volume.

END OF THE SECOND VOLUME.

JUST PUBLISHED.

MADRAS IN THE OLDEN TIME: being a history of the Presidency from the first foundation of Fort St. George to the Governorship of Thomas Pitt, Grandfather of the Earl of Chatham, 1639—1702 compiled from Official Records, by J. TALBOYS WHEELER, Esq., minature quarto, with Fac similies of the autographs of the early Governors of Madras...... Rs. 5-0.

HAND-BOOK TO THE MADRAS RECORDS, with Chronological Annals of the Madras Presidency from 1639 to 1861, 8vo. cloth...Rs. 2-8.

OPINIONS OF THE PRESS.

" It affords us much pleasure to observe that two very interesting and valuable publications are on the eve of being given to the world by Mr. HIGGINBOTHAM. We allude to Mr. TALBOYS WHEELER'S volume entitled "Madras in the Olden Time," and his "Hand-Book to the Madras Records, preserved in the Government Office." The former of these works is a re-print of that admirable series of papers which have for some time past enriched the columns of the *Indian Statesman*. Those papers are so widely known and highly appreciated, that we need say nothing more about them. In the meantime we have immediately to deal with Mr. WHEELER's Summary (i. e. Hand-Book) of the Records of the Presidency, which lies beside us. Mr. WHEELER has had a rich mine opened to him, and has made the best of his opportunity. He was appointed last year to search through the Government Records, and to give an opinion as to the value of them, nor could the task have been placed in better hands. His report on them has been pronounced perfectly satisfactory by the Madras Government.—*Athenæum*, March 2d, 1861.

"The Reporter has performed his task with so much ability, as we said on a previous occasion, and has so condensed the voluminous documentary matter submitted to his treatment, that, to use a pithy old Scotch proverb, we have "great gear packed in little bulk," and can make extracts invitingly short. Mr. WHEELER's toil in wading through the Records above mentioned, with a view to that re-classification of the whole effected by him, must have been enormous.—*Athenæum*, March 12th, 1861.

"We have been favoured with a copy of Mr. J. TALBOYS WHEELER's entertaining work, entitled, "*Madras in the Olden Time*," a history of this Presidency from its first foundation to the Governorship of Thomas Pitt, Grandfather of the Earl of Chatham. This interesting work, compiled from official records in the Government Office, had already afforded us a good deal of amusement, and no little instruction, as it appeared in a fragmentary state in the *Indian Statesman*. It comprises the annals of our Madras Commonwealth during a period hitherto little known or studied, extending from 1639 to 1702 : and we must confess we did not imagine that old Madras could have furnished any thing so interesting. Had the prospectus of such a work been set before us, we should have smiled incredulously at the promise of entertainment ; but we can assure our readers that a perusal of this little history will amply repay them both with valuable information and amusement. Mr. WHEELER has eliminated what is dull and commercial, and has thrown a charm over the early records of our Presidency by his easy and pleasant style, whilst he has also exhibited his subject in connection with the history of the times in a most instructive manner.

" Madras has reason to be grateful for the labours of Mr. WHEELER, and we hope ere long to see a continuation of his researches into times of still increasing interest and importance.—*Madras Observer*, March 14th, 1861.

" Madras in the Olden Time," a compilation from the records of Government by Mr. J. T. WHEELER, has just been published in convenient form by Mr. HIGGINBOTHAM. The student of Indian history will find much to interest him in the old Records for the first time disinterred and arranged chronologically by Mr. WHEELER, for the *Indian Statesman*, and now placed before the public in a compact volume by Mr. HIGGINBOTHAM. The compiler appears to have laboured with great zeal and industry, wading through hundreds of volumes of consultations," and we think it must be admitted by all who perused the several chapters as they appeared in the *Statesman* that the permission accorded by the Government to Mr. WHEELER has been used very judiciously. So far as we are able to judge, we should say that no event of any importance in the history of the infant Presidency has been omitted, whilst the extracts referring to the quarrels of the Governors with one another, with their servants and subjects and with the native chiefs from the Naik of Poonamallee to the great Mogul himself, convey the most vivid description of the position, manners and character of the first settlers, and of the people by whom they were surrounded. As to Mr. WHEELER the least we can say of him is that whilst he has furnished the public with some very interesting and amusing reading, he has added a valuable contribution to Indian History.—*Examiner*, March 2d, 1861.

" The whole period about which Mr. WHEELER writes is between 1639 and 1702, corresponding, as he remarks, almost exactly with that of Lord Macaulay's History. The materials for the narrative have been collected after an amount of labour, which few would voluntarily undertake, from the old Government Records. It was well known that, amidst very much that was uninteresting and having reference only to mercantile transactions, much that was valuable and amusing might be discovered if any one sufficiently indefatigable would undertake the work. A few scraps of valuable matter had been disinterred from among the rubbish which surrounded them, but it was left for Mr. WHEELER to gather up all these fragments, separate them from the worthless material by which they are encrusted, and work them into one, continuous and readable narrative."—*Madras Crescent*, March 23d, 1861.

The *Hurkaru* writing of Mr. WHEELER's work says:—

" We have to acknowledge the receipt of " Madras in the Olden Time," from 1639 to 1702 a seemingly very interesting work, by J. T. WHEELER, Esq. Every page of it into which we have had time to look contains matter of much interest to any settler in the East."

" In conclusion, we may notice the fact two works have issued from one of the local presses of great interest to all who are connected with Madras, and of considerable importance to the student of Indian History. They are both written by Mr. J. TALBOYS WHEELER, the Editor of the *Indian Statesman*, and are deservedly spoken of in the highest terms in two reviews which we quote elsewhere. One is " Madras in the Olden Time" being a history of this Presidency from its first foundation to the Governorship of Mr. Thomas Pitt, Grandfather of the Earl of Chatham, that is, from 1639 to 1702. This Period has been almost ignored by Mill, and where alluded to by him is in many instances inaccurately treated. As the present work is compiled from the Government Records, which were placed at Mr. WHEELER's disposal by the Madras Government, all the facts connected with the early history of the Presidency have been for the first time brought to light in a handy and well printed volume. The other work is a Hand-Book to the old Records of Madras which has been prepared for Government. It deals with the same subject of Madras in the Olden Time, but is of course more official in style : it is nevertheless highly interesting."—*Overland Athenæum*, March 29th, 1861.

" We have now beside us the publication referred to, in the form of a " Hand-Book to the Madras Records," a pamphlet in boards extending to the length of 94 pages, (with Chronological annals extending over 40 pages,) and full of most interesting matter connected with the past history of our Presidency, which we heartily commend to the notice of our readers, as a valuable addition to their libraries. They will learn from it much that even the most studious among them, and those best acquainted with extant books relative to India, never knew before, because he has wisely been permitted to open to them sources of information hitherto concealed, and the nature and value of which was unknown to the possessors of the treasure so long kept under lock and key, in the archieves of Fort Saint George. Regarding the excellence of the Report, and the amount of labour bestowed on the preparation of it, we need add nothing to what we have said already, but we must particularly mention in addition to the Report, as now printed, of thirty-one pages, which are perhaps more valuable for the purposes of reference, although less directly instructive and amusing, than the Report itself, as they contain " Chronological Annals of the British Government at Madras, from the earliest period to the present day ; 1631 to 1861." In those " Annals" Mr. WHEELER has brought his work down to the 5th of March 1861, his record concluding with a notice of the late lamented Bishop of Madras. He has furnished a minute and correct chronological series of past events, not to be found elsewhere, which every one who wishes to learn the past history of Madras will do well to consult.—*Athenæum*, April 13th, 1861.

"MADRAS IN THE OLDEN TIME ; being a history of the Presidency from the first foundation to the Governorship of Thomas Pitt, Grandfather of the Earl of Chatham—1689—1702 ;" such is the title of a work compiled from official records, by J. TALBOYS WHEELER, Professor of Moral Philosophy and Logic, Madras Presidency College. The work first appeared as a series of papers in one of the ablest of our Indian journals, the *Indian Statesman*. Many of our readers will remember that a similar work, entitled " The English in Western India," by the late lamented Phillip Anderson, a Chaplain on this Establishment, appeared as a series of papers in our own columns. The two works are the best we have on 'the Olden time in India.' They are replete with information, amusement, and interest. ... ...
... ...

We could give our readers, if our space permitted,

many more amusing pictures from the work before us. We shall, however, conclude by supplying them with a *tableau vivant* of Fort St. George at the end of the seventeenth century. "They will hear the gun fired at early morning,—and they will see the gradual stir of the inhabitants,—the measured tramp of the European soldier,—the little stately peon with his sword and buckler,—the rush of noisy and naked coolies,—the appearance of apprentices, writers, factors, and merchants in half-Hindoo costume,—the assembly for morning prayers in the little chapel, good master Patrick Warner officiating in his gown and bands, and indignant at the smallness of his congregation,—the opening of the Factory and jobbering crowd of Native traders,—the grand displays of European goods for sale, and packing up of Native Merchandise for export home,—the little school-room and long array of little boys and girls,—the orderly dinner shortly after noon, where all are assembled at the general table from the apprentices to the Honorable Governor himself,—the return to the labors of the desk and ware-house, until the joyous hour of closing has arrived, and the jaded Europeans recruit their exhausted spirits with the pleasures of punch, tobacco, and other persuits which we need not and cannot name. If it is Sunday, all would be changed; for in old times English Sundays were rigidly observed as little festivals. Then Europeans, civilians as well as soldiers dropped their half native attire, and were apparelled in the European fashion of the time. Then for a brief hour or two the Chaplain would be a greater man than the Governor. Then he would denounce vice and popery to his heart's content, and expound the Scriptures by the light of a theological learning which was almost general in those days when the Church was a living reality, but which is fast passing away now. Then the Church could boast of literary giants, such as Walton, Lightfoot, Stillingfleet, Beveridge: thousand time-honored names. She has few men to boast of now."—*Bombay Gazette.*

www.ingramcontent.com/pod-product-compliance
Lightning Source LLC
Chambersburg PA
CBHW031954300426
44117CB00008B/752